Leeward Marine

The Phoenix

ADVENTURES OF A COMMERCIAL DIVER

THE FINAL TALES

C.B. LEE, DSD

"Hope rises like a phoenix from the ashes of shattered dreams"

S.A. Sachs

ACKNOWLEDGEMENTS

I want to thank all those that read AQUAFACS, my first collection of stories published in 2019. LEEWARD MARINE will take the reader on another wild ride from 1989 through 1995. This collection of stories will end deep in the Caribbean with my final project and last of my career as a commercial diver.

Once again, I have to thank family and friends for their support, then and now.

To my wife, Susan, for her patience and especially for her enduring and surviving all the ups and downs through the Leeward Marine years, Love and thanks!

Author's Family- Melissa,Jonathan,James,Susan,Lindsay,Mindy,Kristin- Left to Right –

To my children, Melissa, Mindy, Kristin, Lindsay, James, and Jonathan who had to persevere through another seven years and a move to Florida as my new company continued to push the limits of commercial diving. Still a mystery man for a father, constantly traveling, missing countless events and milestones, the years ticked away. I thank you and looking back on those years I hope you can forgive me for not having been there as often as other fathers.

Special thanks to my brother Jay for his continued support following the demise of Aquafacs. He gave me the encouragement to move forward with Leeward Marine and push on with the dream. His passing in 2014 was a huge loss. He is sorely missed by family, friends and all who knew him. Sail on Jay Lee.

And my siblings, Scott, Greg, and Jean Marie. I thank you all for being there through the years, and special mention and thanks to my brother Dana who passed in late 2019 as I began to write this book. He will never get to read how his contributions and support were instrumental in helping me develop a plan and strategy for Leeward Marine but I'm sure he knew.

Thanks to David Keefe for his help by selling me his company, Puffin Inc. The name would change and go on to become Leeward Marine. Dave and Jay's continued support was key to forming up the new company. Their experience helped me drive forward and continue on for another seven years. With the new opportunity, we went on to pioneer a number of underwater services that are still in practice today.

Special mention and thanks to Paul Mercaldi for all his efforts over the years putting up with the challenges of keeping the ball rolling and looking after the diving crews as they muckled their way through all the ups and down chasing ships all over the world. And thanks to my sister, Jean Marie, for looking after Paul and supporting our cause from Aquafacs through the Leeward Marine years.

Specials thanks to Rita Shepard for initial funding for operations of Leeward Marine. Our friendship continues to this day.

SPECIAL ACKNOWLEDGEMENTS

To brother Scott, Boston University Alumnus, and retired Commercial Pilot with nearly thirty-thousand flight hours, special thanks for his patience and talent reading, consulting, and editing. He urged me to include more detail and color to better flush out the stories. With his help and suggestions, I believe the reader will experience a better understanding of the complexities of the work we performed and in some cases pioneered.

C. Scott Lee, Brother, Storyline Consultant and Editing

Finally, to Erin and Jonathan Lee, especially huge thanks for extending the invitation to visit and help me prepare the final manuscript of LEEWARD MARINE for publication. Erin did the editing while Jon and daughter Chloe prepared the book architecture and artwork for my first book, AQUAFACS. And now, they've once again done a tremendous job with the book architecture, artwork, and final submittal for publication.

Erin , Jon , Max and Chloe at St Mary Glacier, Colorado

In life, we all soldier on and live our own adventures, to all of you that read this book I express my thanks and encourage you to live all your adventures without fear, for we have but one life to live...

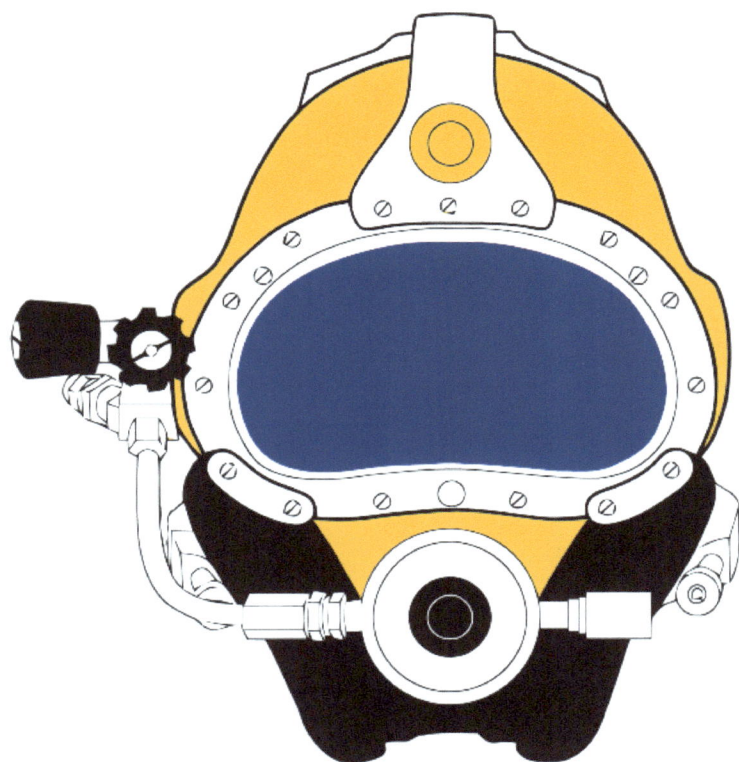

CONTENTS

The stories within are all based on true events and written from my best recollections using a first-person narrative as much as possible. Some people that shared the times at Leeward Marine may have a slightly different view of events as we all experience life from our own perspective. All in all, this book is a collection of stories, written to entertain as well as document more of my times in commercial diving tending to the broad range of ship operators needs and concerns. The Maritime Shipping Community is incredibly tightly held and perhaps the most secretive business on the planet when it comes to their ships.

The creative formation and evolution of Leeward Marine was both a joy and relief. So, with that, I once again put pen to paper to capture some of the highlights of my second act and last chapter of my career as an extraordinarily blessed and lucky Commercial Diver.

Christopher Lee, DSD

PROLOGUE

In 1989, my life as a commercial diver had been filled with travel and adventure. It had been over ten years since completing my training in California at Commercial Diving Center in Wilmington, California. This collection of stories continues my adventures from the formation of Leeward Marine to the close of my career as a commercial diver.

George H.W. Bush was elected President in 1988 and the winds of war in the Balkans and Middle East were on the rise following the Ronald Reagan Presidency. Gorbechev was still the leader of the Soviet Union but found himself on the downward spiral that would soon lead to the end of the cold war and fall of the Berlin Wall.

Winter wonderland in Hamilton, 1992 – Last winter before relocation to Florida

I was living with my wife Susan and now, six children, in Hamilton, Massachusetts.

The increasing demand for oil and widening global trade continued to drive the shipping community forward despite the geopolitical turmoil. The work prospect looked great for me in August 1989 but for the terminal condition of Aquafacs.

Forming a new company to carry on the legacy of Aquafacs without the baggage would be a huge challenge. There would be high risk along with an uncertain outcome, but with my luck and a little faith I had to take the chance. Luck had always been there for me, lighting the path forward. Aquafacs had tragically reached the end, and in a weird kind of way would add to my luck.

Nineteen eighty-nine was an exceptional year. Hurricane Hugo had destroyed most of the Island of St Croix, on September 17th, 1989, shortly after the formation of Leeward Marine . It was unimaginable, the horror of that storm in St Croix that broke the wind gage at Point Eustis on the east end at 210 MPH. We had been back there only once as Leeward Marine before Hurricane Hugo struck.

Our second ship call at the Hess Terminal in St. Croix was three weeks after Hugo destroyed the island. Not even a category five hurricane would stop the flow of crude oil into the refinery.

When I arrived, it was a shock looking down on final approach to the airport, the landscape had changed from lush greenery to brown dirt. There wasn't a leaf on a tree, and the tops of all the palms were gone, only the trunks remained.

Where once there were homes, all that remained were clean building slabs that looked freshly poured. In fact, they were blasted by island sand fiercely strafing the houses powered by the 200 MPH winds, leaving only the slabs behind. The buildings were scattered to the four winds with little debris left behind. The vast majority of the wreckage was blown out to sea and carried away by the tides.

It was amazing that so many houses and buildings were simply obliterated by Hurricane Hugo. After St Croix, the storm moved on to do extensive damage in the Carolinas, flattening the coastal forests.

Remains of waterfront home following Hurricane Hugo, St Croix

For us, St Croix was a special Caribbean Island we'd all come to appreciate and was our best location for working on ships. The Hess Marine Terminal at HOVIC (Hess Oil Virgin Islands Corporation), would have become a faded memory without Leeward Marine rising from the ashes of Aquafacs. Continuing our services was the best way for me to save face with our clients. Considering all the years and hard-fought battles, it was a saving grace.

For the years to come, there were more challenges and a significant increase in technical diving difficulty. The demand and client expectations continued to push the limits. My reputation was what I relied on, not only on the technical diving side but also having forged a bond of trust with my clients. They knew I would keep their business confidential, as such Leeward Marine became much more of a 'black bag' operator. This was a much different place for me. Being constrained from advertising our successes was contrary to my former promotional strategy for Aquafacs.

The new client expectations had a much greater level of danger than what we faced earlier in my career. The following story may help to better understand how environment, being raised in Marblehead, helped prepare me for an unusual career as a commercial diver and fueled my fatalistic views and acceptance of life's twists and turns. .

Looking North from Castle Rock, Marblehead Neck, toward Salem Bay

"Only in Marblehead"

Quote from David Keefe. Halloween, 1991.

$$\approx\!\!\!\approx$$

"Only in Marblehead" explains much of what makes natives of Marblehead unique. The quote was from David Keefe when he and I visited Marblehead on Halloween day, 1991.

The Perfect Storm – Marblehead

Not long after the Leeward Marine adventures in Croatia in August 1991, story included in this book, a weather event occurred that affected the New England coastline and Canadian Maritime. Cape Ann, Salem Bay and Marblehead were severely impacted. It was called the 'Halloween Storm,' better known to us today as the 'Perfect Storm,' made famous by the book and movie of the same name, recounting the loss of the tuna boat 'Andrea Gail' from Gloucester.

Such an important event and this, the true story of my day in Marblehead as the Perfect Storm rolled into town is one to remember. The day left me shaking my head in disbelief. Yet another example of how it's residents cope come what may , through hell or high water since the early 1600s.

Susan and I, in Hamilton, were battening down the hatches when the storm arrived. My friend and former Aquafacs member, David Keefe, called and asked if I could meet him at the Landing in Marblehead and help him check on his sailboat stored out on Marblehead neck. It was on a cradle and located at my family's Ballast Lane property.

Former Lee Family home on Ballast Lane, Marblehead Neck

The seas were growing and with the incoming tide there was a strong chance the waters would overtop the Causeway. The Causeway was the only road to get out to Marblehead Neck and the only egress for the permanent residents in harm's way should the need arise.

I grabbed my cameras and headed for Marblehead. My wife Susan wasn't thrilled and wasn't coming. The winds were stiffening with strong gusts along the way, but traffic was light, so it didn't take long to make the trip. When I pulled into the Landing the tidal surge had already pushed the water level in the harbor up to the parking lot and began flooding it. I parked on the high side toward State Street. Dave was waiting for me out front and we could see from the parking lot waves breaking over the Causeway seawall leading to Marblehead neck.

Beach rock overtopping seawall, Marblehead Neck, Perfect Storm, Oct 31,1991

It hadn't quite been overtopped but each breaking wave crashed with an explosion of white water over the seawall flooding the road. We wouldn't dare make that trip without a good-sized four-wheel drive truck if we had one. Even with that, it wouldn't have been worth the risk. The sailboat could not be washed away as our property was in the center of the neck at a high enough ground elevation to be well above the danger zone. There were, however, many homes that were waterfront and at risk of sustaining major damage as the storm battered the coastline.

Unbelievably, the Landing was still open as the harbor water sloshed around the parking lot and lapped at the floorboards beneath the restaurant. Being open for business it only made sense to get out of the weather and go inside and get a drink. Patrons were seated at the bar as we approached and ordered a couple of Irish Coffees. There were others mulling around playing darts. The Landing once belonged to the Minuteman Dart League. I was a member of their team back in the late seventies.

The Landing Restaurant – State Street Wharf, Marblehead

Turns out, the kitchen was also still open, and they were operating business as usual. It was a surreal sight. Our drinks arrived and Dave asked, "How was the ride from Hamilton?"

"Not good. Gusty winds blowing me around and raining." I replied. "This storm is a 'pissa.' I can't believe the bar is open." Just after I made the comment there was a loud thump from the dining room at the far end of the Landing, closest to the water. "What the hell was that?"

Dave, looking toward the kitchen door said, "I have no idea." just as a second thump could be heard and moments later another and then another.

We stepped outside and saw the tidal surge had overtopped the curb of the parking lot and a swell was rolling up under the section of the restaurant that sat on pilings over the water. The thumping sound was the swell lifting the building off the pilings and dropping it back down as the swell passed. It started as a minor annoyance. The patrons inside at the bar continued drinking and hanging around, ignoring any inconvenience.

We went back inside and sat again at the bar. The music was playing, and nobody was leaving. Seemed to us that the sound from the far end was getting louder and we could feel a slight shudder each time we heard the thumping sound. Moments later there was a much louder thump and the sound of cracking wood. The few remaining die-hard lunch patrons were now rapidly leaving the restaurant through the inside entrance to the bar. The actual restaurant door, closer to the harbor, could not be opened to the outside due to the flood water in the parking lot.

In the bar, the Bartender was paying a little more attention but was still pouring drinks when suddenly the kitchen door flew open and the Chef came running out screaming "Fire! . . Fire! . . Fire!" as he ran out the front door. Now *that* got everybody's attention, but not off their bar stools. The Bartender announced, "Last Call!"

A couple of minutes later we heard the sirens of Fire Engines. The doors swung open and three firemen came in dragging a hose into the kitchen. At this point, the Bartender requested that everybody leave and make way for the Firemen to do their work. Nobody was in a hurry, but they did all move along out the front door. Dave and I were last to wander out, shaking our heads in disbelief of what we just witnessed. "*Only in Marblehead*," Dave said. "could you find a bar full of patrons drinking as the building is being destroyed and the effing kitchen's on fire!" We both laughed at the absurdity.

Outside I asked, "Wonder how things are going at the 'Barnacle'?" After what we witnessed at the Landing, a fair question.

"Don't know. Let's go check it out!" Dave said.

The Barnacle is a very popular seafood restaurant and bar, located up the street about a quarter mile from the Landing. It sits on the waterfront atop a robust seawall and nearly adjoined to a multistory residential condo just north of the restaurant. As we headed in that direction the weather was getting worse and the ocean was pounding the shoreline in front of the houses, densely packed along the harbor front. The level of noise from the waves pounding on the seawall was surprisingly loud and threatening.

FILE PHOTO: Barnacle Cove looking northeast toward mouth of Marblehead harbor

When we moved north from the Landing toward the Barnacle you could see water shooting through the narrow openings between the ancient houses, built in Colonial times. They were built and clustered together, using rollers to move the buildings as close as possible to each other for survival against the cruel weather of New England. That could only mean the waves were breaking on the houses with the force of the water blowing through the three-foot gap between them. The spray was twenty-foot high or better shooting through the gap and into the street as each swell rolled up against the buildings.

PHOTO BY AUTHOR: Seawater flooding street in front of the Barnacle Restaurant

As we approached the Barnacle, we found Police caution tape blocking access to the street and crossing the road a couple hundred feet from the restaurant. It was also still open like the Landing. Patrons were visible sitting at the bar from our location and the dining area still had people sitting at tables not far from the waterfront. The building was enclosed with a glass window wall and had a narrow deck outside.

"Now what?" asked Dave.

I had two cameras slung around my neck including a Nikon with a large telephoto lens. I said, "Hey, I'm the Press here to take photos of the storm!"

"Ya right. Good luck with that!" Dave said with a laugh.

"I'll be right back." I said passing under the yellow tape and heading down the small hill leading toward the Barnacle. There is a rocky beach just south of the restaurant where there is great visibility to look out at the mouth of the harbor. I grew up in Marblehead and never saw such an angry sea. The swells were huge and formed up better than ten-foot high before curling and breaking on the rocky shore. The swells were continuing to build in Salem Bay, and I could see larger sets forming and heading for the mouth of the harbor.

The action was way too close for my long lens. My other camera would be good to shoot the Barnacle as the swells closed in. I steadied myself and began taking photos of the building with the patrons clearly visible through the windows sitting in the bar. There were several patrons visible in the dining room but set up away from the front, I would assume from fear of the surging waves. Looking out, the next group of swells was moving in and were much bigger than the last set. I couldn't believe my eyes how much bigger they actually were.

When the first of the monster swells came in it slammed against the seawall, nearly reaching the restaurant building set well above the rocky beach. The sound of all the beach rocks being sucked in and out by the force of the swells is hard to describe other than a loud rumble, alarming and disturbing as the swells rolled in and out. The patrons were still eating and drinking as I snapped away with my camera. Then it was showtime.

A swell approached that looked like a tidal wave. It came in and appeared to be higher than the building itself. The patrons were only protected from it by a plate glass window wall that would likely break when it slammed against the building. I waited with my finger on the trigger and watched until the wave curled and bashed onto the roof and window wall, blowing out the entire pane glass frontage and filling the restaurant with seawater. The sound of the furniture being crushed by the wave and washed across the room must have been terrifying for those inside, and certain to get the people off their bar stools. Sure enough, the front door opened, and everyone came running out screaming, heading for the proverbial hills to escape the encroaching water.

I held my ground as I saw the next even larger swell approaching. It curled and hit the building reaching the second floor of the condos next door and exploded over the Barnacle. I fired my camera, turned, and ran like hell up the hill with the water not too far behind me.

Dave was waiting behind the caution tape. "You're fucking crazy!" he said. "That last wave almost got you. It pounded the building and landed in the street right where I last saw you before you disappeared in the mist."

"I'm thinking fearless! Got the picture! Nobody will believe this happened without seeing it. Don't see anyone else hanging around taking pictures." I said. "This one's for posterity." Whip! . .

CHAPTER ONE

NEAR MISS OR DIVINE INTERVENTION

St. Croix, USVI - October 29th, 1990

⚓

Murder at Sandy Point

Early on for Leeward Marine, I figured that setting up rapid, direct, and reliable communications was the answer on how to operate and manage the new venture without incurring the additional expense of maintaining a full-time staffed office. Our job was to provide technical diving services and as such, my clients never came to my office for meetings or anything else. They expected me to go to their office if needed, but mostly we needed to catch up to their ships when they made port, wherever they may be, to take care of business.

My being reachable anytime they'd pick up the phone and call was the goal. The ship operators encountered all sorts of issues with their ships that required immediate and confidential attention. They needed a trustworthy vendor both above and below the waterline.

The first piece of my strategy was to set up a 1-800-phone number as the primary contact for Leeward Marine. This allowed my clients to make a toll-free call from anywhere to reach me or leave a message. Port Engineers traveled around using pay phones or remote phones like myself. With that 1-800 number, they were able to reach me using any phone, anywhere, anytime. Doesn't sound now like a big deal, but pre-cellphone it was an innovative plan to provide reliable communications.

Using the same 1-800 number, I called myself toll free to activate my office equipment twenty-four seven to check for phone messages. It gave me a personal remotely operated long-distance answering service.

When out in the field, I would check messages multiple times daily and be able to call back, usually the same day if I weren't stuck offshore somewhere or under water blowing bubbles.

The phone worked flawlessly given the technological constraints of the times. As an owner/operator, it provided the independence needed to be in the field and directly manage a remote office from anywhere we went.

The second major piece of my communications plan was adding a new paging system that claimed to provide true satellite service. They said that with their device you could be reached anywhere on the planet. The company was Skytel with their SkyPager system. What a great idea!

My clients, if they had emergencies or other critical issues, could reach out and find me anywhere on the globe. That could be a game changer! It wasn't cheap, but it worked when I tested it, so it was added to my communications plan. It was the perfect device for me to carry as we continued to travel as that one-way pager would find me anywhere.

There were only about a dozen high level execs in the shipping community that were provided my SkyPager number. I asked them to use this number only in an extreme case and reassured them that for business as usual situations that they could reach me on my 1 800 Leeward line. If they had an emergency or needed immediate attention and they called my SkyPager, it would reach me, and they would get an immediate response as I promised to drop everything and find a phone to call them back. If there was no access to a phone or we were offshore working they would get a call back at absolutely the first opportunity including by way of Marine telephones available on most ships.

Leeward Marine did no advertising. We ran solely by personal contact, and by the need to know principal. Those that needed to know, knew how to find me. By this method I was able to manage the workload and keep the highest level of performance with smaller experienced teams, hand-picked veterans previously trained by me at Aquafacs. They knew how to run fast, work long shifts and succeed in getting the results for the ship operators when they called.

The new Leeward Marine was now operating a lean, mean, Diving Machine for just over a year and I always had my new SkyPager with me .

And so, it was on October 27th, 1990, that my wife Susan went with me on a trip to St Croix. The island had come a long way in the year since Hugo happened in September 1989. Many of the hotels had been renovated and re-opened, but they still had a long way to go, and the linemen from Texas and Louisiana were still finishing re-wiring the power grid.

It was a work trip to inspect the Maritime Overseas Supertanker, *WESTERN LION*, at the Amerada Hess Refinery at the HOVIC Terminal in St Croix. I planned the trip with a couple of extra days built in to enjoy a brief get away for Susan from the grind of managing the household. With me running all over the place as Leeward Marine, it was only fair to get her a little away time. The *WESTERN LION* wasn't due at the St Croix breakwater until sometime in the late morning on the 30th. Arriving the 27th gave us a window to hang out.

We stayed at the Caravelle Hotel in downtown Christiansted and got a late start on the 28th. After enjoying a leisurely breakfast on the waterfront, the rest of the day would be spent relaxing at the pool and shopping later. The weather was perfect. After a great dinner at the Charthouse we sat and planned our day off before the arrival of the

WESTERN LION. Sandy Point Beach, on the west end in Frederiksted, would be a great place to spend the day beaching it. The white sugar sand and sweeping, unspoiled beach line was awesome. We rented a four-wheel drive jeep for our trip, so we'd have no problem getting in and out of Sandy Point.

When we got to the beach it was about ten in the morning. A beautiful sunny day with puffy clouds and a good breeze blowing in from the Atlantic. When we pulled in and parked there was only one other vehicle in the small parking area. The beach was empty other than the one couple lying on the beach a couple hundred yards down. We took a right on the beach and walked north another couple hundred yards. They were now a distant quarter mile, plus or minus, from our special spot on the beach.

While Susan sunbathed, I grabbed my mask and fins and went snorkeling. Not much to look at but sand and an occasional small fish, when I spotted something off to my left. It was a huge starfish.

The starfish was in about fifteen feet of water and when I swooped down and picked it up it was an incredibly bright color and an unbelievable find!

I swam to the beach with the starfish and called out to Susan to come down and bring my camera. When she got to the water, she couldn't believe her eyes! "Oh my God!" she said. "Where'd you find that?"

"Well, I didn't bring it with me." We laughed. "Give me my camera. I want a picture."

She held up the bright orange starfish and I took her picture. At the time there were no digital cameras, so I'd have to wait until I got the film developed and hope it came out. It was a magnificent photo.

She wanted to take the starfish home. I had to explain to her there was no practical way of smuggling a starfish out of St Croix. We wouldn't have enough time to dry it out and pack it for bringing with us. The right thing to do was to re-enter the water and place the starfish properly on the bottom, roughly where I found it. She was so so disappointed, even to this day.

After returning the starfish I joined Susan on the beach blanket. We had a snack and an ice-cold drink before continuing with sunbathing. A short time later, there was a weird sound from my beach bag. It was my SkyPager!

Having carried it around and paid for nearly a year of service, this was the first time it had ever gone off! Now I was worried, especially being deep in the Caribbean. The call was from John Katramados, Senior Port Engineer at Sea-Land, one of the very few with the number. I had to call him ASAP. That was the deal.

Susan asked, "What was that?"

"That was my SkyPager." I said.

"Your what??" she asked.

"It's a satellite pager that can reach me anywhere in the world. I have it so my clients can find me if they have an emergency. The deal is, if they call this number, I promised to drop everything and call them right away. We have to go."

"Go? No way! I didn't come all the way to St Croix to get yanked off the beach because of some dumb SkyPager." She complained.

"We have to go. I can find a phone in Frederiksted to make the call and we can head over to Cane Bay after that and go snorkeling. There's a great Tiki Bar over there to get a couple of Pina Coladas before heading back to the hotel. We have to go, now."

Susan was really pissed, but she knew we had to go. After packing up and heading to the jeep we could see the couple down the beach, and she tried one more time to convince me to stay. I just gave her a look and kept on going to the jeep . . . It was just a little past twelve when we backed out and headed to Frederiksted.

I found a payphone at the Frederiksted pier and managed to make the call to New Jersey to John Katramados at his office in Port Elizabeth.

"Hello John. This is Chris returning your call. You sent me a page on my Sat Pager."

"Hello there. That's right. I need your help. We have a new management team and they're requiring a detailed report on the status of our fleet maintenance program. It's an important project and they need me to reply by the end of the week." He said.

Here I was figuring a ship was sinking somewhere out there, and he pages me for help with a report! Better keep this one to myself.

"Sure John. How can I help?" I asked

John went on to describe the follow up documentation he needed. I had the dates, ships we'd serviced, locations and any other details he might find useful for his report. Easy stuff for me to get him when I got back. Oh well . . . Off to Cane Bay. I would stress the importance of the call to Susan and how as soon as we got back, I would probably have to go to Port Elizabeth, New Jersey.

We had a great afternoon snorkeling, sunbathing, and enjoying the delicious Pina Coladas at the Tiki Bar across the street from Cane Bay before heading back to the Caravelle.

After showering up, I called Dennis, my charter boat captain. He operated a thirty-foot charter fishing boat with a wide-open back deck, perfect for a commercial diving operation. We had used Dennis for years with Aquafacs and he was waiting for my call. The *WESTERN LION* was due the next morning.

"Hello Dennis. This is Chris. How are ya?"

"Great." He said.

8

Caravelle Hotel – Christiansted Waterfront

"You all set for tomorrow? The *WESTERN LION* is due at the breakwater around ten in the morning. Susan and I got in on Saturday and spent some time today out at Sandy Point. It was beautiful out there."

"Oh yeah? What time were you guys out there?" he asked.

"We got out there around ten o'clock and spent a couple of hours, but I had to leave a little after twelve to make a phone call. At least we got in the couple of hours." I said.

"Oh yeah? Well, I was out fishing today at Sandy Point and sometime after one o'clock, I pulled a woman out of the water just off Sandy Point Beach, stark naked with a hole in her neck." He said.

I could feel the hairs stand up on the back of my neck as he told his story.

Dennis went on, "Some character came out of the woods and shot a guy on the beach, dragged his girlfriend up in the bushes and raped her. She told me that when he went to pull his pants up, she bolted to the water. He shot at her as she ran, grazing her neck. When she made it to the water, she swam as fast as she could, straight out, all the while he continued to shoot at her. I came along sometime after and spotted her waving to me."

I could hardly breathe listening to the story. Had that guy been there the whole time we were, just waiting for one of the couples to leave? and then . . .

My God. My SkyPager, John Katramados calling with no real 'emergency,' or was there? What if there was no page from Katramados? Could that have been Susan and I if the other couple left first? It made me ill pondering the situation. Clearly not our time, or my time, but the sheer horror of it all, and my charter boat Captain pulling her out of the water onto the very boat we would board in the morning and pile my equipment on to head to the *WESTERN LION* at Hess.

To this day it sends shivers down my spine when I think about the incident. They caught the guy, and after an investigation and trial sent him to prison for murder. St Croix took Sandy Point off their tourist maps for several years following the tragedy.

It could have all ended for me and Susan that day. We nearly met with our demise. Had we been on the receiving end of the deadly assault there would have been no adventures, no Leeward Marine, and six orphans in Hamilton, Massachusetts in late 1990. The Sandy Point incident was a traumatic experience, just too close for comfort.

Susan on workboat day after incident at Sandy Point

We had wandered through the day completely oblivious that upon leaving the beach it would only be a short time later that a man would be shot dead and a woman pulled to safety by my charter boat Captain in the waters off Sandy Point. Did our departure seal their fate? It still haunts me.

The stark realization of the dangers associated with my work, and the fragility of life, made me think twice about planning future getaways and reinforced my fatalistic view of life. When it's your time, it's your time, simple as that. And with that, I step back a year in time and continue with the formation and adventures of Leeward Marine.

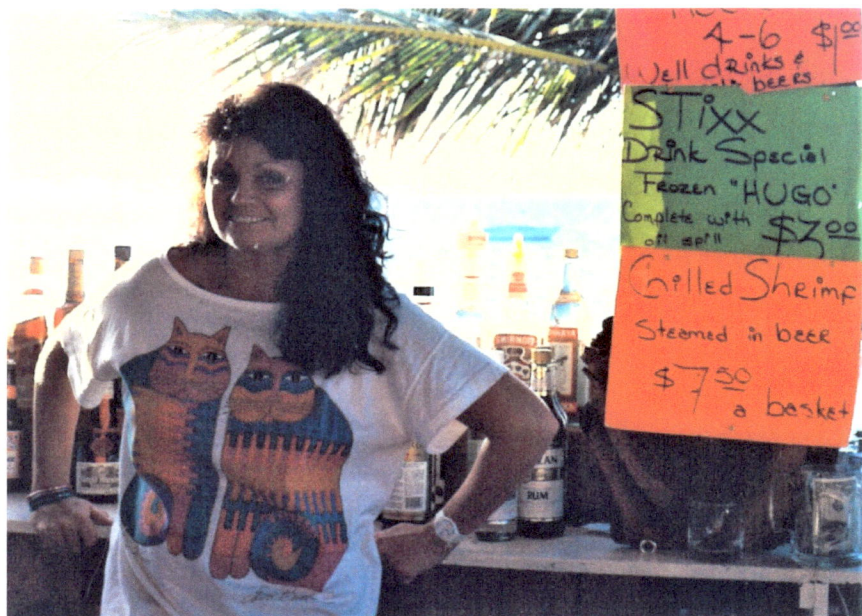

Below is an excerpt from an article about the actual incident

899 On October 29, 1990, Michael Caswell and a female companion were picnicking at Sandy Point, an isolated beach south of Frederiksted. It is charged that the defendant, armed and dressed in camouflage pants, approached them. He allegedly forced the woman to restrain Caswell with handcuffs that he had brought and then took the pair to a bushy area nearby. Firing a bullet into the ground, Roberts purportedly ordered Caswell to sexually assault the woman. After Caswell said that he could not do so, the defendant, it is claimed, raped the woman at gunpoint and afterward shot her in the neck. When Roberts moved away, the woman fled and swam out to sea. She remained in the water until she was picked up by a passing boat some two hours later. The police found Caswell, nude and handcuffed, with one bullet wound to the head and another to his midsection. According to the police, the female victim subsequently identified Roberts as the Sandy Point assailant. After considering evidence presented at the defendant's pre-trial detention hearing, a magistrate found probable cause to believe that Roberts had committed the crimes of murder in the first degree, aggravated rape, first degree assault, kidnapping for rape, employment of a deadly weapon during the commission of a crime of violence, and robbery.

CHAPTER TWO

LEEWARD MARINE - GENESIS

Aquafacs – Last call

Somehow, when there is such a combination of talent, drive, and luck behind a startup, there is a belief that all our collective efforts will be rewarded, as promised, from the beginning. In this case, like so many others, the reward was not what we expected. One of the five principals of Aquafacs, Wilkinson, declared himself sole owner having provided the initial funds for the new venture. Didn't seem to matter about the others who contributed financially and provided the expertise that brought Aquafacs to life.

That member insisted that his family attorney was the most affordable, and best resource to prepare the articles of incorporation and draw up all the paperwork for Aquafacs. He promised that the articles would be properly drawn and clearly define the terms of the partnership and identify all the members of the ownership group. The expectation was that stock would be distributed to complete the process.

There was verbal agreement of the organizational plan, but there was a hitch. Whenever asked for an update on the status of the partnership, the Red Fox, nicknamed by the other principles, always had the same answer; the lawyers are working on it. We had no reason to not believe him, he was, after all, one of the Aquafacs members.

The company continued to grow, and the business development was meteoric, but the excuses continued to pile up. As we executed our amazing rise in the commercial diving field and Maritime Industry, the question, looming large, was where are the shares?

I was out of town and missed the showdown at Pier One when he was called out by my brother, Jay Lee, and George Osgood. They had the scoundrel cornered at our office at Pier One and insisted on their shares of stock. They leaned on him hard. No more excuses!

He refused to deliver. At that point he made it clear he had no intention of honoring his commitment to the group and no stocks would be forthcoming. Finally, he told the truth.

How long did he expect to keep up the charade? At any rate it spelled the end for Aquafacs. It took the Red Fox having no escape to cough up the ugly truth that would destroy the company.

We gathered, without Wilkinson, at Pier One. Jay and George recounted their meeting.

"That son of a bitch! He wasn't getting out of there until we beat the truth out of him!" said Jay.

"I can't believe he thought he'd get away with it. Doesn't make any sense! We were getting more work and industry recognition. Hell, we were even training Navy divers for Christ sake!" George said exasperated.

"That rotten bastard! We've been Wilkied!" Jay blurted out, unwittingly coining a new expression. He said it again, "We've been Wilkied!!," causing us to laugh at the absurdity of the moment. We'd all been 'Wilkied'!

It was a sad moment as the reality began to sink in. Was it all in vain? After the time and effort to propel the company forward against all odds, it seemed criminal. We'd all been conned.

The only thing left was how the partners were going to proceed. Getting a piece of Wilkie was front and center. The lawsuits would fly and Aquafacs would be constrained from continuing until the issues were resolved. They had no interest in continuing anything to do with diving but said they'd support me continuing with a new venture if I chose to, leaving that door open.

As for myself, the turn of events was hard to wrap my head around. There was no Aquafacs before I arrived, or any chance of forming a successful diving company, and yet here we were, a highly successful group, now facing the realization we had a failed organization and a snake in the grass that we all had to deal with.

The meeting ended with talk of lawsuits and the breakup of Aquafacs. At this point, there would be no more ship calls. Wilkie would have to cease and desist after being warned by Attorney Dave Keefe to not take any further action with Aquafacs due to impending legal actions.

Later, mulling it over, I was convinced that Wilkie's ultimate goal was proving his worthiness to inherit his family fortunes and the mansion on the bluffs in Swampscott, worth millions, overlooking the North Atlantic. You can call it sour grapes, but there had to be a reason or some logic behind his actions.

There were a bunch of ships out there, sailing along, fully expecting to see a diving crew when they made port per their normal maintenance schedule. I felt compelled to find a solution to keep that ball rolling and meet our obligations. There had to be a way to meet the commitments.

The Road Forward

It was 1989, and after a five-year evolution of the Aquafacs group the company would be forced to cease and desist at the pinnacle of success.

We had traveled the world and pioneered innovative services for ship operators, developed propeller polishing on large diameter propellers with 3M, and put divers inside the cargo tanks of Supertankers performing 'In-Tank Inspections', the first ever on the planet. The list of accomplishments goes on and on.

Having developed the confidence and trust of our clients, we were the first they called if they had problems below the waterline. The number of inspections and repair requests were continuing to grow. They counted on our creative thinking and common sense to help keep their ships operating and away from the drydock.

Now, everything we worked so hard to develop was all up in the air and at risk of total collapse unless the legacy and good will could be salvaged. Containing the fallout from the breakup of Aquafacs would be a delicate affair if the full story became known.

After a long conversation with my brother Jay, and David Keefe, the big question was whether it would be possible to stitch something together to capture what was left of the business by spinning up a new venture.

"That rat bastard!" said David. "I put a bunch of time and money into this thing. I didn't expect to get effed by Wilkie. Just goes to show, get your paperwork straight before getting into something like this, no matter how good it looks. I just can't understand how he was able to con all of us!"

"Hey, we're all locals and know each other with the exception of Captain Bernie." I said. "Wilkie was one of our tennis and yacht club pals for Christ sake. Not sure how he figured to get away with screwing everybody?"

Other than me, there was no interest from anyone else to participate in a new venture . During our meeting, Jay and David came up with a simple, straight forward plan.

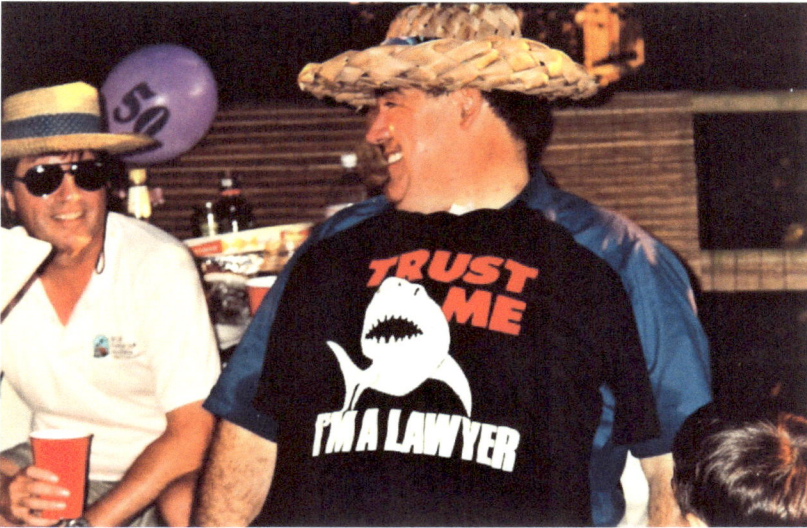

Jay Lee with David Keefe to his right

Step One: David Keefe would sell me his Massachusetts registered corporation, PUFFIN Inc. That would become the new corporate vehicle.

Step two: Register a name change. I came up with a clever marine combo, 'Leeward Marine.' With a re-branding, the venture would stand apart from Aquafacs and have room to breathe.

Step three: Reach out to the clients and inform them of an organizational change. Sell it to them as a simple name change that would seem reasonable as many companies evolve.

Step four: I would make personal calls to the clients as soon as possible, provide them the details, and pitch the new organization.

It was Step four that gave me the biggest challenge. They must be convinced that nothing would really change other than the name. My request would be simple, all future work orders would be requested with the new company name, Leeward Marine. It would be important to move as quickly as possible to preserve the client base.

Other than that, all else would remain the same. Scheduled work and existing programs would continue, and the rates would not increase. The only difference would be the invoices and tee shirts would now say Leeward Marine. . . .

CHAPTER THREE

THE START UP – LEEWARD MARINE

Leeward Calling

I started the process of contacting my clients and delivering notice of the change from Aquafacs to the new Leeward Marine company. When I told each of them we had an organizational change and would now be operating as Leeward Marine, there were few questions other than validating the schedules and confirming that we would continue to meet our commitments. I said this would be a simple name change with no change of diving personnel and pricing. Also, our excellent service would continue uninterrupted.

It was a huge relief getting no push back. It shouldn't have been surprising having always maintained a good personal relationship with my clients. Many had become friends over the years. Eventually, if the details of the blow out at Aquafacs came to light, I would be able to deflect from the ugly truth and highlight the actions and performance of the new Leeward Marine. But for now, I was simply prepared to take the reins and drive forward as planned.

Author

VLCC WESTERN LION -- St. Croix

It was in late August 1989, when the newly formed Leeward Marine would have its first official job on the Maritime Overseas, *WESTERN LION*. I reached out to my old friend Joe March and explained my situation and leveled with him on the issues that brought about the new company formation. I asked him to keep it confidential and for his help to continue the work we had ongoing with Maritime Overseas.

Joe had become a great friend along the way since our work together in the Canary Islands in 1984. We had met many times in St Croix and shared evenings at the Domino Club enjoying the mountaintop Tiki Bar with the gentle breezes, great drinks, and Cynthia's smoked Kingfish. Joe agreed to inform Keith Duncan, VP Maritime Overseas, about the re-org at Aquafacs and Leeward Marine now continuing the work with me leading the new venture.

Duncan told Joe that he had no problem with the organizational change and was happy to hear I was steering the ship, probably pun intended. Joe had gotten back to me and confirmed the schedule to meet up with the *WESTERN LION* in late August after she got done offloading two million barrels of crude in St Lucia per the usual lightering process. Supertankers heading into the Hess Refinery in St Croix were constrained by the water depth and had to reduce their draft to no more than fifty-five feet to enter. That meant offloading crude oil in St Lucia until the tanker draft met the fifty-five-foot limit before departing for St Croix. When they arrived in St Lucia with six million barrels of crude oil they were drafted at seventy-five feet +/-.

Joe said he'd firm up the schedule once she was inbound to St Lucia. That was great news! We were almost off and running. Next was the call to Amerada Hess to re-gain access and favor to work as Leeward Marine at the HOVIC terminal in St Croix. That would have to come directly from the Hess Marine Group and Joe Gehegan. I reached out to Dick O'Boyle, the agent that represented us previously, and let him know about the organizational issues and Leeward Marine picking up the mantle to continue the programs.

Although surprised to hear it, Dick O'Boyle was all about continuing as usual and preserving his commissions for work he referred. I assured him Leeward Marine would continue to honor the deal.

O'Boyle cleared the way with Gehegan at Hess. He told O'Boyle to have me get ahold of John Fredricks at HOVIC and let him know we were coming and had his approval. Oh boy, here we go again with Fredricks. Over the years, he had been unfriendly and difficult to work with. Thankfully, Fredricks seemed a little less hostile when I called him about Leeward Marine. Not sure why, but it was a great thing we were getting back into HOVIC without a hassle. He probably got a call from Gehegan. This was the key to success for the new start up and a huge step forward.

HESS OWNED QUARTER MILE LONG SUPERTANKER AT HOVIC TERMINAL - ST CROIX

Joe March called and said the *WESTERN LION* was three days out of St Lucia. That gave us one week until she'd make St Croix. Plenty of time for planning and getting some of the old crew back onboard to get things rolling again. They were just as happy as I was to be re-starting. The uncertainty of their employment following the Aquafacs disaster weighed heavily, causing them all to consider updating their resumes. It was still touch and go as the new startup was a shoestring venture with little capital. I was able to piece together the equipment we needed and tweaked my logistics strategy and obtained credit to keep the ball rolling.

The team heading for St Croix would include myself and three others. Arne Backlund, Steve Humphries, and Kai Holleson were the core of the new dive team. Any one of the three were well trained and qualified to lead a crew back to St Croix on behalf of Leeward Marine as we developed.

We flew to St Croix the day before the ship arrived and got our access re-established at the HOVIC (Hess Oil Virgin Islands Corporation) Marine Terminal.

When Aquafacs dissolved, equipment had been abandoned in St Croix. We planned to inventory and use the equipment left behind at the Marine Terminal. In storage, we should find a hydraulic power pack and hoses for the propeller polishing machine along with diving hoses and accessories. The only items we assumed would be missing in the St Croix cache we brought with us, diving helmets, diver radio comms, cameras, and a propeller polishing tool head that I salvaged from Pier One before Aquafacs folded.

After we cleared security and made our way into the HOVIC terminal we found the equipment. It was all there, just as we'd left it the last time on the island. The *WESTERN LION* would be at the breakwater around eight AM the next day, August 30th, and we'd be ready.

Joe March would not be there for our first trip. It was disappointing, but we had attended to this ship several times over the past few years, so it was a routine ship call. We'd have Dennis, our boat Captain, meet us with the workboat at the sulfur dock.

Massive amounts of sulfur were produced as a byproduct of refining crude oil and was loaded for export at a special dock located at the far end of the inlet to the refinery. Dennis planned to be there around ten o'clock, allowing time for the giant tugboats to bring the WESTERN LION through the breakwater and tie her up at Dock One. The crew would load out the gear while I boarded the ship after she cleared US Customs.

When I was finally able to board, the Italian Captain and Chief Engineer recognized me from one of our previous visits. I mentioned we would be ready within the hour and planned a propeller polishing and inspection of the rudder and stern quarter per our usual plan. They were happy to see us and agreed to tag out the engine room with notification that divers were in the water working on the propeller. On a twelve hundred foot long, three hundred foot wide Supertanker, the stern quarter was a huge area to inspect and contained many things they wanted looked at. All was good.

The boat was ready and equipment online when I made it back to the sulfur dock. We moved a half a mile to the stern of the WESTERN LION and tied off to the starboard side of the enormous rudder. That was the side closest to the dock and provided the most shade from the glaring Caribbean sun.

We were required to notify the HOVIC Port Captain anytime we put a man in the water, and also when we completed the work and had the man back on deck. So once again it was showtime, this time, Leeward Marine.

"Port Captain. Port Captain. Leeward Marine." I called out on the radio.

"Go Leeward." Said the Port Captain. Music to my ears.

"We're tied alongside the rudder on the starboard side of the *WESTERN LION* ready to put a man in the water." I replied.

"You're cleared to proceed Leeward. Please call back when you're finished. Port Captain out."

Boy did that feel great, back at HOVIC, like riding a bike, you never forget! Time to get to work.

We finished up seven hours later and after notifying the Port Captain, returned to the sulfur dock where the crew began to unload the equipment. It was a routine job and no complications along the way. I went back to sign off with the Italian Captain and Chief Engineer. Just another perfect day in Paradise, and a great day for Leeward Marine. 'The Start Up !.' . .

Dennis took off in the workboat back to Frederiksted and we went on our way back to the Caravelle Hotel. It was time to celebrate and take the crew out for dinner. They all wanted to go back to the Chart House for Rasta Ribs, the rib bones they re-cycled from all their prime rib dinners, sauced up and served St Croix style, they were incredible. After a couple of rounds of drinks to celebrate the new Leeward Marine, off to the hotel we went. The Phoenix was now rising!

We flew back to Boston the next day. Mission accomplished!

CHAPTER FOUR

HURRICANE HUGO – SEPTEMBER 17, 1989

St Croix

A couple of weeks following our first job as Leeward Marine, on the *WESTERN LION*, Hurricane Hugo devastated the island of St Croix. The damage was horrific with many houses blown away leaving nothing but slab foundations where they once sat. Gigantic Mahogany trees were twisted into knots along the road leading into the rain forest on the west end. The two hundred and ten mile an hour winds completely wiped out all the vegetation, palm trees lost their fronds and every blade of grass, gone, from the tornadoes and wild winds of Hugo.

We arrived three weeks following the storm to meet an incoming ship that despite the wreckage, was scheduled to offload at HOVIC following a long return voyage from Valdez, Alaska. With the exception of generators, almost all power was out to the island due to downed power lines. Only a few hotels were open powered by generators with limited power for the people who had to be there other than the residents.

The waterfront in Christiansted was a total disaster zone. The Caravelle Hotel where we usually stayed, had a large sailboat crash through their seawall and now lay in their swimming pool. It would be months, maybe years, until the island of St Croix would recover.

HOVIC had massive backup generators and was still capable of discharging a Supertanker at Dock 1 and unload its typical four million barrels of crude oil. Not surprising, it was the *SEAL ISLAND*, one of the Hess fleet that was inbound. The really critical issue was whether the Hess refinery on St. Croix was able to continue operating. At the time, it was considered the largest refinery in the Western Hemisphere. They had to continue production as soon as possible after the storm to keep from upsetting the supply of petroleum products to the mainland, especially the Northeast US. Without the Hess St. Croix refinery online, gas and heating oil prices could spike and severely impact the economy and pricing in the marketplace.

When we arrived at the HOVIC Terminal, we saw the five-story administration building near the entrance. It had been stripped clean of all the exterior walls and roof with only red iron columns and poured floor slabs remaining. The Marine Terminal Building was destroyed but still standing. The Administration and Security Offices were in makeshift quarters at one of the refinery out buildings that survived the storm. There was a temporary entrance gate where we were waved through and directed to the new security office.

HOVIC Marine Terminal Destroyed by Hurricane Hugo

Along the way to the Security Office someone said, "Holy shit! Look at those storage tanks. They're completely collapsed. What happened to the oil ? Don't see any spills anywhere."

LARGE STORAGE TANKS DESTROYED AT HOVIC BY HUGO

There was no visible sign of any spillage of crude oil. Seems impossible, but did the storm suck up all the oil and carry it off with those 200 mile per hour winds? No oil in the water or at the docks, was it a miracle, or did they have some sort of a catastrophic environmental plan should such a monster storm materialize? Apparently not. Nobody at the Marine Terminal knew where it went!

Housing for the crew was now a big deal with virtually the whole island powerless. The Hess terminal had assembled a housing trailer park with simple accommodations. It had power, running water, toilets, and showers, what else could we need ? Our new home for a few days. We were grateful to be invited to stay there. We dubbed it 'The Hess Hilton.' .

28

The Seal Island was due for inspections and propeller work per her normal schedule. Due to the long voyages between St. Croix and Valdez they wanted to keep the maintenance going. Incredibly, we were able to complete our scheduled work on the ship without any difficulty with the only difference being the stark accommodations.

SEAL ISLAND AT HOVIC TERMINAL ST CROIX

Amazingly, we were still able to get a rental car when we arrived and did a tour of the island to see the extent of the damage. Power poles were down everywhere we looked, and the island was trashed. The north side, on the way to Cane Bay, had giant mahogany trees twisted like pretzels in freaky looking tangles. Must have been tornados that did that. The road through the rainforest was impassible. We hoped the Domino Club and the beer drinking pigs made it. It was depressing seeing the level of devastation close up.

In Christiansted, the Caravelle Hotel was closed and severely damaged. It would be a challenge to get that large sailboat that crashed inside the pool removed. The waterfront with all the shops and the Charthouse Restaurant were smashed to pieces. No Rasta Ribs for some time to come. The boardwalk that surrounded the waterfront was gone with only a few pilings and planking still visible.

Christiansted Waterfront with wreckage from HUGO

As we were leaving, we saw signs of heavy equipment being delivered and dozens of line trucks parked on the way into town. Louisiana and Texas linemen and construction workers would be arriving and overtaking the island to restore power and critical infrastructure and water supply. With any luck they might be able to get some of the hotels back in service. They'd need that to support the crowd of utility workers surely heading their way.

We made our way to the airport and headed back without incident. What a mess. There was no way of telling when we would be back due to the massive undertaking to restore the island. The supertankers would continue their supplying of crude oil so there was little doubt we'd be back; the only question was when?

St Croix - The Road to Recovery

It would be a couple of months after Hugo when we started getting back into a regular routine of ship calls at the Hess Marine Terminal in St Croix. The Lineman and Utility crews were hard at it rewiring the power lines. General Contractors were rebuilding houses and restoring the buildings that had somehow survived the complete destruction we saw around the island in the residential neighborhoods.

Hess continued to maintain the temporary housing and allowed us to use their accommodations whether we were on island for them or another client delivering crude oil to the refinery. There was a nearly frantic effort to get the hotels and other 'Tourist' attractions up and functional. We would move out of the 'Hess Hilton' lodging and patronize the local hotels as they became available.

Achieving a level of restoration that was acceptable to tourists would be a huge challenge and had a long way to go. In the meantime, leave it to entrepreneurial exploitation to develop creative ways to entertain the hundreds of workers stranded on St Croix.

In Christiansted, the town that offered the largest draw for tourists over the years, the waterfront hotels and restaurants would take a long time to be restored and made functional. A block or so up from the water there were former popular eating and drinking establishments that were more easily brought back to a useable condition.

One of those buildings was converted from fine dining to an enormous 'strip bar' large enough to handle the huge crowd of rough and tumble construction workers and linemen, mostly from Texas and Louisiana. Needless to say, the new 'Caribbean Gentlemen's Club' was crowded seven days a week with the help being rotated in from as far away as Atlanta.

There was a certain gravitational pull that drew all off island workers to that place and we were no exception. After working on a Supertanker at Hess during the day we'd hit the food truck in downtown Christiansted and then drift over to the Club for a couple of cold beers and a little social activity. It is here that my story turns an improbable event from twelve years earlier into something with odds that likely exceed even the largest Powerball Lotteries.

Before leaving for Commercial Diving School in 1978 I attended a Birthday Party for one of the Smith sisters in Old Town Marblehead. At the party, my long-time friend Robert 'Bo' Johnson and I had managed to tie one on and debate our upcoming careers. He was on his way to a career in the Merchant Marines and I was leaving for California to pursue a career in Commercial Diving.

As we finished up the evening we had a toast to celebrate our sure to be successful endeavors. We both had large Brandy snifters and clanked them together to execute the toast when to my horror the large crystal glass snifter slipped from my chest high grip and fell to the hardwood floor four feet below. I cringed expecting the glass to explode and spray the room with Brandy and shards of glass, when to both of our shock the glass landed solidly flat on its base without breaking or spilling even a drop of my Brandy! We both stared at the glass before breaking out laughing and proclaiming it must be a sign! Then off we went.

Maybe there is some cosmic connection that drives us forward and somehow we are destined to follow paths that will bring us back together some day. And so it was, as I looked across the bar at the new 'Gentleman's Club' I saw a familiar looking guy leaning against the bar wearing a ballcap and looking three sheets to the wind. Holy shit! It was Bo Johnson!

Back to what are the odds. Two men head out to start careers on the Ocean Seas. They travel the world for twelve years, one as a Merchant Marine Officer, the other a Commercial Diver, never seeing each other or having any communications. Twelve years later they are brought together ten feet apart in the bowels of the Caribbean at a temporary Strip Bar. What are the chances? The odds have to be astronomical, how many millions to one?

After being certain it was Bo I walked around the bar and bumped into him. He turned around. "Hey. Remember me?" I asked.

He was having difficulty focusing but finally he recognized me. "Chris Lee! Holy Shit! Is that really you?"

"Sure is! Been a while since I dropped that Brandy snifter. It's been twelve years. How've ya been? Maybe a better question is what the hell are you doing here?" I said laughing at the total absurdity of the moment and the realization of how unlikely an event to meet at this time at this place one hundred and forty-four months after our fateful toast.

"I'm working on a ship docked over at the Hess Marine Terminal. What the hell are you doing here?" He asked.

"Waiting for you!" I joked. "Did you see a big son of a bitch tanker over there? That's what I'm doing here. We travel all over the planet chasing Supertankers and ships around."

"No shit! Wow." He said. "That's unbelievable!" I could tell he was starting to come around to his senses.

We spent a few minutes catching up, but we had to get going. I told him we'd be over there in the morning and I'd stop by. If he heard any radio chatter with Leeward Marine it was us working.

His ship was stationed there for a few weeks. Our job was the usual in and out and we would only have that one get together during our trip. After that I never saw him again until mid-December 2019 in Fort Myers, Florida nearly thirty years later when we had more time for a meal and a couple of beers. Plenty of time to marvel about the coincidence of our meeting in St Croix after all those years, or was it something destined to be? Was our fate sealed as soon as my Brandy snifter hit the hardwood floor at the Smith sisters party in Marblehead?

Bo and I stay in communication. He now lives and works in Marblehead during the summer and returns to Fort Myers for the winters.

Author and longtime friend Bo Johnson - Ft Myers- Dec 2019

CHAPTER FIVE

SEALAND ATLANTIC CLASS

SeaLand, the largest of Leeward Marine clients, operated fifty-five containerships including twelve nine hundred fifty-foot long Panamax ships. They were a special fleet of ships designed as the longest and largest capable of passing through the locks of the Panama Canal. As such, their official design class was called 'Panamax.'

SeaLand called these their 'Atlantic Class' as all twelve had been operating the transatlantic routes to Europe, feeding the insatiable desire for goods from America along with the return trips full of highly valued imports that were in constant demand.

Being they were the largest containerships capable of navigating the Panama Canal from the Atlantic to the Pacific, they would also be the ready reserve fleet for the expanding trans Asia trade. With their enormous capacity, they gave SeaLand a unique capability in both the Atlantic and Pacific.

We had all twelve of the Atlantic Class in our Sealand maintenance program. Leeward Marine continued providing propeller polishing every six months and underwater inspections and repairs as needed. They were all qualified to use the *UWILD* program (Underwater Inspection In Lieu of Drydocking), that allowed them to stay in service for up to two years between drydockings.

The underbody of the ships had been previously marked and painted during their drydocking cycle for underwater inspection. The frame numbers and all other required landmarks were painted on raised welds with highly visible bright white paint. It was great having enough markings to keep from getting lost down there while inspecting and documenting the condition.

950-Foot-long SEALAND ATLANTIC CLASS ship - Inbound to PORT ELIZABETH, NJ

Their enrollment in the *UWILD* program not only gave them a competitive advantage but created maintenance issues that kept us busy during the long interval between being hauled and serviced.

The massive ships plied the North Atlantic for their two-year cycle and suffered significantly more operating challenges. Some of those were structural in nature. Their rudders were prone to develop horizontal cracks below the pintle pin. That's the pin that allows the rudder to turn and holds it in place. The punishing stresses of the North Atlantic Ocean on their rudders caused the cracking. It also caused cracking of the protective fairing plating at the leading edges of the rudders. Those plates were to allow the ocean to pass smoothly over the rudders surfaces as the ships made way up to twenty-five knots.

The plates, should they break free from the leading edge of a rudder, would greatly increase the pressure and stress, raising the risk of a catastrophic rudder failure. That could endanger the ship or at the very least, cause an incredibly long tow job from the middle of the Atlantic.

Of the twelve ships we were monitoring, three had sustained enough damage to their rudders to warrant repair, Sea-Land Integrity, Sea-Land Performance and Sea-Land Atlantic.

Welding repair of Rudder - Freak Wind Incident, Port Elizabeth

The *SEA-LAND INTEGRITY* was inbound to Boston from Northern Europe and due to arrive on November 13, 1989. We planned to repair the rudder after discovering cracking on the plating during her the last trip. The damage was photographed and documented in a report to the Marine Engineers at SeaLand. They were provided our scope of work for repair and approved the plan.

All the cracking and impacted area was on the Starboard side of the rudder. After consulting with the Engineers, they theorized the eastbound trip to Europe, must be causing substantially more stress due to the heavy loading onboard and the prevailing currents and conditions of the North Atlantic crossing.

For planning purposes, we were tracking the schedule when the ship would be back. Everything would be ready for prepping and welding the cracks as soon as the ship arrived back in Boston to discharge containers. There was a logistics problem, however; the time to discharge cargo in Boston was usually no more than six hours before heading outbound for Port Elizabeth in New Jersey to complete its journey. That would not be long enough to complete the work.

Port Elizabeth was the location of the main terminal for SeaLand for the Northeast. It was located on the east side of the New Jersey

Turnpike, directly across the highway from Newark Airport, a location that provided excellent access over the years. It was there that they would offload the remaining cargo and load the outbound containers for the next voyage to Europe.

SEALAND MARINE TERMINAL, MARINE ENGINEERING HQ, PORT ELIZABETH NJ

The Port Elizabeth cargo operation would require a longer ship call to complete. For us it added up to a full two-day window of opportunity. We figured it could take both stops to get the work done to secure the plating without rushing the welding.

When the ship arrived in Boston we had underwater burning and welding gear at the ready and wasted no time getting down to business. I checked in with the Captain and Chief Engineer while the crew rigged up all the welding and diving equipment.

They docked the ship at the container terminal in South Boston with the starboard side to the dock per our request. Our crew was highly trained and experienced to handle the welding and repair which allowed me to support and supervise the service.

Arne Backlund and Kai Holleson would be the primary dive team with Steve Humphries being the third man if needed. Paul Mercaldi rounded out the crew as the primary diving tender for the project, maintaining the air compressor, welding and hydraulic machines, a lot to handle.

Dive team members: Kai Holleson, Paul Mercaldi, Arne Backlund, Left to Right

During the brief stay in Boston we made good progress in preparing the steel and were able to start welding the extensive cracks on the starboard side of the rudder. Predictably, the ship didn't stay long, and wrapped up its cargo operations in the usual six-hour timeframe. The Harbor Pilot and tugboats showed up to take her out. That was it for us until catching up with the ship a couple days later in Port Elizabeth.

We packed up and hit the road for New Jersey to continue the work on November 16, 1989. The ship was at the dock when we arrived early in the morning to get started. Unfortunately, due to the tide that ripped down the Hudson they arrived during an outgoing tide forcing them to tie up port side to the dock. Our work would be on the backside of the rudder from the dock and could cause complications. For safety we decided to hang a man basket on the starboard side that could be set up for our guy to work out of underwater and be able to better control the tools, hoses and welding cables needed to complete our repair.

After checking in with the Captain and Chief Engineer, again we went to work. During the setup of the welding equipment, it was discovered that we left the box of specially coated welding rods back at the shop. The coating was essential to waterproof the rods for underwater use. This was a *showstopper.*

Fortunately, we had worked so many times in the New York area that I had a vendor nearby that carried the welding rods and Broco rods for burning steel underwater. Irritating as it was, it would only cost me a two-hour Gofer round trip to get a new box of rods. The crew had plenty to do, I would standby until everything was set up, the man basket in place and first man in the water before leaving for the fool's errand an hour away.

Traffic was always a nightmare around Newark and this day was no different. The good news was they had plenty of twenty eighteen coated rods once I got to the supply house. I bought several boxes and left for the return trip to Port Elizabeth. Wouldn't cause much of a delay considering what we had left to do and having a much longer working window.

When I got back to the dock I saw the crew mulling around and wondered why they weren't hard at it. I jumped out of the car and said, "What the hell's going on here?"

Paul Mercaldi spoke up, "You're not going to believe it, but while you were off getting the welding rods we had a freak wind that blew the ship right off the dock! All the stern lines parted. Sounded like gunfire as the ship began to swing off the dock and straight out to the channel in a matter of seconds. Kai was in the man basket on the other side of the rudder and went for the ride."

"Bullshit !" I said.

"Seriously! I managed to save the comm box. I could hear Kai screaming 'What the fuck is going on . . .?' As the comm box came flying by like a football, I caught it and gave it a good yank breaking the wires off." Paul explained, proud of himself for having made the catch. "We had a wrap on the air manifold, so the hose pulled away from the connector to the umbilical and went over the side with Kai on the end of it somewhere. I thought we killed him. "

Paul continued, "Kai bailed out and we saw him safely floating on the surface about a thousand feet straight out in the channel.

Kai Holleson following incident on SEALAND INTEGRITY

We lucked out as there was a small boat nearby that we were able to hail. They plucked him out of the channel and dropped him back here."

"Where the hell is he now?" I asked.

"He went over to the men's room at the terminal. Had to change his suit." Paul said with a chuckle.

I was taking everything in when I noticed our hydraulic machine was not where it had been when I left. I asked, "Where's the hydraulic power pack.?"

Nobody spoke, they all just turned and looked over at the channel.

"No Effing way ! You're telling me it's on the bottom somewhere ?!" I said in disbelief. "So, the hydraulic power pack was ripped off the dock and into the bay, running ? Jezzus !"

Looking around I saw normal looking cargo operations. It was surreal. Now what? Salvage?

The crew was waiting for my return to get direction on how to continue. I needed to speak with the SeaLand Port Engineer and Chief Engineer, but with a few minutes of direction the crew could prepare to start a salvage operation. I asked Arne Backlund to use our standby Scuba gear to drop to the bottom of the seawall and hopefully find the end of the air umbilical with a Superlight attached and the hydraulic machine close to the dock. The man basket was still attached to the starboard side of the rudder and made the nearly half mile trip out to the middle of the channel and back.

Luck counts. Arne found the hydraulic machine and hoses right away. The crew dropped him a line and hauled it up. It was a couple of hundred pounds but not that hard to lift with a bunch of guys on the lift line. He didn't see the air umbilical anywhere. I asked him to swim over and check in the basket. Eureka, the Superlight remained in the basket after Kai bailed out. It made the trip out and back and was safely in the basket. Arne swam back to the edge of the dock with the air hose. He then went back to the basket and hand signaled the crew to start hauling in the hose while he guided the expensive diving helmet back to the seawall. It had survived in fine shape. No damage just soaking wet, it's usual condition anyway. At least we could get that back online within minutes and just maybe, we would be able to get back to work sooner than I expected.

I left to track down the Port Engineer, Bill Davies, at the terminal building. He was in his office.

"That was quite a hell ride your guy had out there! We were damn lucky nobody got hurt when that ship blew off the dock. Our guys are all OK and your guy must be one tough son of a bitch. Handled himself well and your crew did a great job getting him picked up before he landed in Bayonne." Said Bill.

"I know. What a freak thing that was. The only worry Kai had was how he'd be able to call for a ride from Bayonne with no coins for a payphone. Not to mention wandering around in a dive suit dripping wet." I replied.

Bill said, "That crazy wind blast overpowered our tension winches. When that happened, the strain popped all the stern lines and the ship swung out with the stern a thousand feet out in the channel within a minute or so with your guy hanging on the rudder. Never seen that before ! One other thing, we just heard the same storm collapsed an elementary school fifty miles north of here and killed a bunch of kids. They're still working at the scene now. So, where does that leave us.?" He asked, concerned about getting our repair completed.

"Well, we had some good luck salvaging our gear and the crew tells me they'll be back online shortly. Hopefully, we can pick up where we left off and put in a little overtime to get things done." I said.

"Overtime?" He chuckled, knowing there was no overtime, only whatever it takes to get the job done. Compensation was never the issue.

Bill asked if there was anything they could do for us. There was something he could help us with. They had a huge maintenance shop for all the trucks and equipment at the terminal. I asked if they could help us flush out the hydraulic powerpack and see if we could get it running again. We just might need it before we wrapped things up. He said they'd be happy to help.

Time to light it up out there again on the rudder repair. Arne Backlund took over the welding duties. He strung the welding leads over to the man basket and after loading up a bunch of the new welding rods, he was ready to go. "Make it hot." He said to Paul who was manning the single pole knife switch used to energize the current for welding. Hearing that, we just might come out of this OK, despite the unbelievable calamity.

Kai was tasked with getting the machine running, figuring he could use a break. Their mechanics would handle the flushing and try to bring the machine back to life. Two hours later he returned and said they'd got it running. Amazing. The mechanics delivered it back to us with a forklift at the stern of the *SEALAND INTEGRITY*.

We worked well into the evening and hit a local Diner on the way to the hotel. Our gang would have to stay overnight to complete the welding. It would take another long shift. A six AM wakeup call would start the trek down to the Port.

The job went well on day two and we completed the scope of work by early afternoon despite the setbacks. Plenty of time to beat the traffic across the George Washington Bridge and back to Boston. We might make it back by dinnertime.

STITCH PLATES WELDED OVER CRACK ON RUDDER – Photo by Author

I couldn't help thinking about what Bill Davies said. He described the incident for Sealand as an 'Act of God' down at the dock. The elementary school kids, innocent victims of the freak windstorm, was that an 'Act of God'?

Not sure the families of the children would see it that way. Story can be found in the NY Times archives from the front page on November 17, 1989 authenticating the tragic event.

Lost at Sea - Propeller Blade – Atlantic Class

Not long after the incident on the *SEALAND INTEGRITY*, we got an emergency call from Bill Davies. Another ship in the Atlantic Class, *NEDLLOYD HOLLAND*, had developed a major vibration in the stern and had to drastically reduce speed in order to mitigate the impact as she made her way across the North Atlantic from Europe to Boston. When I spoke to Bill they were three days out.

The cause of the vibration was a mystery. The only moving parts back there were the propeller and the rudder. Either one could be the culprit and the issue for us was to determine which. The one thing we were confident in was with the large amount of vibration the ship would have to be drydocked to repair whichever of the two choices we found to be the cause.

They planned to offload all the container cargo in Boston and limp their way to a drydock once they determined what needed to be fixed. I planned to meet the Port Engineer and do the inspection as soon as the ship arrived.

950 Foot ATLANTIC CLASS SHIP - NEDLLOYD HOLLAND at South Boston Terminal

We got the call that the ship would arrive at the Port of Boston and be alongside at the South Boston Terminal around mid-afternoon. Hearing that, I suggested to the Port Engineer we meet for lunch first and then head over to the ship when it was docked.

The Sealand Port Engineer was Ed Washburn Jr., a Kings Point Alumnus and really young guy for a Port Engineer. His father was a

Chief Engineer on one of the Sealand ships that operated the southern routes that used San Juan as their hub.

We met at the famous seafood restaurant, Pier Four, on the waterfront just west of the South Boston container terminal. After a great lunch on the deck we left to meet the ship. Our feeling was the degree of vibration was more than likely from the propeller but until we got a look it was only a best guess.

When we arrived at the terminal the *NEDLLOYD HOLLAND* was already at the dock and tied up. She arrived earlier than projected and we were now late getting there. The Chief Engineer was pissed and had called New York to complain. Being pre-cellphone days, there was no way to reach us to let us know the ship had arrived. Ed Washburn would take the heat for our delay.

While Ed was dealing with the Chief Engineer, Paul Mercaldi set up our gear in record time and I dressed in and prepped my stills camera. Time to make the jump.

Paul handed me my Superlight. After clamping the helmet on and a comms check I stepped off the dock and made the ten-foot drop to the water. Ed Washburn and the Chief Engineer were both topside listening in as I made my way to the propeller.

Having made the trip so many times down to the propellers, I stop only when I see it or bump into it. There is no way to miss a five bladed twenty-six-foot diameter propeller between the rudder and the stern tube of the ship. On this trip I was still working on the camera settings and figured there was enough time before bumping into the propeller. When it felt like I'd been gliding along much longer than usual, looking around I found myself in open water without a propeller or ship in sight.

"Paul, take up my slack." I asked without saying I had no idea where I was. As he pulled in my slack the ship and propeller appeared ghostly in front of me in the dirty water. "All stop. Found the problem. There's a blade missing! It broke off at the hub." My glide carried me through the open space it made above the shaft. The missing blade that broke off came to a stop at the twelve o'clock position. I simply passed through the opening created by the missing blade.

"Missing blade?" asked Ed Washburn. "Can you tell if it looks like it hit something?"

"It's pretty clear that it broke off after cracking and going through a series of continued cracking. There are markings like tree rings showing the layers of fracturing that finally gave way throwing the blade. I'm taking photos of the cross sections. It's dramatic in appearance." I said.

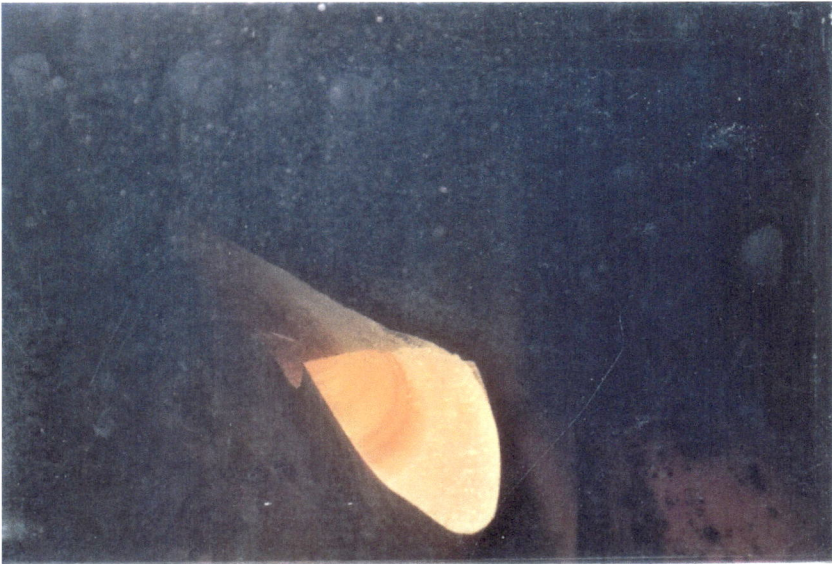

Picture of cross section of missing propeller blade with discolored ring like markings

"Holy shit! I've gotta run and give John K a call. He needs to get a drydock lined up and a replacement propeller sent to the shipyard.

That's a big deal with a twenty-six-foot diameter prop." Said Ed Washburn.

"Roger that. I'll take a few more pics and wrap it up down here. Paul, we need to wrap up in a hurry and find a one-hour photo place here in South Boston. I'll get a pic of the manufacturers stamp. Might help them sort out a replacement. Standby."

We'd go on to develop the film in South Boston and hand off two sets of photos to Ed Washburn for their use. John Katramados lined up the drydock to change out the propeller and had a spare at the warehouse in New Jersey. They would load it onto the *NEDLLOYD HOLLAND* at the terminal as she passed by on her way to drydock.

Ed Washburn would be a busy guy taking the ship through drydock. John Katramados assigned Ed to handle the propeller changeout and getting the ship back in service as soon as possible.

In the end, I'm sure our sins of being late to arrive when the ship ended up at the dock in South Boston faded quickly. We would go on to see the ship again when she returned to her normal rotation to clean and polish the new propeller her next time in Boston following the propeller changeout. Another great opportunity realized on the Atlantic Class and they would continue . . .

CHAPTER SIX

OPERATION DESERT STORM

Military Sealift Command (MSC)

I feel there is a need to provide a brief historical account of the times leading up to this Leeward Marine Story. It was nearly thirty years ago. It may be a bit boring and with a slight bias, but hopefully this will allow the reader to understand how and why we ended up in Portland, Maine for this project, along with other Military Sealift vessels in New York/New Jersey.

The story begins more than forty years ago under President Carter's administration. As old as it makes me feel, anyone in his early forties would have been no more than toddlers at the time. Without a strong interest in history the reader may find this whole era perplexing. With that said, I offer my recollection of the times with supporting dates and events to help follow along.

Iraq was a major oil producer and became an important US ally against Iran following the incident at the US Embassy in Tehran when Iran raided our Embassy in late 1979. They held hostage the US Embassy personnel for over four hundred days during the last period of the Carter administration. We need a little deeper dive, pun intended, into the weeds to provide more details and an important historical understanding of how it was that we got to Portland, Maine ten years later. This is written from my perspective having lived the experience and is supported by accurate dates and statements of fact..

Iran was in the midst of a revolution to oust the Shah, Mohammad Reza Shah Pahlavi, who was installed and supported by the US in

August 1953. Coincidently, my birth year, I was three months old. The Shah was forced to flee Iran in January 1979 for many reasons but mostly for his iron fisted rule, brutality, and no love lost for the US having been the ones backing him since 1953.

Left behind was a governing council and a guy, Shapour Bakhtiar to hold things together as they awaited the return of Ayatollah Ruhollah Khomeini, an extreme Muslim cleric. Khomeini returned to Iran in February 1979 after 14 years in political exile.

In November 1979, the US Embassy was raided by a group claiming to be college students and followers of Ayatollah Khomeini. They were successful taking control of the embassy and holding hostage fifty-two American diplomats. They would remain captive for four hundred and forty-four days until finally being released following behind the scenes negotiations by the Carter administration. They were released on January 20th, 1981, the same day Ronald Reagan was inaugurated as the 40th President of the United States. A remarkable coincidence!?

With the incoming Reagan administration left to sort out how this could have happened, and how to administer justice for the fifty-two hostages and for those lost on a failed rescue attempt under Carter, a plan began to emerge. The US would form an alliance with Iraq to include military assistance and support for a war between Iraq and Iran. It began with Iraq invading Iran in September of 1980 over a disputed waterway along the Iraq Iran boarder at the upper reaches of the Persian Gulf. Off and on the war lasted until August 1988 in the closing months of the Reagan Presidency.

Saddam Hussein having established a brutal regime in Iraq, was more than ready to join this alliance and fight as a surrogate for US interests. There is evidence that envoys, including Donald Rumsfeld from the US spent time in Baghdad working out the arrangements. How many remember hearing about the Iran Contra scandal that occurred during this period under Reagan? Well, the story goes on and on until Iraq and Iran fought the war to a standstill, ending it with a shaky UN negotiated cease fire agreement on August 20th, 1988.

George HW Bush, VP for Ronald Reagan, was elected shortly after the war ended in 1988 and became the 41st President of the United States after Reagan left office in January 1989. In less than a couple of years into his Presidency, war broke out again in the region.

Lacking good access to the Persian Gulf and with only a tiny sliver of waterfront available, Iraq was otherwise land locked. Turkey, Syria, Jordan, and Saudi Arabia formed its northern, western, and southern boundary with its enemy Iran forming their eastern boundary and the eastern shore of the Persian Gulf across the waterway. Saddam Hussein needed more water access to the Persian Gulf to support his oil exports and maritime trade to the world.

And so, it was, that on August 2nd, 1990 Saddam Hussein, President of Iraq, invaded the neighboring country of Kuwait. He claimed to have received signals from the US that it would not interfere. Hussein moved on Kuwait and completed his invasion in two days.

The Bush Administration denied it ever gave any signal to Saddam Hussein and immediately called for them to withdraw. Saddam Hussein refused, and a huge debate raged in the US while Bush set in motion an action plan.

President George HW Bush, with a strong push from the Saudis to intervene, went about forming a coalition of nations to unite and force Hussein out of Kuwait. He must retreat to his original borders or else suffer the consequences.

So finally, brief history completed, here we were, Leeward Marine, called into service in mid-December 1990 in Portland, Maine. Our mission was to help breathe life into a moth balled ship that was being readied for the fight. That moth balled fleet was being re-activated and made ready to join the Military Sealift Command to transport a large volume of military hardware and supplies to the Middle East. This was the part of resupply planning and execution for what would become 'Operation Desert Storm.'

We received a call from Richard O'Boyle, our Agent in New York. He said there was a fast-moving project to restore a fleet of ships that had been laid up at various locations around the country. They were kept in reserve just in case they might be needed for a large naval supply mission in support of a military campaign. One of his clients, DiMaria Shipfitters, Port Elizabeth, NJ, was assigned an old breakbulk cargo steamship that was moved from layup to Portland Maine where they could work on making the ship ready for service. No small task having been in wet storage for decades. They needed our diving assistance to remove all the protective cover plates used to preserve the ship while in wet storage along with cleaning the ship and propeller. With all the covers removed they would have cooling water and discharges for generators and pumps needed to reactivate the vessel.

SS JOHN BROWN: SIMILAR TO MSC SHIP, PRIOR U/W SURVEY BY AUTHOR IN VIRGINIA,

We assembled a great crew and planned for what could be a couple of weeks or more in Portland, Maine in the middle of winter.

Freezing temperatures and the need to work long shifts would require deploying a hot water system and suits. This was a new thing for us as our work on large ships, even in extreme cold was managed with comfortable dry suits. This was different.

The need for total dexterity of hands and body was predictable due to the many hours of dive time twisting wrenches and who knows what other tools we might need to complete our task. The big issue would be to maintain body heat and avoid hypothermia in the icy waters. Working those long shifts in the water for hours on end would be a challenge. We figured a four-hour minimum for each diver in the water.

My issue of concern was more about production and not what you might think. Being all warm and comfortable down below versus blowing snow and single digit temperatures topside, just might slow things down. Making sure our divers were focused on the work and not enjoying the hot tub temperatures that comes with your suit being flooded with a perfect hundred-degree water from above, could be a big problem and not easy to manage from up top. Making the choice of blowing bubbles and wallowing around down there or working topside in a blizzard was a no brainer, give me the bubbles.

Needless to say, there would be no problem getting a volunteer to be first to suit up when we'd start each day. The answer I figured could be easily handled by temperature control. The unit we built for the project had an accurate controller. If we lowered the temp every once in a while it might send a subtle message or encourage a shift change to suit up another diver.

To buy a ready-made hot water system for commercial divers was expensive and not much to it. Basically, a modified steam cleaner with a temperature controller and shut off valves for water supply. We bought and assembled our own system. Rather than generate steam our machine would simply be used as a boiler, set to supply hot water at a specified temperature with an adequate flow rate to keep a constant supply to the diver three hundred feet at the end of an air umbilical. Simple, the only x factors were ambient conditions, water temperature and setting the happy temperature for each diver, differing by several degrees.

My preference would be to keep things more toward the slightly warm side instead of the bath water temp I was sure would be most popular.

In one way, the use of the hot water system made the suit selection easy. The best was a full body surf suit, eighth-inch neoprene. A body harness of soft poly tubing entering at the back of the neck with branches to both arms ending in the light weight gloves, then following down the middle of the spine bleeding warm water along the way and branching again into both legs with the ends entering the top of the booties . The comfort level is hard to describe going from a Portland, Maine blizzard to hitting the icy water and feeling the warmth of the water supply . We were ready to go.

After final testing of all our tools and equipment we loaded out for Portland, not much more than an hour away. The ship was at the dock just south of the lobster docks on the waterfront. It was roped off and well secured by guards and barricades. After calling the Chief Engineer on the ship to confirm we were on the list of vendors, we entered the facility and scoped out where we would set up.

Before we could do much of anything, I had to meet with the gang working onboard trying to get the ship fired up. Turns out the lead was someone I met from work in New Jersey in the past. Joey, a towering steam fitter, was just the man for the job. With long wild red hair stuffed into a wool ski hat he was quite a sight, coveralls already covered in grease and oil. He came out to the dock and helped us find a spot that would remain clear the whole time and allow us to reach the entire ship.

The crew started getting the dive station set up and the water supply hooked up for the hot water machine. It would take a fair amount of time to get the dive station, hydraulic tools, and hot water machine online. For transportation, we used our large box truck. It doubled for protection against the foul weather for the crew, and security for all the electronics and equipment we'd need to store at night. Who knows what we'd find once we got underway down there.

We brought hull cleaning machinery, propeller polishing tools and abrasives, hydraulic tools, and wrenches to supply the five-man crew. Counting myself, we had four divers and one tender. My team would do all the diving unless we ran into an issue. In that case, you know who, would be getting dressed in. Gives me chills thinking back to those days in Portland.

Joey and his crew needed the covers that sealed all the openings to the hull for cooling water discharges removed as soon as possible starting with the ones that supplied the main and standby generators. They had shore power to feed the ship but needed to get the backup generators serviced and online due to long lead times if they had to be replaced or special parts ordered. We had Arne Backlund scheduled to be first in for us. He got the cover locations from Joey and told him to tap the hull next to the location and he would tap back confirming before dropping the cover. We had a plan to start.

Paul Mercaldi had the crew helping him to get the stage set. It was time to light up the hot water system and get it warmed up before Arne got dressed in. He had a handheld thermometer to measure the temp at the dive suit end. When we had ninety-five degrees topside we figured it would be OK for Arne to make the jump and adjust the temp up or down depending on the ambient water temp impact on the supply line.

Arne suited up with warm water flushing his suit, "Ahhh . . . Comm check, testing" he said.

"Yeah, great. We hear you, you asssshole! We're freezing to death up here while you're getting a Swedish sauna in that suit!" Paul said sarcastically. Probably jealous, having to work in the frigid weather. He was wearing a P Coat he made off with from the Navy years earlier when he was stationed in Alaska. The hooded jacket hanging to his knees was designed by the military for survival in the Arctic.

"Just like pee!" said Arne. He would know, a commercial diver's onboard hot water supply, often used in wetsuits to warm up and fend off icy water. Paul would know only too well about that having the chore of flushing out suits, usually cold and ripe with the smell of urine. I would often hear him bitching about divers not being able to control their bladders. I was one of the offenders. Whatever it takes to survive down there !

Paul tossed a bunch of slack in the water and told Arne he was clear. Arne stepped off the dock and dropped ten feet or more to the water. Bah whoosh, he was in and dropped below the surface. "Wooo, turn up the heat ! It's freezing down here." Arne said.

"Hold your horses!" said Paul. "I have to go out into that effing blizzard to adjust the controller." Meanwhile we began logging the dive time and activity logs for our records.

Arne was already well on his way to locate the first covers to be removed and didn't bother to respond to Paul's blizzard comment. "I'm at the first cover. Let them know to tap the hull and I'll confirm."

Joey gave us a radio to reach him. He had his guy tap the hull. I could hear it through Arne's comms. Arne tapped back to confirm. "Ok topside. There's a heavy layer of marine growth but I think we can get to the bolts okay. I'm ready to work the cover. When I get it lose I'll come back for a tag line to tie it off before pulling the last bolt."

"Roger that." Paul said. All we could hear was heavy breathing and grunting as he strained to loosen the bolts. "How's the water temp?"

"Fine." Arne responded, a man of few words. Twenty minutes later he had the cover bolts all out except two, one at each end backed off an inch or so. The plate was not moving. "I'm coming back for a hammer and bar to pop that cover loose. Take up my slack"

Paul pulled Arne's slack back to the dock while the crew rounded up a pinch bar and three-pound hammer. They lowered them to Arne and off he went back to the cover.

Thump, thump, thump. You could hear him hammering away on the cover. "Let go you son of a bitch !" Arne muttered, not known for his cursing. He continued to beat on the pry bar to break the seal. "There you go you bastard, finally!!" He exclaimed. "Coming back for the tag line." The cover was not very heavy, estimated to be between fifty and a hundred pounds. Arne would tie the line through one of the bolt holes and then remove the two last bolts allowing the piece to swing away toward the dock while the crew hauled it up and out. Joey said he didn't care about the bolts but wanted the cover plates salvaged if at all possible.

After the crew hauled in the cover plate they marked it with a yellow lumber crayon to identify it later. There was one more same size cover that Joey needed removed before we got into the dirty work of cleaning the hull and propeller, both with heavy marine growth, barnacles, and sea grass. The remaining covers we needed to remove would uncover more pumps and intakes that could become clogged with the debris from cleaning the ship. We needed to get that done as soon as possible

Arne went right back to work on the second cover plate. He knew what he was up against. This time things would be different. The crew fired up the hydraulic equipment and handed off an impact gun to loosen the bolts. They attached a flotation buoy to compensate for the heavy weight of the impact gun. He didn't want it on the first cover plate in fear he might snap off one of the bolts. Happily, the bolts securing the plates were in good shape.

It didn't take long to get the bolts loosened and removed. He still needed the hammer and bar to break the suction . Two covers down and plenty left to go. It was time for Arne to take a break and come up while the operation shifted to cleaning . There was a lot of work to do and even with the relatively small size of the ship we figured it could take days to complete.

We had to keep the hot water pumps running when we brought Arne out. He popped off his diving helmet and the steam surrounding him and out through his suit was a sight. He had a shit eating grin again and we all knew why, standing there with the wind and snow blowing. He was the only one toasty warm and he knew it. The good news, I saw a great working hot water system that would be invaluable

It was closing in on midafternoon in Portland and daylight was beginning to fade. Light snow continued to fall, and that persistent wind made it brutally cold. We didn't want to get into night work our first day out and there was a lot of work ahead of us, securing equipment to fend off the freezing temperatures.

The extreme cold could impact all of our diving gear and the hot water machine that had to be kept from icing up. We let Joey know we were winding down for the day and would be set up and ready to rock n roll early in the morning. He was pleased to see we had come prepared and ready under tough conditions. There was a lot of pressure to get this ship fired up and ready.

Before leaving for the day, Steve Humphrey and Kai Holleson assembled the hull cleaning equipment and made up the hoses. The machine required a small air line to go along with the hydraulic lines to operate a forward thrust controller on the machine. They taped that to the hose bundle and tested everything before giving me the thumbs up for tomorrow. In the meantime, Paul was tending to the dive suits and hot water machine making sure we had a small constant water flow. It would be cold water as there was no need for keeping the boiler fired up . The small, continuous water flow would prevent the machine from freezing up.

The light was fading fast as nightfall approached. By five o'clock we completed securing everything for the night. The chill factor was extreme. We all needed to get out of the weather and back to the hotel for a hot shower. We'd go over our progress and planning for the morning during dinner.

Thank God the Drydock Tavern was still in business down the street from the ship, it was a welcome return for us, having been there many times when we worked in Portland years earlier cleaning the floating drydock for Bath Iron Works. We'd be ordering up the lobster bisque, the best thing ever after freezing all day. We were not disappointed. In Portland, Maine their version of bisque was more like 'lobsta chowda' with large chunks of lobster filling the bowl , tails hanging over the edges and loaded with a rich steaming broth.

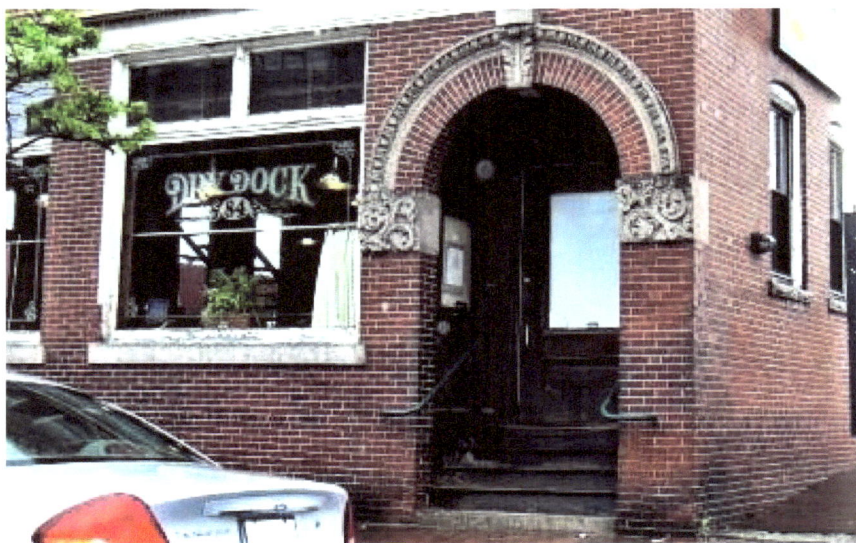

Drydock Tavern, Favorite Decompression Stop, Portland Maine

Not much planning needed for the morning. We had put the time in before ever getting to Portland laying out our plan of attack. Back to the hotel after the DD Tavern, a welcome night's sleep lay ahead.

The six o'clock wakeup call seemed way too early, especially with it still dark outside with no sign of daylight. I flipped on the TV and watched the weather report. The snow had stopped, and it was forecast for the sun to come out. My concern was the wind was still blowing and the temperature was in the high teens. It was going to be a cold one out there on the dock.

Downstairs we rallied and grabbed a coffee on the way out. Our plan was to hit a restaurant for a hearty breakfast and then on to the ship. There was a hint of a lightening sky to the east as we entered the greasy spoon breakfast stop. Somehow the warmth of the place and hot coffee seemed to slow our march to the freezing dock. Oh well. Time to go.

We got back to the ship and opened the box truck for another perfect day in paradise when Paul came running over. "We've gotta problem!" he said nearly out of breath.

"What's up?" I asked.

"You're not going to believe this, but someone turned off the water to the hot water machine and it's frozen solid. "He said.

"Come on! You've gotta be shittin' me! How the eff could that happen? Did you check to see if anything burst inside the machine?" I asked, as it was after all, not much more than a coil of copper tubing with water flowing through it, heated by a diesel flame heating from the center.

"No." said Paul. "I came right over to tell you what I found."

"Let's check it out. Get us one of the spare water hoses and running water. We need to find Joey and let him know there's going to be a delay getting started today. Sure glad we got those covers off yesterday. Get the hose hooked up and fire up the boiler on low to see if we can thaw out the coils. While I go find Joey." There was no way to tell whether we were going to be in trouble or not without tearing the cover off the machine.

Fortunately, we loaded out the cold-water dry suits. We used two types, a quarter inch neoprene UniSuit and a vulcanized rubber over canvas suit that used a heavy fleece liner for insulation. It was made in Sweden, and appropriately named a Viking suit.

In both cases the suits would slow down the operations, and due to the rough conditions of the scope of work, there was a high probability of tearing the suits. That could be an expensive proposition. The suits were repairable but had to be kept as waterproof as possible due to the icy water. For hull cleaning purposes, Arne had great machinery control no matter what suit he was wearing if we had to go that route.

When Joey heard what we were up against, he said with the two covers off they could continue inside, so we had time to do what we needed to do. With that, I thanked him and returned to the dock to hear what they found out with the hot water machine. Not good.

The facility was protected twenty-four hours a day by security guards. Turns out, during the overnight shift, one of the security guards needed water to make coffee. Seeing our water hose, he removed it to fill his container with water and shut it off when he reconnected the hose. No flow whatsoever through the coils overnight. The crew undid a cover on the machine and could see the coils had burst rendering the unit unusable. What an idiot ! Maybe it was me that was the idiot for not insisting on a sign like 'Don't touch the Effing Machine'. . . . Now what?

Arne would have to start the day in a Viking suit to begin cleaning the hull while I figured out how to replace the hot water machine.

My luck would hold. It turns out there was a Grainger Supply store in Portland, and when I called they said they had what we needed, an exact replacement unit. That was the good news. The bad news was it was going to cost close to two grand as I expected. Oh well, we'd bury the expense somewhere in the job under miscellaneous supplies. After explaining my situation, the Grainger guy agreed to deliver the unit to us as soon as his driver got back from another local delivery. Two hours later the unit was delivered.

While all of this was going on, Arne had dressed in and started the hull cleaning. He wasn't happy not having that bath water machine, but he knew we were fixing the problem. With a couple of hours running start, he had made a mess of the water around the ship. A good sign, showing progress was being made. It would take a bunch of machine time to clean that hull.

Paul continued to run the dive operation while the crew started working to convert the new machine. We stripped out the needed parts from the broken machine and set about building the new hot water system. It took us about an hour to make the conversion. If things worked well the plan would be to dress in the next guy with a hot water suit after taking a lunch break. I got on the comms "How're we doing down there ?"

"Fine." The usual simple response.

"Bet you'd be happy to hear we got the new hot water machine up and running." I said.

"Great. Take up my slack I'm coming out."

"Hey wait a minute! Who says? You love that Viking suit." I said. Arne mumbled something that sounded like Swedish. I'm not up on my Swedish but I'd bet he was cursing me out. "Alright. Come on up. We'll get some lunch ordered. There's a good sub shop down the street."

I got everyone's order and took the chase car to get the subs. Arne made sure not to make the mistake of ordering a tuna fish sub, remembering the last time, years ago, when we were cleaning the Portland Drydock up the street. It damn near killed him, gagging, almost causing him to throw up in the diving helmet down below. He said it was trying to fight its way back to the ocean. Truth is, it could have been a major emergency had that happened under the dock.

It would be a good afternoon, even with the freezing temps. When the sun came out it was actually bearable. This time of year, with limited daylight hours, it did pose a challenge. Once we got past the weather, we got into the production side of getting the ship cleaned up and ready. Things were going well, with the only hiccup being the water shut off incident. The new machine was running perfectly and 'lesson learned' by all not to mess with the diver's equipment!

We made great progress cleaning the hull, moving our way from bow to stern, leaving the propeller for last. As we cleaned areas and exposed covers, we removed them. Three days into the cleaning the crew cleared an area that had a very large cover. They didn't measure it but estimated it to a full four by eight feet with dozens of bolts securing it to the hull. We hit a snag. There was a bolt that was completely seized and would not loosen, even though we were using robust hydraulic nut busters that had worked beautifully on all the other covers.

Turns out that this cover was protecting what they call the 'main sea chest,' housing a variety of intake piping for the main engine and other pumps in the aft quarter length of the ship. This was all on us to solve and my crew needed direction.

Well, I guess it was my time to try out the new hot water system. When the crew stopped laughing, after hearing me say I'd check it out, they helped me get dressed in and made another water piping harness as they were all custom fit for each diver. The situation was a little tricky and made me uncomfortable. A four by eight-foot sheet of steel plating would be extremely heavy. Being hung up on one bolt, if it snapped it could pose a serious danger as it would fly back and forth as it fell away to the bottom. It would be up to me to find a safe solution that would allow us to recover the plate and not hurt anybody. Probably need a small crane to handle the weight

They fired up the hot water machine and tested my new water body harness. Everything was a go. Time to dress into my eighth-inch surf suit, freezing my butt off, taking care not to pull any of the tubing out of line. Paul started the water flow, thank God. He threw my slack over the side and when it was time to jump off the dock I took a second look. Somebody pulled the plug on Portland Harbor. It was nearly twenty feet to the water. We had a ladder long enough to get out, but the get in piece was a long drop. I had to make the jump, nobody else did a woosie down the ladder entry. "Holy shit!" It seemed like slow motion, stepping off the dock and waiting to hit the water.

Long jump to water, PORTLAND MAINE, MILITARY SEALIFT COMMAND

Bah whoosh . . . looking up after popping to the surface, the whole crew was hanging over the dock cracking up laughing.

"Nice jump there !" said Arne over the comms still laughing. "When was the last time you did one of those ? You wouldn't get much of a score in a diving competition!"

"Ef you ! If you guys could have figured this out I wouldn't have to show you my special high diving moves ! Slack me off so I can go take a look at that effing plate."

"Jeezus!" I said when I saw the plate hanging on the one bolt. The plate was hanging down four to six inches on one side. "This thing is a serious hazard. Let me check something out here. Standby."

The plate was really heavy but at the farthest point from where the seized bolt was, there was plenty of up and down movement. It made sense, that with the weight of the plate and with enough up and down action it might be possible to shear the bolt and drop the plate. At this point, salvaging the plate was the least of my concern. They needed to get this ship moving and if this ship didn't end up in a scrap yard after this deployment somebody else could figure out the next cover . . .

"Alright topside. I've got a plan. Take my slack and walk it forward fifty or sixty feet and take it up until I tell you to stop. I'm going to snap that bolt off and let it rip. Be ready to take my slack up in a hurry to help me clear the zone. That plate is going to be squirrely. Let me know when you've got my slack positioned."

"You're good to go." said Paul.

I grabbed onto the edge of the plate and wedged myself against the bottom of the ship to get better leverage. Getting some good movement and pushing down forcefully, put all the stress and pressure on the bolt. Nothing happened.

Repositioning, I said, "Alrighty topside. I'm going to kick down on this son of a bitch and it's going to go flying. Get ready to haul up my slack. I'm going to ride that plate until you pull me off it. Can't have that flying back at me! You got that ?"

"Yeah." Said Paul. "We're ready."

"Okay! Here we go . . ." I gave that plate as much down pressure as could be mustered and with an extra bump, 'pop' the bolt sheared. "Take up my slack!" I said frantically holding on to the plate as it sailed back and forth on its way to the bottom. Suddenly I was ripped away from the plate from above. Man, oh man. That was pretty hairy and not exactly my favorite ride, but we dropped it off ! "I'm coming up."

Climbing out, I had my Arne moment surrounded by a cloud of steam. No way to avoid that shit eating grin. I was ready to jump back in and take a shift but from the looks, that wasn't going to happen. Oh well.

I had to let Joey know, that one got away. He wouldn't care. Probably wouldn't even ask what happened, but I sure the hell knew. What a ride!

We would continue for another three days finally finishing with the propeller cleaning and polishing. Photographic documentation and select video of the stern quarter showing the rudder and propeller condition was completed for our client and that was all she wrote !

Joey was happy when we showed him the video as the crew began packing up and getting ready to go. Our original projection was up to two weeks to complete, we finished in one, even with the machine incident. . Nice work.

Dick O'Boyle, our agent, called a few days after we left to tell us how happy they were with our help and he had another ship waiting for us in New Jersey.

ADM Callaghan - (T-AKR-1001) Port Elizabeth, Military Sealift Command

The ship was in Port Elizabeth, New Jersey, and had an interesting history and design. 'Admiral Callaghan' was the name of the ship. It was a seven-hundred-foot twin engine RoRo, (roll on roll off), and conventional, lift on lift off, ship for cargo operations. The ship was the first all-gas-turbine vessel constructed for the U.S. Navy and powered by twin General Electric LM-2500 marine gas turbine engines generating 25,000 horsepower each.

The concept for a RO-RO was the ability to rapidly load and deploy massive amounts of military hardware into a conflict zone. An enormous ramp formed the stern of the ship and could be lowered to the dock and then used to drive anything on wheels or tracks, in the case of tanks, onto the craft and parked on the multiple decks like a giant parking garage. Excerpt below from Maritime Administration piece about the ADM Callaghan and the role of the Ready Reserve Fleet, RRF. Our efforts in Portland, Maine on a break-bulk cargo ship also contributed to the 78 RRF vessels referred to below.

ADM Callaghan was one of 78 RRF vessels that were activated to support Operations Desert Shield/Desert Storm[4]. The vessels involved were roll-on/roll-off vessels, break-bulk cargo ships, tankers, and barge carriers. More than seventy-five percent of the RRF provided sealift to support the U.S. effort's in the Persian Gulf between August 1990 and April 1991. The ships transported 750,000 short tons of dry cargo, which was one-fifth of the total dry cargo sealifted during the conflict. The Ro-Ros proved to be the most effective vessels and they delivered nearly twenty percent of Central Command's material and other support during the first phase of the operations. Having participated in several operations and exercises since Desert Shield, ADM Callaghan remains an active vessel in MARAD's RRF in Alameda, California.

We worked on one other 'special' ship in NJ for the MSC, Military Sea Lift Command. It was one of MSC's eight fast sealift ships (FSS), the fastest cargo ships in the world, with unofficial speeds in excess of 33 knots when fully loaded. A typical FSS load could include more than 700 Army vehicles such as M-1Abrams tanks, Bradley fighting vehicles and fuel trucks. Normally they are kept on a 96-hour standby. The first FSS was ready to deploy in only 48 hours after being called up for the Iraqi operation. There are many other distinctive features on this ship that were probably classified, and we chose not to name the ship or comment on its unique nature.

ADM Callaghan Ship Call

So off we went, from Portland to Port Elizabeth in January 1991. This would be the second of three ships we serviced to help make ready for deployment to the Middle East for MSC. We arrived at the Naval facility where we found the ADM Callaghan was already at the dock and beginning loading operations. Security was much more robust and required background checks before receiving passes to enter the facility.

Leeward Marine, as a company, was in early development but we were known to MSC through our Agent Dick O'Boyle and the work we just completed in Portland, so access didn't become too big an issue. I'd like to think it was my track record and reputation with Aquafacs that carried the day but that would be wishful thinking. O'Boyle was connected. This was after all, the Military Sea Lift Command . . .

The ADM Callaghan was a fully functional active vessel and our participation was primarily inspection plus propeller polishing of the twin propellers for the first time underwater. They needed that for maximum efficiency, especially with the gas turbine engines driving the ship.

After Portland, the crew liked the sound of this one. We estimated no more than two days on site at the outside when asked how long it would take to complete the scope of work. It might be possible to complete in one long day if we had good access. The 'Callaghan' did have two propellers, but they were smaller than single screw vessels of similar length and tonnage. The other thing working in our favor was our scope of work for inspection was located entirely on the stern quarter.

When we arrived alongside, the dock area was a crush of vehicles including a bunch of M1 Abram Tanks. With all the volume of traffic it was incredible that there was any open space for us to set up safely. We needed help from the traffic controller to cone off an area forward of the ramp location. Our final set up spot would end up approximately a hundred feet forward of the ramp to create a safe zone for operations.

The crew jumped right into screwing equipment together once we got positioned. Time for me to go topside to find the Captain and Chief Engineer. With all the action going on it was a sure bet they'd be busy, but still looking for us to show up. They needed our inspection report and the cleaning and polishing of the propellers done before they could leave. The propeller cleaning and polishing was something they were looking forward to, having heard about the new 3M system now available. We wouldn't disappoint them.

I met briefly with the Captain in his office. He was happy to see us and offered assistance if we needed it. The Chief Engineer was completely swamped and unavailable. The Captain would let him know we were here. No danger of an accidental gas turbine engine firing up and spinning a prop. Both props would be static until much later in the process. We would, however, have to endure the loud sounds and noisy commotion of the loading process as they filled the ship.

Sound carries well underwater and seems to have a surround sound effect making it very difficult to tell where it was actually coming from. That could be a little disorienting for the uninitiated, especially with cloudy visibility.

After returning to the dock, we had a brief meeting to discuss what needed to be done and how we'd proceed. My turn to lead the charge, scope things out down there and take a bunch of photos before we started the real work around the stern quarter. That might take a while and a couple of rolls of film. Maybe even video if there was anything worth filming.

The weather was considerably better in Port Elizabeth so we wouldn't use the hot water suits. That would save us time on this job. Now dressed into my favorite Uni-Suit, it was time the show started. Paul had the dive station set, comms checked and my Nikonos stills camera loaded and ready.

Stepping off the whaler at the top of the wooden fender system into Newark Bay, it was a lot shorter drop to the water than at Portland. "Holy smoke topside! We have great effing visibility! I'm guessing ten feet. Drop me the stills camera. I'll go check this bad boy out."

Starting on the port side, outboard from the dock, the rudder and propeller both looked in great condition. The propeller was in serious need of a cleaning and polishing but other than that, no damage or issues of concern were observed. Same condition on the starboard side. It took the better part of two hours to complete the pre-service inspection and documentation. We had set up in an excellent location, just right to reach the entire stern quarter. That fact alone would help speed up our service.

FILE PHOTO: MSC ADMIRAL CALLAGHAN

They just started loading the M1 Abram tanks when I finished up and was heading back to the ladder. The noise level was deafening. The sound of all those M1 Abram tanks tracking their way up the steel loading ramp vibrated the water below and was painful to the ears. Cleaning and polishing the propellers was up next. Too bad you can't use ear plugs down below. Not sure who'd be pulling the short straw on this one.

With the ship being twin screw, it would only take a few hours per propeller to clean and polish 'em up. The good news, with the photos out of the way except the finished propeller shots, there wouldn't be much left to do once they finished them. The other good news, no video would be needed. There was no real value and it was not a requirement other than if we found an issue. What they really wanted was to get loaded up and get underway.

We finished up, wrapped up and got out of there without any fanfare. The Captain thanked us, and I wished them luck as we parted company. Next stop for them was the Middle East.

Doesn't seem like that much, having kick started three ships on their way to the war zone, but we had made our contribution. Two of the ships were a special breed of military transport and we were honored to help out. See reference link Page 286.

CHAPTER SEVEN

CROATION WAR - HESS OIL TANKER

BLACK OP SURVEY

⚓

August 12 – 22, 1991

My old friend Joe March, from Maritime Overseas, called to set up an inspection for the VLCC '*WESTERN LION*' when she arrived back in St Croix following another run to Valdez and back. She would be at the Hess terminal the week of August 11th, 1991 after lightering in St. Lucia. The ship had a rudder issue and required close monitoring to avoid a potentially catastrophic failure.

Typically, the rudder of a supertanker is a gigantic balanced type that is held in place by two enormous pins. The design is a bit of a challenge to explain but is the focus of their problem and ours to track.

The entire weight of the rudder is supported inside the hull by the rudder stock. It passes through a hull penetration known as the rudder carrier where the weight is transferred to the ship's hull. The stock, after passing through the hull, is attached to the top of the rudder with a gigantic nut.

The lower pin passes through the rudder horn, a casting attached to the hull that hangs down and fits into a notch on the lead edge of the rudder. The lower pin is secured by another huge nut inside of the rudder, below the horn, and provides the lower pivot point for the rudder to swing side to side to steer the ship.

Big trouble can happen if the clearance from the bottom of the rudder stock and rudder horn is somehow less than the engineering calls for. The risk is the entire rudder could close the gap between the rudder and rudder horn and making contact. If the rudder drops down with enough hard contact on top of the horn the ship will be unable to steer. The size of the rudder assembly, and a quarter mile long Supertanker, make this condition hard to imagine and yet here we were having to take measurements every trip. Simple enough, right?

Normally we attended the ships twice a year for propeller maintenance and routine hull inspection of the stern quarter. When the rudder condition was discovered on the *WESTERN LION*, Maritime Overseas negotiated to keep the ship operating by monitoring the condition and measuring the gap between the rudder and horn after every round trip to Valdez. We were asked to meet the ship in St. Croix and provide the measurements and report on any change to the gap until the ship went back into drydock.

The *WESTERN LION* was due to arrive on Wednesday the 14th. I planned my travel to bag a couple of days off before the ship arrived. Staying at the Caravelle and lounging at the pool was just what I needed to catch up on a little R&R.

Arriving in St. Croix on Monday night, I spent Tuesday lounging at the pool and ordering Banana Blasters from the hotel bar, a local version of a Pina Colada with a little extra kick. Discharging crude oil from a Supertanker took three days or so in port at St. Croix to complete. The inspection of the rudder was a thirty-minute exercise, not counting the set up and break down of the diving gear, no big deal.

Back in the room, when I went to order another drink, the light was blinking on my hotel phone.

"Oh!! Mr. Lee! Mr. Lee! I have ten messages here for you from New York. They said it was extremely urgent. The last call was from somebody named Joe Gehegan. He sounded very gruff. I told him I'd give you the message as soon as I could." Said the lady at the front desk.

"Okay, okay. Give me the phone number for Joe Gehegan. Everything will be fine. Thank you very much." I said.

Oh boy. . . The shit hit the fan somewhere. I dialed the number for Gehegan in New York. It was his direct line and he picked up on the first ring.

"Gehegan."

"Hi Joe. Chris Lee here. Heard you were looking for me ?" I said.

"Yah. Where are you ?"

"Down in St Croix at the Marine Terminal."

"What are you doing there?"

"Waiting for the WESTERN LION, gotta a rudder inspection. What's going on?" I asked. Joe was the VP for Amerada Hess, Marine Division, and very close to Leon Hess and the Hess family.

"I need a survey."

"Okay. What can we do for you?"

"There's a problem. The ship is in Croatia."

Aw, shit! I thought. They just started a hot war over there with Yugoslavia coming apart with the decline of the Soviet Union. Serbia and Croatia were at war for control of the country, and this was a major shooting conflict. People were dying over there, and I heard the State Department ordered all US citizens out.

"Jeezus Joe. There's a mess over there. It's been all over the TV." I said.

"Yeah, I know. We have the *GROTON* over there in drydock going through some repairs and a paint job. It's part of a normal cycle and we can't get the Coast Guard or ABS in there to certify the ship to get her out of there. The Feds have ordered all US citizens out. Coast Guard isn't going in but said if we could get someone there and perform an underwater inspection, they'd allow a one-way trip to St. Croix. What they need is a survey and general condition letter stating there were no issues of concern. I need you guys to help me out." said Joe.

"Alright. So, who do you have over there and when do you need us?" I asked, this being Tuesday afternoon around 2:00PM.

"Friday, by noon. Captain Vince and his crew are all on board." He answered.

"Ok Joe. I'll get ahold of Joe March over at Maritime Overseas and catch the *WESTERN LION* next time in St. Croix." I could sense his high level of concern.

"We're gonna need a lot of help with logistics. With the Feds ordering everyone out it won't be easy getting in, especially with a crew and 2000 lbs. of gear to complete the scope of work." I had no time for thinking this through and not exactly sure what the right path was. Never had to sneak into a war zone before.

"I'll catch a flight out of here at 6:00PM tonight back to Boston. I need you guys to have your freight forwarder at my shop in Hamilton by 10:00A tomorrow. We'll have all the boxes packed and ready to load out. You guys will have to figure out how to get it there." I said trying to sound confident and maintaining my cool. "We'll need pre-paid airline tickets waiting at Logan, and a clear path into Croatia, hotel accommodations and also a rental car. You guys will have to cut all the red tape to get us there and back. If you can do that? We're in."

"Rental car?" he asked, leaving a pregnant pause. "What are you going to do with that?" .

"Need that Joe, to get around and have wheels if we run into any technical issues and need to track something down over there." Thinking to myself, it might give us a running start if things turned south. Gehegan didn't offer any sort of rescue plan if the fighting got to Rijeka and I didn't ask. I knew that Hess wouldn't leave that crew in harm's way, and with only myself and Holleson we'd grab onto their coattails. I convinced myself Hess would swoop in with a corporate jet and exfill the crew if it got that hot in Rijeka.

"Agreed." Click, the phone went dead. I wondered how many people were listening in to the conversation. I gave Joe quite a laundry list of things to do to get us onboard.

I called my travel agent and got my late afternoon flight confirmed back to Boston. What the hell did I just agree to? I came up with the idea that a single, highly qualified crew guy, would minimize exposure and the high risk of heading into a hot war zone. I volunteered Kai Holleson and had Gehegan sign him up with the pre-paid ticket and trip to Croatia. Now I just had to call him and make sure he was onboard with the plan. Going to Croatia, and into a hot war zone, might be a stretch for anyone to consider.

"Hello Kai. You up for an adventure?" I asked, filling him in on the action. Kai was single and the right guy for the job.

"No shit? Rome tomorrow afternoon? I'm in. Not sure about Croatia but if you're going, I'm going." He said.

"This is a pretty serious deal here. Are you sure? There are risks. I did ask who they had over there, and the regular crew was onboard. I figure if things get too hot Hess will swoop in with one of their corporate jets and scoop us all out of there." I said, not sure I believed my own BS. Maybe wishful thinking but that luck I've been counting on has followed me all these years.

"We'll be fine. I'm in!" Kai said.

"Okay. Meet me in the morning at the shop, seven o'clock. They have a freight forwarder schedule for ten o'clock. Our flight leaves at four PM at Logan. Not sure what to tell Liz but we'll be back in a week or so." I hung up and ordered another Banana Blaster. I'd need it as I stuffed everything in my bags and headed for the airport in St. Croix.

My mind was racing as I traveled on the flight back to Boston. Considering all the risks, I was about to ship a quarter of a million dollars' worth of diving equipment and the best camera, video, and ultrasonic equipment available at that time into a war zone. As for myself and family, all insurance would likely be null and void heading into a war zone once the US ordered everyone out. Should anything go horribly wrong, Susan would be on her own with the six kids. I began to wonder if Gehegan had asked everyone else and I was the only one that said yes. I had to mentally shut this off and change my thinking to more like, I always wanted to see Rome, or not being surprised Joe called as I was the best on the planet at what I did, especially in Black Ops on the commercial side of things. I liked that much better as I dozed off.

When I got home the stark realization set in that I had no control. It was an act of faith with Hess at the wheel. A huge gamble that Hess had the juice to actually make it happen. I told Susan years ago if I ever didn't come home, sue everyone, and don't quit until they make it right.

I called Susan at a payphone in Newark asking her to pick me up at Logan. She wasn't thrilled but had plenty of time to meet me at the airport and I needed more time to come up with a story to tell her without freaking her out. She knew I went down to St. Croix and for a ship call and now coming back early there had to be a reason. She hadn't asked on the call. Probably too annoyed she had to pick me up at Logan.

We had a routine when I was inbound to Logan. This was pre cell phone so she had to track the flight by phone, calling the airline, and I would meet her at baggage claim on arrival. It worked so far, and I hoped it would tonight with the crazy mission that lay ahead.

I didn't have much luggage, so we didn't have to wait long to get out of Logan and head home to Hamilton. I traveled so often in the last six- or seven-years Susan didn't find this any more unusual than any other pick up following a far-flung job. I always had a good answer and almost always true. In this case it would have to be true, just not quite flushed out with all the minor details, like heading into a war zone.

CHAPTER EIGHT

CROATIA - INTO THE WAR ZONE

≈≋≈

The Scramble to Croatia

It was Thursday, August 14ᵗʰ and I had slept like a baby until my alarm went off at five thirty. With six kids in the house and school looming a couple of hours from now, I hung out, making breakfast, and helping Susan get everyone off to school.

I retired to my home office and told Susan I had reports and billing to do, a true statement, but no Croatia conversation.

I left for the shop a few minutes later. My crew was there waiting. Kai had called everyone and asked for help. This was the most serious mission Leeward Marine had taken on so far and we had little time to sort out all the equipment that had to be boxed up for shipment to Croatia. We needed all hands on deck. What exactly do you ship into a war zone in a former Soviet Union backed country coming apart at the seams ? Short answer, everything, sort of. You couldn't count on finding spare parts over there.

At 10:00AM the freight forwarder showed up as scheduled. We had everything crated up and ready to go. I'll never forget looking at their taillights as they drove away, not confident I'd ever see my equipment again. Next stop, some dock in Croatia, maybe. It occurred to me for a second that if the equipment didn't arrive we'd be having a great vacation if we didn't get killed.

Oh well, too late to worry now, it was time for Kai and me to pack up and catch the red eye to Rome.

I asked Kai if his girlfriend Liz could run us into Logan. That would allow me to get out of town without having to explain too much, didn't want to panic Susan. Liz agreed. We'd pack light. Every piece of the diving and surveying equipment was crated and shipped. We planned to look like a couple of tourists, at least until we hit the Slovenia / Croatia border.

Kai and Liz showed up at my home in Hamilton just after one o'clock. I told Susan I'd be gone for a few days and I'd call her. After saying a quick goodbye, we headed to Logan Airport in Boston. Travel arrangements had been made by Hess and tickets were supposed to be waiting at the Alitalia counter.

Logan Airport was always a mess with traffic that defies description. When we arrived at the International Departures Terminal Kai said his goodbyes while I grabbed our bags and had them ready to go on the curb in front. I had deprived myself of a more proper send off from Susan in fears she'd figure out we were up to something other than the usual chaos of chasing ships around. There was no way I was going to tell her we were heading to Croatia.

We arrived at Logan. No need for a Skycap, we were traveling light. There was plenty of time to check in, providing the tickets were there. We entered the terminal and tracked down the Alitalia counter. It felt strange standing there hoping the agent would have our tickets. In our business, travel was always well planned in advanced, leaving no chance of missing a flight. Our clients relied on us to meet their ships that were in port with short turnaround times until they sailed off to the next port of call with little to no margin of error

The flight was listed as on time for Rome, our first of two legs. Our second leg would get us from Rome to Trieste, a city in northern Italy. I took a good look at a map of Italy at the counter to check how far it was to Rijeka. Trieste was in the most northeast located city in Italy near the border with Slovenia. Then what? Gehegan said they'd have all the arrangements made.

"Can I help you?" asked the agent as we stepped up to the counter.

"I hope so." I said nervously. "You should have tickets for Lee and Holleson to Rome. They were pre-paid and supposed to be here for pick up."

She smiled and said "Just a minute. Let me check." And she walked over to another counter. In 1990 computers were around but limited and there wasn't much of an internet. I could see something in her hand as she headed back to our counter. "You must be special." She said continuing that smile she had when we first walked up. "These were hand delivered by a travel agent about an hour ago."

"Great news ! We're not that special, just in a hurry to get to Rome. Never been there and they say it's great this time of year." I said.

Her smile faded. " I'm sorry to say, you won't be seeing much in Rome. You have a connecting flight to Trieste and that may not be easy to make. In Rome you'll have to clear customs before catching your connecting flight. Looks like you'll have enough time if they don't have much of a delay getting into Rome." She said looking concerned. "Do you speak Italian?"

Great, do I speak Italian? Seriously. "No, but we'll figure it out. I'm sure they have English speaking help there. Thanks so much for your help."

She smiled again "Here's your tickets. Have a good flight and good luck."

Phew. At least we'll get to Italy. The flight was due to depart after four o'clock and was an overnight trip arriving in Rome around seven AM local time. We headed to the gate and waited with an hour and a half to go before departure. Kai was a rock-solid professional with a calm demeanor, thankfully. He could tell I was pretty concerned.

"You alright?" he asked.

"Yeah sure. We've got this. Worst case is we get a free trip to Italy, well actually to Croatia." I joked. "If our gear doesn't make it through Zagreb it might be a short trip."

We waited. I was reading a good book and Kai was napping when the announcement came over the PA that the flight was ready for boarding.

Our plane to Rome was a 747 jumbo jet and from the lounge area it looked like a lot of people getting ready to board. With all of my traveling and flying 747s, it was actually looking like light loading. When we got on board the plane it was only a little over half full with lots of empty center rows. Empty row equals full bed. It could be a short flight to Rome.

As we climbed out of Logan I looked down at Boston and felt confident. If we made it to Croatia and our equipment was there we'd rock this and get Hess what they needed to get that tanker out of there. The deal was amazing. The Coast Guard, unofficially, agreed to accept our findings from Croatia and grant Hess the authorization to proceed directly to St. Croix where they'd dispatch their team to inspect the ship per usual protocol. We would also be required to meet the ship back in St. Croix to conduct an instant replay of our survey work from Croatia. What a deal. What a trip. Started with a phone call from Gehegan, a scramble out of St. Croix to Boston, on to Croatia to do our thing, back to Boston and finally returning to St. Croix two weeks after the ship sailed from Croatian waters. Calling it a whirlwind tour would be an understatement.

Red Eye to Rome and on to Croatia

I was able to get a little restless sleep on the flight to Rome. When we touched down it was early Friday morning the 15th and we knew we had a challenge and foot race to get through customs and find our connecting gate and flight to Trieste. Fortunately, the flight arrived fifteen minutes early. We'd need every one of those extra minutes.

The airport in Rome was confusing but had good signage with a lot of graphics . Customs turned out to be not as big a deal as I expected. That was the good news. The bad news was we had to leave the International Terminal and catch a bus to the regional terminal where our flight to Trieste was showing as on time and would require luck and a foot race to make it.

The bus was crowded and seemed to take forever to get to the regional terminal. When it pulled in we ran to the gate and arrived with only minutes before they closed the flight. Our luck was holding as we settled in for the connecting flight. We had checked our personal gear through to Trieste.

That would be the next hurdle but not a showstopper. All of our critical equipment and material had been included in the air freight. In that case it was black or white. It either made it and we were good to go, or it was a bust and our personal gear wouldn't be so important, could always buy a toothbrush somewhere.

It was a really short flight to Trieste. When we touched down our bags had made it from Boston, great news. Fatigue was beginning to set in. As we turned toward the exit, I saw a man standing there with a sign that said, MR LEE. I had been told there would be a car waiting that would transport us into Croatia. Must be our lift.

The driver was friendly enough but didn't speak English. Good thing he knew where he was going because we surely had no idea how to drive into a war zone. His car was an extra heavy looking Mercedes four door sedan. I wouldn't have been surprised if it was armored.

We departed the airport and the driver took off at a high rate of speed. I was getting deliriously tired as we whipped our way out of Trieste and started the climb toward the Slovenian border.

When we reached the boarder there were two men with AK47s slung over their shoulders. One of them asked for our passports. Our driver collected them and handed them over. The guard stuck his head in the window and looked at me, looked at my passport, looked at Kai, looked at his passport.

He leaned back out of the window shaking his head with a shit eating grin as he flung the passports back to our driver. That look is something I'll never forget. That guy probably thought we were CIA. Who the hell drives into a hot war zone?

Photo from Passport Carried by Author in Rijeka, Croatia

We were up in the mountains in Slovenia. Our driver was beginning the downward leg speeding toward Croatia, flying around the winding mountain roads I started to notice road construction. They were filling and paving the roads. I looked at Kai and said, "Hey, I thought we were heading into a war zone. What's with all the construction?"

He looked surprised by my comment and said, "They're filling in all the fucking potholes and damage done from being bombed, you idiot! You see those funny looking steel things along the side of the road? Those are tank traps."

I was losing focus from the lack of sleep and stress from making the trip. Time to snap out of it. Kai's comments were a serious wake up call. I'd rest later.

Our driver continued down through the mountains into Croatia passing everything in front of him. If there was oncoming traffic he'd lean on the horn and squeeze his way through. It was really hard not to say something. Guess I had to accept it's a matter of fate if we arrived alive.

That driver knew what he was doing, and with speed, the bad guys wouldn't have time to get a good shot. That thought changed my feelings entirely about his driving.

I began to root for the guy like rooting for a Grand Prix driver every time he leaned on the horn, the only difference being we were passengers and our lives depended on his skills. I could see we were finally coming out of the mountains and houses were visible in the distance.

Our entire trip had been carefully planned by Hess. We rolled into the City of Rijeka.(ree-EK-uh). The city was a good-looking modern place with a normal appearance, nothing seemed unusual, at least as how I envisioned it, clean and well kept.

The strangest thing I thought, was seeing the people going about their day, sitting in cafes, shops open and the usual hustle and bustle you'd expect to see. Thought this was a war zone!?

Our driver wheeled his way around the city and pulled into an official looking building.

The sign indicated it was a ministry of something or other. He asked for our passports before he got out of the car and headed into the building.

Not understanding even a word of the language, all we could do was sit and wait while he went in. Twenty minutes later he returned with a grin on his face and handed us back our passports with an insert added.

STANICA MILICIJE ZA GRANIČNE
POSLOVE I POSLOVE NA MORU   Reg. broj № 647065
            (naziv organa)

P R I V R E M E N A   D O Z V O L A
ZA KRETANJE I ZADRŽAVANJE NA GRANIČNOM PRIJELAZU

Dozvoljava se _CHRISTOPHER BRIAN LEE_
                        (Prezime i ime)

Državljanstvo _USA_   Vrsta i broj osobne isprave

_H 2/28 32_

RIJEKA

kretanje i zadržavanje
            (Naziv graničnog prijelaza i mjesta graničnog prijelaza)

radi _poslovno u MB, GROTON_

Dozvola važi od _220891_ do _10. 9._ 19_91_ godine

U _RIJEKA_ dana _220891_ 19___ godine

            (M. P.)   Potpis

Obrazac br. 2 — RSUP 419/80   30

Original work permit for diving in Rijeka, Croatia

We could tell it was some sort of work permit. It would become my first Croatia history lesson. Turns out, this area was where the Romans would escape the oppressing heat and grueling summer conditions. Caesar would move to the mountains and areas around Rijeka every year until the weather became bearable again in Rome. Our issue was the bottom of the seas around Rijeka were littered with Roman artifacts.. No SCUBA diving or any other diving was allowed unless officially sanctioned by the state.

Our driver pulled out, and about five minutes later we were sitting in front of AVIS Rent a Car. Alrighty, good old AVIS, my preferred rental car vendor at the time. He indicated the he would wait until we got our car and then have us follow him to our hotel. Clearly our guy knew every move on this special journey.

We went into the Avis office and identified ourselves.

File photo: Identical car to our Canary Yellow 1990 Yugo sedan

They looked pretty serious as they finished up the paperwork and had me sign the documents. I had no idea what they said but did it really matter? Other than presenting a driver's license he didn't ask for a credit card or anything else and handed us a key. No surprise it was a YUGO, a canary yellow Yugo. Great, I thought, makes a good target, easy to spot.

Our driver left Avis and waved for us to follow. Guess we had an escort. All our personal bags were still in his car. Seemed like we were heading south and after turning a corner we could see the Port of Rijeka in the distance and, low and behold, there was our ship laying against the long dock. Our driver pulled into a small hotel and pulled up out front. He got our bags out and motioned to us to follow him. He was helping us with the check in; with no language skills it was a welcome gesture.

The hotel was clean but not as welcoming as you would expect in the US. Stark would be an understatement of the surroundings. It did have a great view however, overlooking the city and was close to the port, two or three miles north of our shipyard destination.

Time for us to part company with our driver. Both Kai and I shook his hand and thanked him. I gave him a fifty-dollar bill from the wad of cash I brought along never knowing when you might need it. He smiled and wished us luck ! We'd need it. At least we got there.

We were asked by Gehegan to report to the ship by noon on Friday. It was just a few minutes past as we hopped in our Canary Yellow Yugo and headed to the port, close enough. I'd say, more like miraculous. And now, did the equipment make it ?

Barge section of ITB Groton in drydock at Victor Lenac Shipyard, Rijeka, Croatia

CHAPTER NINE

ITB GROTON RIJEKA - CROATIA

There was no problem finding our way to the port and the Viktor Lenac Shipyard. Gaining access to the ship repair yard and drydock area was not a problem as Security was made aware to expect our arrival. The Hess ITB (Integrated Tug and Barge)'*ITB GROTON*' was in two sections when we arrived. By design, the cargo section was separate from the engines and wheelhouse section referred to as the 'tug.' The cargo section, called out as the 'barge' was more like a ship hull than barge. When joined together by massive hydraulic ram connections they married up to form a hybrid ship. From a distance it was not easy to distinguish the difference.

The barge was still in drydock being finished up and painted. When we showed up they were about a week away from being launched and reconnected to the tug that lay alongside the dock. It was the tug that would be the subject of our inspection and servicing to comply with the agreement Hess made with the Coast Guard (USCG) and American Bureau of Shipping (ABS)

Kai and I pulled up to the *GROTON*, parked at the end of a fifteen-hundred-foot dock in our canary yellow Yugo and were met by the Chief Engineer. When he got done laughing he said, "Good to see you guys! Where the hell did you get that clown car?"

"Hey, don't laugh. Just try to get an Avis Rent a Car in an effing war zone! I asked Gehegan to agree to it before signing up to help you boys get out of here." I said.

"Son of Bitch" The Chief said. "Wouldn't get us one! The Captain was pissed. Cheap bastards."

"Not sure what to tell you. Wasn't thrilled with the color of this damn Yugo. Like a moving target in an arcade if we ever have to make a run for it! Better than no wheels at all, I guess. Where's the Captain?"

"Can't be far away. What's he going to do, ride a bike?" He joked. You could tell the humor was probably the only way to handle the stress of sitting there. I had already seen contrails from bombers overhead heading into the hot zone on the backside of the mountains, not much more than fifty miles east of the Rijeka toward Zagreb.

"Don't suppose you've seen our equipment show up?" Being sure of the answer already not seeing our crates anywhere.

"Nope. Let's go find the Captain." He said.

ITB Groton Tug Section, dockside in Rijeka, Croatia

It was after lunch and I had a game plan to start first thing in the morning. The rest of the afternoon we'd shake out our gear and get set up for tomorrow, assuming it showed up sometime that afternoon.

We found the Captain up on the bridge of the tug. I knew him from working on the ship a bunch of times in St. Croix. "Hey there Vince! What the hell are you doing over here?"

"Wish I had a good answer. These cheap bastards figured they'd save a bundle going to this shithole shipyard. Must have gotten a great deal. Look around. Ever seen anything like this?" Vince said. Vince was an older guy not far from retirement and quite a character with a strong Jersey accent and no shortage of colorful language.

"I did notice the welders over there were using vice grips and pliers for stingers!" I responded. Stingers were the handheld end of welding leads that hold the rods. "So, I'd call that a creative solution to a war induced shortage?"

"Hell no! Just the same bullshit we've had to deal with since we got here. Thank God we don't need any welds ex-rayed." Vince was clearly not a happy guy. Throw in a hot war and there was no doubt he was ready to get out of there. "Hey, there's Steve, the Devoe paint guy. He's a funny bastard. Every morning he tee's up the painting crew and then takes off touring the City and mountains. I told him he's a crazy fuck. These guys are killing each other and when they see you, you're a great target. He just said, "I'll take the chances. Gotta check this place out."

Steve was coming onboard. Probably saw the canary colored Yugo alongside. When he arrived on the bridge, Vince introduced him to me and Kai.

"Nice car! What are you guys doing here?" Steve asked.

"Vacation. Great deals to Croatia these days!" I said.

"Ah, another wise ass from Boston by that accent. We'll get along fine. I'm from Baltimore."

"Sorry to hear that. Explains why you're over here." We laughed. It did seem totally absurd, looking around at the mountains and surroundings in Rijeka. "We're here to get Vince a one-way trip out of here to St. Croix. Kai and I have to do an underwater survey to punch a ticket with the Feds to get him out of here. So, I hear you're the paint guy and tour guide for Rijeka."

"That's right. What are you guys doing for dinner? Found a special place east of here. Family style cooking with a twist."

I looked at Kai. "Feeling adventurous? If our equipment shows up it won't take that long to shake things out and I'm getting hungry."

"Sure thing. I'm assuming it's safe." Said Kai.

"Absolutely. I've been there so many times over the past two months they treat me like one of the family." Steve said.

Just as he finished speaking, I saw a small, beat up, pick-up truck dragging a trailer behind it heading our way. Sure enough, it was our crates. Thank God. Really rather come back some day to explore the countryside but for now we had to get down to business.

"Looks like we're all set on the equipment piece. We'll shake it out and be ready to go. Too late to start working a survey. After that we're all in. How about you Vince?"

"Thanks, but no thanks. That shit gives me heartburn." He chuckled.

Kai and I went down to the dock to receive the gear and drag it aboard. We were told that there were serious issues with theft around the shipyard and our stuff would be high on their list if they spied it, message heard. The crates looked in good shape.

After hearing about the theft problem, we decided to pop the covers and inspect the crates. If they looked alright with no obvious damage, we'd screw the covers back on and wait until morning. If they somehow stole any of what we shipped, it would be a disaster. We only packed a few small spares and batteries.

Kai unscrewed the covers. Our luck held. Everything looked OK, so he screwed the covers back on. Time to find Steve. Something about dinner tonight.. He was still hanging around up on the bridge.

"All set for tomorrow Vince. Everything looks good on the equipment side. If you're ready, Steve, we're getting pretty hungry. The four wheeled Canary awaits." I said.

"Sure I'll fit?"

"Can you walk there ? Who's the smart ass now?" I said.

We piled into the Yugo and headed out of Viktor Lenac Shipyard for a restaurant in the hills a few miles east of us. When we pulled up you could see the place was busy. It was a neighborhood joint and looked clean.

"You're going to love this place." Said Steve as he led us into the lobby. "Josip!"

"Mister Steve! Mister Steve !" Josip greeted us with a big smile and really strange laugh. He and his wife Ana owned the restaurant and seemed to be wearing some sort of ethnic looking clothes.

"Hello my friend. I bring you my friends from Boston. I told them you had the best food in Rijeka!" Steve wasn't kidding. Josip was genuinely happy to see him, and us. He laughed that strange laugh again and led us to a table.

I asked Steve about the special clothing they were wearing. Steve told us that was the special part of this restaurant he told us about. Josip and Ana were from a part of Croatia called Lika, not to far south of Rijeka. Josip wore a Lika Hat, cylinder shaped with a flat top. It was bright red in color on top with black sides and black tassels on the back. Baggy pants and shirt finished the look. His wife, Ana, was wearing matching clothes with a peasant look and head scarf.

File Photo: Lika Costume, similar to dress worn by Josip and Ana in story

Steve ordered up the house special of lamb and veggies in a stew along with some sort of dumplings and a round of Grappa, a local favorite liquor. The food was great just as Steve said and after a couple of Grappas we had to twist off and get back to the hotel to get a good night's sleep. Tomorrow would be showtime.

Steve was a guest aboard the *GROTON*. We dropped him off at Viktor Lenac and found our way back up the hill to the hotel. It was still pretty early but a welcome relief to hit the bed. Everything was looking good going into tomorrow.

The Adriatic – Gin Clear Rijeka Waters

We left early in the morning on Saturday for the *GROTON*. Breakfast aboard would be the best way to start our day. Vince was in the galley when we showed up. This would be a good time to fill him in our plan for the next few days and how we'd fixed him up to get out of there. Our scope of work, as it was required by the Coast Guard, was long and involved with a few measurements to confirm and extensive photographic and video documentation.

The hull of the ship had been marked and painted per the Under-Water Inspection in Lieu of Drydock program and they expected us to document every piece. The tug section was not drydocked and serviced in Rijeka and thus fell under the in-water inspection protocol. I had visited the *GROTON* the last time she had been through drydock in the US when it prepared for the program. In the dry, it was possible to photograph all the markings painted on the hull and specific features of interest located on the underside of the tug. All the intakes and discharges, the stern quarter with propellers and rudders, and any pre-existing anomalies or damage to the shell plating were identified and videoed by me. There's more going on down there than meets the eye once she's afloat.

Only the barge needed drydocking for re-piping and mechanical work on deck. The tanks and hull would also need new coatings and paint. Our new pal Steve had quite a chore there.

The Chief Engineer, Jack , showed up in the galley, grabbed a cup of coffee and sat in our discussion. There wasn't much anybody needed to do aboard the vessel. She was powered up by shore power and had water supplied from the dock so there wasn't much if anything running that we needed to be aware of. Should be smooth sailing once we got underway.

From the dock the water looked exceptionally clear. That would be a good thing to capture the video requirements of the survey. Underwater photography was a lot more forgiving when it came to water clarity. We'd soon find out.

The tug section of the *GROTON* was no more than two hundred feet in length. The ITB Class of vessels were a twin-screw pontoon design with port and starboard engines, propellers, and rudders. The design allowed us to set up in a notch forty feet +/- across at the centerline and approximately thirty feet forward of the stern and formed between the pontoons.

At that length we would only need one location for the diving equipment and cabling for the video system. We prepared the dive station with an air filtration system we brought in order to use barge air from the ship as our air supply for breathing. A three-hundred-foot umbilical with an auxiliary video line taped on was coiled and ready to go with my Superlight hooked up. We didn't have a backup air supply other than a small 'bail out bottle' attached to our diving harness. That was a seventeen cubic foot air tank that would normally be enough to get free and ascend should an emergency occur below.

A ladder was placed on the outboard, port side pontoon, inside the notch out of the way of any tugboat or other traffic that might show up in the channel. The *GROTON* was tied in the outermost location of the dock at Viktor Lenac Shipyard. We were ready to light it up.

There was plenty of room for the tender to manage the diving and technical piece on the deck area of the notch aft of the wheelhouse. Kai and I would switch out tending duties for each other. Under the circumstance we opted to not bring a third crew member. All systems checked; it was showtime.

I would start the survey effort having the memory of wandering beneath the *GROTON* in the dry. The water was on the chilly side so quarter inch wetsuits were the call. After dressing in and coms checked, I started down the ladder and entered the water, the first time in the Adriatic for me. Kai lowered the Nikon stills camera. I planned to start by taking general condition pics while scoping out the underbody.

There was something strange as I dropped down to the portside propeller. The water clarity and visibility was the clearest I've ever experienced. It was gin clear. As far as the eye could see, it was like standing on the dock, not under the hull of the *GROTON*. Freaky clear, as I dropped below the rudder and looked forward along the bottom of the tug. The entire hull was visible and literally as clear as it was on the drydock. I could see the entire underbody.

"Jeezus Kai. This in unbelievable down here! I have never seen clearer water or better visibility. This makes the Caribbean look like a frog pond. I can see clearly the entire underbody of the tug and looking in the distance, I can see the entire length of the dock all the way to the end, an incredible sight. Slack me off. I'm heading forward to the front of the tug and working my way back. When I get this done I'm coming up."

"Roger that. Can't wait to get a look!" said Kai.

I moved forward under the port side to the forwardmost point of the tug. It was uncomfortably clear if there is such a thing. Low on the outer shell I could see every hull marking from stem to stern. I began to wonder how good my video gear was and if it would capture just how clean and clear the conditions were.

After a good look below and blowing through my first roll of film I made my way back to the ladder. Kai pulled in the slack and when I climbed out and unclipped my harness, he took my Superlight so I could climb over the handrails and onto the deck. I couldn't help but smile. We had this. Still a long slog to cover the bases, but with these conditions, if our video equipment and everything else held together, we'd come away with stunning photos and videos to take with us back to St. Croix in two or three weeks.

Time to Strategize

It was coming up on lunchtime following my preliminary inspection and photo run. I wanted to take some time to plan the upcoming survey in light of the conditions. These were Hollywood quality. We might be able to shave some time off the overall survey and use the incredible visibility to shorten the video piece of the program. It might add up to as much as a day saved, better yet, a day sooner that we could get the hell out the war zone!

We mapped out our path to completion and figured we could wrap things up in four days, plus one to roll up and get out of there. If we could execute a new shorter schedule we would be spending six days on the ground in Croatia instead of the eight-day original projection. I would need to consult with Captain Vince and ask him how much time and trouble it would be to change our travel plans to get out of Croatia early. It might take Vince a few days just to make the arrangements.

We didn't have time at lunch to discuss our departure plan with Vince. He was tied up and would be stuck taking a late lunch. After work would have to do. Time to put the video system online and give it a whirl after lunch. Kai would be our cameraman and I would direct the survey from above. That would give me an idea of how good our video would be given the unbelievable water clarity. It might provide another opportunity to shorten the overall production if we had longer views that were acceptable to fill the requirements.

Kai dressed in and we discussed the plan to begin the video at the port side all the way forward and work our way back. This would be a long and involved taping. It would take the better part of two days to accomplish. The raw video would come back with us for editing. A final copy would be prepared for submittal to Hess in New York and for handoff in St. Croix when we met up with the ship in a couple of weeks or so.

Once Kai was in the water, I lowered the video camera and he started forward as I payed out his umbilical.

"This is unbelievable!" Kai exclaimed

"OK topside. I reached the front of the portside pontoon." Said Kai.

"Roger that. Turn on the camera and let's get a look before you begin the intro."

"Ok. How do we look ?" the video feed to our mini monitor and recorder was absolutely amazing.

"Fantastic view. Back away slowly to about ten feet forward facing back toward the pontoon. I want to test the clarity and see if we can use longer views for hull markings." I said.

"Roger that. How we looking?" He asked.

"I have great detail and lighting. Between the ambient lighting and onboard lights, it looks like broad daylight down there. I don't think we've ever had this kind of background. Time to get the intro done and start taping." I said.

Our video system had a long play 8mm tape, internal to the camera, and topside we had a battery-operated mini VCR with a six-inch screen, an advanced piece of technology for the time. It recorded in VHF format giving us dual recordings. We would leave the VHF tapes onboard in case the *GROTON* needed them. The 8mm cassettes would travel with us back to Boston for editing and production purposes.

"Alright Kai. Let's get the intro done and follow the plan we discussed." I said

"Roger that. Setting to record." Kai said. "This is Kai Holleson with Leeward Marine. Today's date is August 17th, 1991. We are surveying the underbody of the *ITB GROTON* tug at the Viktor Lenac Shipyard in Rijeka, Croatia. We will conduct the video in accordance with the rules outlined in the *UWILD* guidelines. The *GROTON* was painted with hull markings applied during their last drydocking and is qualified under the new process. . . . ." Kai droned on as he slowly moved aft along the port side pontoon. He had done this many times before and did a great job narrating as he moved along. This would be a great start to our video production. I would get my turn with the video camera, but to make sure we were getting dialed in, I needed to have Kai lead us off.

We made great progress Saturday, but we had a long way to go. Sunday would be our first full day continuing the video production. Hopefully, we'd be able to wrap that up and spend Monday and Tuesday with all the photography and other items required for the sign off. If we continued as things were going, we just might be able to get out Croatia Wednesday, well ahead of schedule.

Sunday morning, we were able to get some time with Captain Vince to discuss our progress and plan for our departure. Video production would likely finish up Sunday and we could see our way to completion by the end of the day Tuesday. With that, all we'd need to do is pack up and stow our equipment aboard. There was no way we were taking anything but personal bags, film canisters and video tapes with us when we made a run for it back to Trieste.

"Good morning Captain." I began. "Looks like we'll be done early. If we continue at this pace we will be done two days early. If we can get out of here Wednesday that would be a good thing. I'll have plenty of time Tuesday after we get done to write up the letter to get you on your way."

"That's great news." said Vince. "You'll need new tickets and travel arrangements for Wednesday if that's what we're talking about. If so, I need to start that process today. We need the car and driver to get you out of here back to Trieste and new airline tickets to Boston. I can do that if you're confident we'll be done."

"I'm very confident we'll have things done. The only other issue will be to work out a plan to safely stow our gear for the trip to St. Croix. When you guys get there, we'll be waiting with the Coast Guard. Brian Swensen will likely be there as well." I said.

"Great. Swensen, just the guy we want to see." Vince responded sarcastically. Swensen could be a real hard ass. As Senior Port Engineer for Hess, he had quite a reputation and was not well liked but commanded respect. He knew his business. "Okay. Get with the Chief Mate about your gear and I'll get the ball rolling on your departure plans. Probably be pretty early out of here to make it to Trieste in time for a connection to Rome and the States. I'll let you know as soon as I get something."

"Thanks Captain!" I said just as the door opened and Steve from Devoe Marine stepped in.

"Am I interrupting?" Steve asked looking at Captain Vince.

I said "Nope. We're just finishing up. We're a couple of days ahead of schedule and trying to get out here on Wednesday."

"You guys can't leave! At least not until we get the gang together for a sendoff dinner ! I found a mountain top lodge north of here with incredible food and a great bar. The scenery from up there is like a postcard overlooking Rijeka. How about Tuesday night before you take off? What do you think Captain?" said Steve.

"We've been working our ass off to get out of here. That would be a great idea. We've got crew due to arrive Wednesday to make ready for our trip to St. Croix so Tuesday will be the last chance to do something good before we get out of here. We plan to marry up the tug and barge Friday and sail sometime over the weekend." Said Captain Vince.

"How about you guys? You up for it?" Steve asked.

"You bet" I said. "My treat." figuring five officers from the *GROTON*, Steve, myself, and Kai making eight total. We could do that. I learned from our first outing how affordable things were in Croatia.

"Alright. I'll let them know we're coming Tuesday for dinner." Steve said as he turned to head out to catch up with his crew. They had to hurry up and get everything done to get the ship set to sail.

Kai got our equipment online and ready to start. It was my turn to continue the video production. I knew just how far away I could be and still capture amazing picture quality. After a brief introduction with time and date and a few details about the *GROTON*, I was off and running. We worked straight though to lunch before I came up for a break. It was amazing down there. I planned to continue after lunch and hopefully finish all the taping.

We took a long lunch break to plan our photographic documentation that was likely to be our focus for Monday and part of Tuesday. With having to pack up and stow our gear we had to finish the underwater survey piece by lunchtime on Tuesday. It wouldn't take me long to write up the compliance letter that was required by the Coast Guard. Then it would be off to the mountain top for an evening out.

After lunch I got back to it and spent the afternoon carefully covering the details and hull markings the Coast Guard would be looking for. When I finished, Kai hauled in the video camera and began rolling it up while I took a spin around looking for what we had left for Monday and Tuesday morning. We'd stick around for dinner onboard and head back to the hotel.

Monday morning came early as we pulled alongside the *GROTON*. Kai would lead off the photo run while I charted the path and kept a photo log for use later. We hit the galley for coffee and breakfast and started a conversation with the Chief Mate about where we could stow everything after we finished up Tuesday. He said he had limited space with all the materials and supplies being loaded out for the trip to St. Croix but assured us he'd make arrangements.

Luck was on our side starting the day; the weather had clouded up. Normally that would not be helpful, but with underwater photography your strobe light is much more effective with less ambient lighting. Our photos would be stunningly clear, with great detail. Good thing as we had several hundred shots to take to complete our plan. Given the conditions we should get the majority done Monday, but we would run over to Tuesday Morning

We were tracking right along on schedule at our lunchtime break and Kai would complete the day on a roll. Speaking of rolls, we used 36 exposure, Fuji film rolls. That would allow us to get everything we needed on ten rolls for processing back in Boston, easily handled for our outbound trip. We would pack and carry our camera equipment, film rolls and video cassettes. Everything else would take the cruise to St. Croix aboard the *GROTON*.

Back at the hotel Kai and I went over everything we had done and used a checklist to make sure we didn't miss anything. Before we got into that, we noticed the TV was on in the hotel lobby and there was something bad going on in the USSR. They showed crowds in the street and soldiers massing somewhere outside Moscow. Not having anyone to translate, we could only assume things weren't getting any better over there as Croatia was in a full-scale war with Serbia and it looked like the Soviet Union was coming apart at the seams.

With only half a day of work left for Tuesday we had to be one hundred percent done to hit the mark. I would draft the brief report and letter Monday night knowing there would be no surprises down below Tuesday . Tomorrow night we were off to the mountain top for the Captain's dinner and an extra early start to getting out of there Wednesday morning.

Tuesday morning, August 20th, we got an early start out to Viktor Lenac Shipyard. Taking the turn to the dock where the *GROTON* was tied up, we saw a large ocean-going Soviet tug. Apparently, it had limped into port overnight. Nobody seemed to know why, but after what we saw on the TV at the hotel Kai and I felt it was highly likely that it was connected. When we got aboard the *GROTON* we asked if anybody heard anything about the commotion in the Soviet Union. Short answer was no.

No time to worry about Gorbechev other than it only reinforced our determination to hurry up and get the hell out of there. For the sake of speed, Kai would finish up the photography. Being considerably younger, he was also considerably faster. We had to blow and go.

Great strategy, he flew through the last of the photography before eleven o'clock and climbed out after I hauled up the camera gear. Time to pack and get everything stowed after lunch. We would work with the Chief Mate to pack everything in a chain locker on the aft deck. It was a lockable space with steel doors and weatherproof seals once the door was dogged shut.

Captain Vince met with me after lunch to review the findings and hand off the certification letter that would buy them the one-way trip to St. Croix. Wasn't a lot to talk about. Everything below looked great and with the gin clear water this was a walk in the park except for that whole Croatian War thing. Vince and crew were looking forward to our outing that night. 'Devoe Paint, Steve' had been talking it up since we set things up. Got to say I was ready for the adventure, but even more ready for the ride out of Rijeka in the morning.

CHAPTER TEN

FAREWELL RIJEKA
THE MOUNTAINTOP

━━⌘━━

The Mountain Top Lodge Captains Dinner August 20ᵗʰ, 1991

When we had everything stowed, and wrapped up our ship call with the *GROTON*, we ran back to the hotel and got cleaned up for dinner. After that, we returned to the ship and met up with the crew. Steve would lead the way to the mountain top lodge. He had a larger vehicle and carried the majority of the gang. We took Captain Vince in our canary yellow YUGO, squeezing him in the back seat.

Mountaintop Lodge Venue, Captain Vince, far right, Devoe Steve, 3ʳᵈ from left

Around five o'clock, Steve headed out and we followed heading north out of Victor Lenac Shipyard. It took a good thirty minutes to wind our way up the mountain road heading out of Rijeka to the lodge.

When we arrived, it was a rustic looking place but very clean with a bunch of cars parked out front. We were not alone by any means. Seemed odd for a Tuesday night at the top of a mountain in the middle of a war zone.

Front entrance to mountaintop lodge and restaurant

When we walked inside it was clear why there were so many cars. The bar was loaded with people talking and pointing at the TV over the bar. Some guy was marching around a bunch of tanks in Moscow and jumped up on top of one with a bull horn.

File photo: Boris Yeltsin standing on tank in Red Square with bullhorn during coup

He was speaking angrily in Russian with the crowd cheering as he spoke. It was Boris Yeltsin, Russian SFSR President. Didn't look good. We came to find out there was a coup underway in the Soviet Union and Gorbechev was nowhere to be found. Great start to our Captain's dinner.

The owner of the lodge greeted Steve and our group. He managed a smile despite the fact his country was at war and now the Soviet Union was coming apart. He led us to a table pre-set for our party. By appearance you'd never know there was anything wrong. The lodge was beautifully situated at the top of a bluff, most of the way to the top of the mountain overlooking Rijeka and the waters of the Adriatic. The sun was setting and the city below was lit with night lights and the glow of the City.

The Captain sat at the head of the table with the Chief Engineer at the other end . The rest of us filled in with Kai on the opposite side next to the Steve and the First Mate. I sat in the middle between the Second Mate and First Engineer on the other side to make sure I had good access to mingle with all the crew.

The table was set with two large bottles of Grappa on swinging frames for ease of pouring, one with fruit at the bottom, the other with wheat or some sort of grassy looking material at the bottom. There were already appetizers spread out on the table; breads and cheeses, along with sausages and salamis made from local game that were hunted on the mountain. Trophy heads were mounted and hanging on all the walls in the dining room. Wild Boar, Deer , Sheep and Brown Bear, would all be served in one form or another.

The scene was surreal. All those men remained huddled in the bar watching events unfold in Moscow as we poured our Grappa and started in on the Wild Boar and Bear salami appetizers. The Captain and crew were all in good spirits knowing they too would be getting out of there soon.

The jokes started and we learned there was still no winner of the betting pool proceeds, waiting for the first crew member to get lucky with one of the local Croat Babes. So far, nyet.

As the dinner unfolded, the main course would be leg of Lamb and Wild Bear with blueberry sauce served family style. When I say leg of Lamb, it was the whole leg and carved at the table.

The Chief Mate picked it up off the platter and made a dirty joke about what he'd like to do with one of those hot looking Croat women while pretending to take a bite. Totally inappropriate, but we all laughed like hell at the theatrics and the size of that leg of lamb! The Wild Bear was served sliced on a large platter with the sauce poured over the top. There were sides of potatoes, carrots, and beans nicely prepared to accompany the exotic meats.

Now we knew why Devoe Steve was so insistent. "We've got to do this!" he said, pushing strongly for the outing when he heard we were getting out on Wednesday.

Photo by Author – Actual Leg of Lamb, subject of Chief Mates humor

Seemed like we sat there for hours eating and drinking the Grappa and enjoying the venue. Our troubles faded away with the ambiance of the lodge. Neither the war nor the Soviets could invade our special occasion.

The owner finally came out and asked how we were doing and waved to someone in the back. A moment later a man arrived with a green striped watermelon and set it down in the middle of the table. Our host reached over and pulled the top off the watermelon. You couldn't see it, but the top had been sliced to remove it. Inside it was filled with fresh balled melons and a generous layer of sorbet on the top. Dessert?

It was a shocker, an unexpected delight following a meal, the likes of which only Steve knew was coming our way. Given our venue, at the top of a mountain in the middle of the Croatian War, it was an extraordinarily special occasion. I was honored to host it for the Captain and Crew of the *GROTON*. Time for the check.

Watermelon filled with fresh fruit, sorbet, and whip cream

I needed Steve's help when the bill showed to figure out how much I owed. Fortunately, they were prepared to accept credit cards. Steve went over the bill with the owner and came back to get my credit card. I asked Steve how much? He said, ninety-five dollars US including the tip. I was shocked. For eight guys, that was just slightly more than ten bucks a head. How cheap was that for all that great food and drink, not to mention that watermelon?!

We left the lodge and headed back to the *GROTON* to drop off the Captain and Chief Mate. Steve would follow us back to the ship with the rest of the crew. It would be a short night for us. Our ride out of Rijeka was scheduled to leave at the crack of dawn from the

GROTON. We said our goodbyes to the Captain and Crew and thanked them for all their help. We might not see them in the morning. If our car was waiting, we weren't going to waste any time.

Back at the hotel we packed up and had everything ready to run. A quick shower in the morning and off we'd go. Our wake-up call was set for 4:00AM.

Making a Run For It

It was still dark when we left the hotel . Viktor Lenac Shipyard had not yet come to life, but we could see taillights of a vehicle parked at the *GROTON*. It had to be our ride. I'd arranged with Captain Vince to leave him my rented YUGO and suggested they hang on to it until they cast the lines for St. Croix. It would give them a few days to run around before getting out of there. Vince agreed to arrange the drop off with Avis.

The Mate was standing watch. We gave him the keys and with a firm handshake we wished him well and said we'd see them all soon in St. Croix.

Our driver loaded our gear in the trunk and mumbled something in broken English. Broken is better than none when it comes to language. He drove off slowly out of Viktor Lenac Shipyard. We knew that wouldn't last. It was still dark out, but dawn was approaching. We settled in for the hour and a half hell ride to Trieste. Once we cleared the mountains to the Slovenian border we'd be out of the war zone.

Sure enough, we cleared the City and our driver rapidly accelerated as he sped up the mountain roads. Didn't take much more than thirty minutes to reach the Slovenian border. It was a huge relief and time to let our guard down a bit. Our travel arrangements were solid and without some major interruption we would easily make our connections in Trieste to Rome and hopefully on to Boston. We had a great chance to be home in our beds not too long past midnight Eastern Standard Time back in the States.

We arrived in Trieste early for our flight and had no issues making our connection to Rome. When we got into Rome we had a transit to the International Terminal and had time for lunch before boarding. Kai was enjoying himself recounting our dinner outing at the mountain lodge and the First Mates leg of Lamb jokes the night before. He said if he'd been in Croatia longer there was no doubt he'd have won that 'Lucky Pool.' I reminded him he was engaged, and Liz wouldn't be happy with that.. He chuckled and agreed.

I was able to make an international call and let Susan know we were in Rome and good to go for our Boston flight.

"You're where?" She said. "What the hell are you doing there?"

"It's a long story. I'll tell you when I get back." I said giving her the flight number on Alitalia and asking her to call for confirmation on our arrival time, just like we always did. It would be late, but I needed a lift. Kai's fiancé, Liz, would pick him up as they had planned on arrival at Logan as well.

Touchdown Logan, 11:30P. We needed to clear customs before grabbing our gear and heading for home. The girls were waiting at baggage claim and after hugs and kisses we were finally on our way home.

I was exhausted and relieved. We had succeeded in our mission to Croatia and lived to tell about it. It would be a quiet ride back to Hamilton. Thursday would be just another school day for the kids in the morning. Other than knowing their father had been traveling again for business, they would have no idea I'd been in a war zone on the other side of the Atlantic.

114

I promised Susan I'd get up and help get them on their way but after that I was going back to bed. I'd tell her the whole story when I got up.

When I told Susan the story, she just sat there and finally said, "I had no idea. You ran out of here and said you'd be back in few days. That was over a week ago! Croatia? Seriously, there's a war going on over there! What if you got killed ? What would I do?" I knew the blast was coming and I deserved it, but if I told her before we left it would have been worse.

Departure day from Rijeka

CHAPTER ELEVEN

ITB GROTON - ST. CROIX - AT LAST

Planning and Logistics

Reality would set in soon enough and the planning would begin again to meet the *GROTON* in St. Croix. In the meantime, we had work ahead of us before the ship would be back.

We had accomplished our mission in Croatia and with somewhere around three weeks to go before traveling to St. Croix. We had several routine projects to slog through. There was a couple of SeaLand propeller polishings in New Jersey and a short trip to San Juan to inspect a ship with a damaged propeller.

Hess Marine called with an updated arrival schedule for the vessel. She sailed from Rijeka on Saturday, August 24th and was scheduled to be at the breakwater in St. Croix on September 12th They were anxious to get the tanker back on track delivering fuel products to the Hess Terminal in New Jersey.

Our upcoming work, although important in tying this off with the Coast Guard and American Bureau of Shipping, could not slow down their loading and sailing schedule. Joe Gehegan had made it clear to Brian Swensen and he made the call to let me know.

I contacted my travel agent and had flight reservations for a three-man crew to St. Croix. Arne Backlund would be added to round out the crew with me and Kai Holleson. We flew to St. Croix on September 11th and checked into the Caravelle Hotel in Christiansted.

The Port Captain at the Hess Marine Terminal in St. Croix confirmed that *GROTON* would reach the breakwater by mid-morning on the 12th. Gave us plenty of time for a leisurely breakfast and slow start for the upcoming survey. The ship would have to clear customs at the dock before we could board the vessel and coordinate with Captain Vince. The Coast Guard had two men dispatched to cover the inspection. The American Bureau of Shipping would count on the Coast Guard findings and use them for their compliance certification. It would come down to just two Coasties and us to run through the instant replay of what we'd seen in Croatia.

When I got back from Croatia, I watched all the video and processed the photos into our usual comprehensive Under Water Inspection In lieu of Drydocking Report. We would have copies of the video tapes and reports with the photographic documentation with us when we met the ship.

We arrived at the HOVIC Marine Terminal and met the Coast Guard at the gangway to the *GROTON*. Once the Customs guys cleared the vessel we boarded the ship and tracked down Captain Vince. He was in his office with Brian Swensen. Swensen had met the ship when the tugs went out to bring her into the terminal. They both seemed glad to see us. Brian asked me to step out with him and let Captain Vince and the Chief Engineer meet with the Coast Guard.

"I gotta tell you, you guys did a hell of a job over in Croatia. The crew is still talking about that Mountain top lodge. Gehegan was pretty happy he was able to track you guys down. He was in tough shape with this one." Brian said.

"Hey, when I get a call from Joe Gehegan I know there's a big deal going on somewhere. I was shocked when he said the *GROTON* was stuck in Croatia. I'd been watching it on TV since the war broke out. When Joe asked if we'd do it, I agreed but there was one huge issue, logistics. Like, how do you ship a ton of equipment and crew into a hot warzone that the US State Department had already made a no-go zone and ordered everyone out?" I responded.

"Yeah, I know. I was sitting there when you called him back. He already had everything figured out until you asked for a rental car. I nearly laughed out loud. It had been a big source of contention with Captain Vince. He wouldn't authorize a crew vehicle." Brian chuckled.

"Thank God for Avis. Who knew, Avis Rijeka? When we got to Avis in Rijeka the only thing they had was a Canary yellow YUGO. Figures, you want a getaway car if things get out of control and they rent you a bright yellow target in a shooting gallery!" We both laughed.

"Already heard about it from Vince. He looked over the side when you guys pulled in and saw that clown car. He said to the Mate, what the fuck is that? Can't be the divers!" that cracked me up.

"No sweat. We redeemed ourselves! Everything worked out and the crew got a great night out before we left. There was something that did freak me out. At the bar in the lodge we went to for dinner, there was a crowd of people watching the TV. Seemed pretty strange to find a crowd on a Tuesday night, especially in a war zone.

There was some Russian guy standing on a tank in Moscow with a bullhorn yelling to a crowd. I didn't really get the whole story until I got back to Boston. Turns out, it was a coup in Moscow. Are you shittin me? I'm on a mountain top in a hot war zone while Gorbechev is being kidnapped and Yeltsin's on a tank with a bullhorn! I'm damn glad I didn't know the whole story! Just being in Croatia was enough for me." I said.

Brian's smile faded. "I know all about it. We were watching closely in New York. Gehegan was asking for contingency plans and was looking at me to come up with something. We all got lucky with that one."

"Nice to know you were thinking of us!" That brought the smile back.

"No harm no foul!" He said. "Gehegan had a corporate jet on standby in Italy and the US Navy was looped in. We had the crews back, even you guys. I told Gehegan, worst case you guys could swim to Italy. He thought that was pretty funny!"

"Yeah sure, we're great swimmers. Guess I owe you a drink for that one! Swing by the Caravelle later if you have time." I said.

"Time to get to it with today's survey. You guys have a plan?" he asked.

"Sure do. The crew will rig everything up while I get the VCR and monitor set up. I've got several hours of the clearest video we've ever produced. If I can corral the Coast Guard guys and pitch them on getting a cup of coffee and checking out the video, we just might be able to shorten this whole instant replay by a bunch. I'm going to give it a shot." I said confidently.

"Great idea. Anything we can do to get done as soon as possible would be a big deal." Brian said liking the plan.

The way I saw it, the survey planned for today was more for checking the box than giving any more details for review. If they would sit and watch the tape the Coast Guard guys could see how great the conditions were, and fast forward or rewind at will to blow through the video. I had high hopes they'd watch the tapes and take less time running through it again today. Instant replay was a waste of time in my opinion, but what the hell, they were paying for it.

Back on deck, the crew was almost finished rolling out the video equipment and setting up the dive station. I check in with crew and told them to get everything a hundred percent ready to go and then standby. I was going to see if I could sell the Coasties on a video show from Croatia. They gave me a WTF look and just shook their heads.

The dive control center was set up in the galley on the deck level of the *GROTON* on the port side, close to the aft door hatch. Monitor, VCR, and diver comms plugged into the VCR were set and ready. I tracked down the Coast Guard guys, still in Captain Vince's office on the second deck. The lead guy was named Rick and his sidekick Joe. Jeez another Joe, great, easy to remember.

"Well, gentlemen, we're all set down in the galley. Coffee's on and the crew is set up and ready on deck. I asked them to standby." I said.

We moved down to the galley and I turned on the VCR and monitor continuing my sales job on checking out the existing tape. "We did a comprehensive survey when we were over in Croatia. It was our first trip ever working in the Adriatic. I gotta say, I've never seen clearer water and conditions like that before. We've spent a bunch of time down here in the Caribbean and have been spoiled by the conditions, but at the Viktor Lenac Shipyard in Rijeka the water was gin clear.

I had as close to unlimited visibility as imaginable working underwater. I could see the seawall nearly a thousand feet down from where the *GROTON* sat. There was an almost unsettling degree of clarity. The tapes I brought back are of the highest quality and clarity that we have ever produced. I'd like to flip one the tapes in the VCR and have you get a look at it. It's amazing." I finished.

Rick said, "Great! Let's have a look. We were disappointed we couldn't make the trip. They pulled the rug out once the State Department made their declaration. Joe and I were all set to go. What a mess over there!"

"It was a little surreal to us. Rijeka was not in the area of the active fighting, but it was unnerving watching the contrails from the bombers and aircraft we could see to the east of our position. Other than that, there was an eerie sense of calm in Rijeka." I said.

"How long were you guys over there?" asked Joe.

"Six days. We were always very conscience of our surroundings . It seemed a lot longer than the six days. Not to mention watching TV over there with Boris Yeltsin on a tank with a bullhorn. Jeezus!" I said for dramatic effect.

"Great timing!" said Rick. "Let's see what you got."

I popped in the first tape. It had a brief intro I had done from the dock showing the *GROTON* sitting alongside at Viktor Lenac and then the shift to the stunning underwater video. I handed Rick the remote for the VCR and said , "I'm getting a coffee. This is a great show!"

Rick paused the video so he and Joe could also get a fresh cup of coffee. We sat back down, and Rick hit the remote and the tape rolled.

All I could hear were comments like, wow!, and holy shit! look at that video. Rick and Joe fast forwarded the video slowing only when they saw something of interest. We'd filmed everything.

They sat for over an hour watching and taking notes. When we finished the first tape I put the second one in and hit play. We had condensed everything into two cassettes. Both Rick and Joe were very focused on the production. It was spectacular, at least for something as boring as the underbody of an oil tanker.

They continued to fast forward through the second tape and finally finished the video. "Man, that was amazing !" said Rick. "What do you think Joe?"

"I've never seen anything like that. The visibility and water clarity was amazing!" Joe said.

"That's what I said. We're ready today to do it all over again, but I figured you'd be interested to see these before we got started." I said in a way leaving open a conversation on what we planned to do now. "What do you think?"

Rick said, "I've seen enough. There is no way we're going to see anything better than that. What do you think Joe?"

"We've got a lot of other work to do onboard, but we should probably at least have a quick look at the propellers and aft hull marking to confirm we actually got a live look at the ship."

"Agreed." Said Rick. "How about getting someone in the water to get a look around?"

"You got it." I said heading for the door to tee up our crew. "Showtime!" I said as I gave them the details. We'd do a good intro and then I'd have Kai on a limited production to capture what the Coast Guard guys asked for. I would hand off the tape and an extra copy I made of the Croatia taping.

It only took about twenty minutes worth of dive time to complete the limited taping. Swensen would be happy. Now we could roll things up and enjoy our stay in St. Croix. Drinks and dinner in Christiansted sounded like a plan.

View between pontoons of typical ITB in light ballast

I finished up with Rick and Joe and after handing off the video tapes they said we were done thanking me for showing them the Croatia video. Saved them a bunch of time. Perfect. Now to find Swensen and Captain Vince.

Brian Swensen had disappeared somewhere, but Captain Vince was in his office. I told Vince we were done.

"Done? You just got here." He said.

"Hey, all that work we did in Croatia paid off! Tell Swensen we'll be at the bar in the Caravelle later if he's looking for me. Thanks so much for all your help!" I said.

"You guys did great! I'm out of here tomorrow. Got a lot of vacation time I need to take. I'll be seeing you again sometime later" Captain Vince said, and with that we shook hands and I headed down to the dock. The crew had already rolled everything up and packed it to ship as luggage for departure. We were going to take a 'reward' day in St. Croix before heading back. We'd earned it.

Back at the Caravelle we hit the bar and had a toast to having survived the ordeal. Dinner would be our favorite, Rosta Ribs at the Charthouse down on the boardwalk in Christiansted. What a relief.

After dinner, Brian Swensen came by the Caravelle and joined us for a nightcap. He'd been in touch with the Hess office in Mid-Town Manhattan. They were very pleased and asked Brian to pass along their thanks. Wait until they see my bill, I thought.

Brian had to take off, but we were sure to see him again with having a steady run of upcoming maintenance projects on Hess ships and others in St. Croix at the HOVIC Terminal. We'd be leaving in the morning for Boston.

SPIRIT OF '76 Painting Image - Original hangs in MARBLEHEAD Town Hall

Looking SW across Marblehead Harbor from Corinthian Yacht Club

Yacht Club Launch drop off at Landing Wharf – Marblehead -

Author's wife Susan and daughters Melissa, Kristin, and Mindy on right, 1982

Author with Children- Jon and Lindsay foreground with James and Kristin, 1991

Author with Father James and Mother Louise in Venice, FL

Authors Father, Founding member,Marblehead Festival of the Arts – in 1962, Photo by Author at Celebration Parade in 1990

Susan Proctor - High School Photo -Met Author in 1976 – Married 1979

Day at the Beach –Cormorant Beach Club - St. Croix, USVI

Author with son Jonathan – Dolphin Habitat rehab – NE Aquarium, 1990

Jonathan sleeping on the job - NE Aquarium - Boston

Brother Dana Lee out on workboat, Hess Supertanker Ship Call, Port of LA-

Hess Oil Virgin Islands (HOVIC) Marine Terminal – ITB Tankers at the docks

HESS VLCC SEAL ISLAND–Discharging Crude Oil - Dock 1 – HOVIC – St. Croix

HESS VLCC ST LUCIA – Newly Arrived– Dock 1 – HOVIC – St. Croix

950-Foot-Long Panamax, SEA-LAND INTEGRITY, Port Everglades, FL

Stern View, SEA-LAND VALUE- Panamax, European Bound from NJ

SEA-LAND EXPEDITION Containership - San Juan, Puerto Rico

SEA-LAND CRUSADER - San Juan Marine Terminal

134

Author on the Condado Beach - San Juan, PR – Caribe Hilton in Background

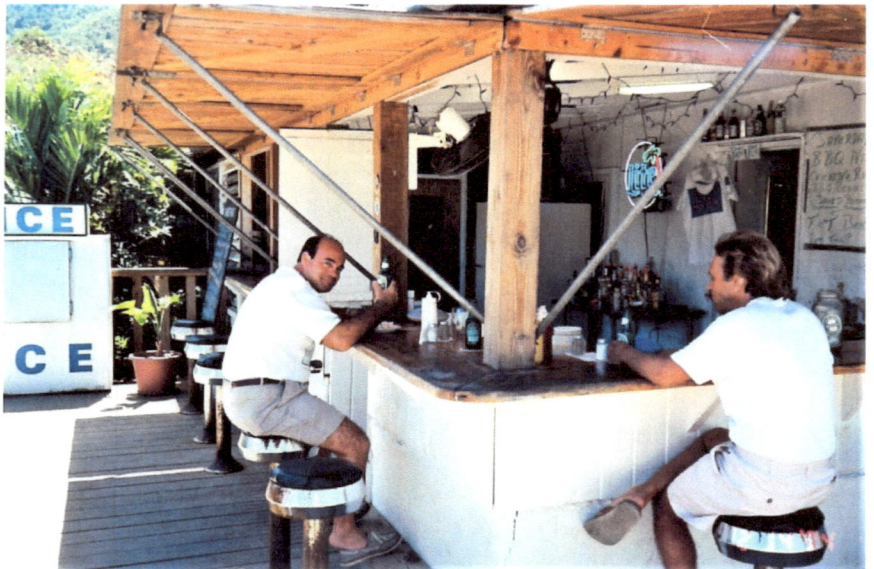

Author with Arne Backlund – Photo by Kai Holleson - Sundowner Bar - St. Croix

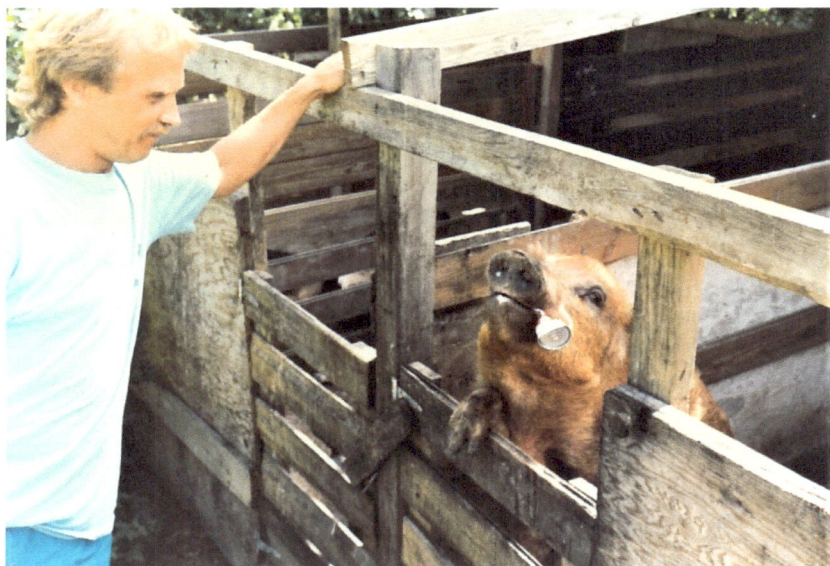

World Famous Domino Club, Beer Drinking Pigs, St. Croix, Still Drinking Beer to this day

Kai Holleson and Paul Mercaldi - Happy Hour in Old San Juan – Photo by Author

136

Selfie - Author's Reflection on 30-foot diameter propeller blade after servicing –

Author preparing to depart St. Croix after successful ship call

Author, Paul Mercaldi and Kai Holleson – Active Ops -HOVIC – St. Croix

Lucy Backlund, Paul Mercaldi, Arne Backlund left to right - Siesta Beach, Sarasota

Kai Holleson and Author on Tugboat - Port Arthur Texas- Photo by Paul Mercaldi

Propeller machining in process - Machine reflection visible on blade

Author sitting on highly skewed propeller – Port Arthur Texas

CHAPTER TWELVE

SEALAND CONSUMER - SAN JUAN
Propeller Repair

⚓

Puerto Rico - US Territory - Caribbean Trans-Shipment Hub

San Juan, Puerto Rico was one of our favorite places to travel to work on large commercial ships. It was a central hub for shipping to the Islands of the Caribbean and South and Central America. Many of the products produced south of the border are trans-shipped through San Juan and outbound to the US, Europe, and the World. The Port of San Juan has an easy approach and access on the northern coast of the Island.

El Moro was the Spanish fort that protected the approaches to San Juan during the early days in the New World following the voyages of Columbus. Overlooking the access to the port with a deadly location for cannon placement, it was the scene of many a naval skirmish as the British, French, and Dutch sailed the Caribbean and challenged the Spanish.

Spain had been highly successful laying claim to much of the New World. Their infamous collection of Conquistadors had raided and slaughtered many of the natives of the region. Taking all the gold and treasures from the Incas and Mayans in the name of the King of Spain made them a target for all those seeking fortune and glory. El Moro would be impenetrable, even famed English Captain Sir Francis Drake would sail back and forth taking pot shots at the fort knowing there would be no winning the battle for San Juan.

Now when you look out at the Atlantic from El Moro, it's easy to imagine the cannons blazing, firing on Drake and any others daring to challenge El Moro. The feeling is palpable when standing there. Today, commercial ships take that turn to port as they round El Moro and head for the inner harbor. Quite a sight from up on the bluff.

File Photo: Spanish Fort, El Moro, overlooking approaches to San Juan Harbor

SeaLand had a major shipping operation in San Juan, and we were often called to service their ships when in port. Surveys, repairs, and propeller polishing's were routine and always a crew favorite. Many were mundane ship calls but there were a few stand outs worth penning for this collection of stories.

First up, SEALAND CONSUMER. On one of her runs out of San Juan, she left to make a delivery to Venezuela. Outbound they ran over a large steel channel buoy, a highly unusual occurrence. As a result, the ship developed a vibration following the incident. That indicated they had damaged the propeller but considered it insufficient to hold up the trip. They called ahead to New Jersey to report the incident and have a dive crew standing by when they returned to San Juan in a couple of weeks.

Bill Davies, SeaLand Port Engineer, called to request that we meet the vessel in San Juan and be prepared to investigate the vibration issue. He felt that they may have damaged the propeller blades and was hoping it may be mitigated by fairing or cropping to reduce the vibration to keep the vessel in service. Last thing he wanted to hear about was a drydock. He faxed the latest arrival schedule to San Juan.

We made arrangements to meet the ship. Not knowing the extent of the damage Arne Backlund and I flew to San Juan to check. We had two more guys on short notice to make the trip if we found the propeller was serviceable. They would transport the hydraulic tools and special equipment to crop and balance the propeller and abrasives to smooth out any damage to the lead edges of the blades. It didn't make sense to send a four-man crew, fully loaded, with no information other than a field report of vibration.

After arriving in San Juan, we heard from SeaLand that the ship was delayed due to making less speed to help tamp down the vibrations. We'd just have to cool it and wait. The vessel was due outside El Morro in the morning.

We'd just have to make the best of it. It was a Saturday night, and anyone that has spent any time in San Juan knows the town is a great place to have a good time. Casinos and dining along the Condado for one, but there was another world-famous venue just outside Old San Juan. The place was called the Black Angus. Now, this place was 'one of a kind.' As the name suggests it was a restaurant, a very special restaurant. Not a steak house as the name suggests, but rather a Chinese fast food takeout serving patrons of the bar from the back of the house. The main bar and business was actually the most famous brothel in the Western Hemisphere, so it was said.

Well, there we were with choices; gambling and hanging out on the Condado or hitting the Black Angus to work on our Spanish. We went with the Angus.

The Black Angus had a horseshoe shaped bar that sat about fifty guys. It was quite a sight. There was a giant black bull with red eyes sitting in the middle of the bar behind the bartenders, and the lighting was set low with red wallpaper and a black ceiling to finish the décor.

Being a Saturday night, the place was packed when Arne and I got there. As our eyes adjusted, we could see there were at least as many women as men in the bar. All the women you might find there were very friendly and primarily from Central and South America. Over the years, we'd been there a few times, not that we kept count, but when we were working in San Juan before Leeward Marine, it seemed like a safe haven, especially with the special likes of typical Commercial Divers.

I found it to be a great way to keep the crew from wandering off when out on the road. Hard to take care of business if you find yourself one crewman short on any given morning. Not to mention getting stuck having to bail them out of jail in the case of an extreme event. Fortunately, the strategy worked by keeping the crew entertained, no bail required, and nothing extra allowed in a crew member expense report.

We had a simple routine if we went to the Angus. Sit at the bar, order ice cold beers and check out the scenery. Needless to say, the women *were* very friendly. It was amazing how much taller and better looking you seemed to be once you reached the bar, and all your old jokes were somehow funny again!

It was not uncommon to have a new friend on each arm vying for your attention. The women were all fully clothed in the bar. Not surprisingly, wearing the fashions one might expect in such a place. The Security was good, and patrons were well mannered. I found they were all great Spanish tutors, and only too happy to help when asked.

I did take advantage of the opportunity. It was always a good ego booster for the cost of a couple of cold beers. The girls would laugh like hell at my crappy Spanish. Anyway, it served as a good diversion from the grind of the work ahead and the dirty waters of San Juan harbor. .

Back to Saturday night. The only place you could squeeze into the bar and get a beer at the ANGUS was the far, inside end of the bar. I just ordered myself and Arne a couple of Medallas, a local PR favorite beer, when out of nowhere there was a booming voice with somebody hollering my name! CHRIS LEE! CHRIS LEE!

"WHAT THE HELL ARE YOU DOING IN HERE ?!" It was the loudest I've ever heard my name called out, or maybe it was just our location that made it seem louder. Sounded like a bull horn only steps away from where we stood. It was so loud the surrounding bar fell silent as this hulk of a man came into focus out of the crowd. Holy shit! It was Ed Washburn, the Chief Engineer of the '*SEA-LAND CONSUMER.*'

He was laughing like hell as he made his way over to us. "I'm going to charge Bill Davies overtime for having to track down the divers at the whorehouse!" He howled laughing. It was a shocker. I had to laugh realizing how absurd the whole thing was. What are the chances of getting called out in that kind of way, and in that kind of place, in the bowels of the Caribbean at the most famous brothel in the Western Hemisphere?

"Thought you guys were due here in the morning." I said, trying to keep my cool.

"You shittin' me, it's Saturday night in San Juan! I made sure, vibration or not, we could make a few extra turns and get here in time to get to the Angus. And look what I found!" he said, once again nearly in tears laughing.

File Photo: World Famous 'Black Angus Night Club,' San Juan

"Okay, okay you got me this time." I said. "What happens in San Juan stays in San Juan, right ?"

"Sure. Bill Davies would probably back charge me after checking my expense report for cash expenditures. He'd know it was from the Angus and throw it back on me. You know he's been here more than a few times over the years !" the Chief Engineer chuckled.

"Great to see you Ed!" I said. "We'll get a good start in the morning now we know you're here. Thanks for the thrill! What are you drinking?" I asked as the bartender showed up. This would be a good time to buy him a drink and hit the exit. I tapped Arne's arm and motioned to the door. He was *still* laughing having witnessed a classic. In close company, he tells the story to this day.

SEA-LAND CONSUMER - *Propeller Damage*

Early Sunday morning, Arne and I showed up at the ship at the container dock at the far end of the Port of San Juan. We needed to get a look ASAP to figure out what we were up against and if we could make a repair. The alternative would be off to a drydock and replacement of the propeller. That would be a huge deal. Based on what we heard they were likely in need of a new prop but that could be scheduled during a normal cycle if they could make it. Ours was to give them a shot at it if possible.

We checked in with the Chief Engineer, our pal from the 'Angus.' When we showed up he was still enjoying his 'gotcha' moment from the night before.

"Morning Chief. I'm gonna get in there and scope things out. There's no guarantee we can fix that thing, but I'll take a bunch of pics and see. We have a crew on standby to join us here if we get a chance. At least enough so you can reach your normal drydock schedule." I said.

Ed Washburn said. "So, I guess if you can't help us, we can find you at the 'Angus' if we need anything? Better get to it !" I had a feeling we had only just begun the razz from our Black Angus encounter!

San Juan harbor is not the cleanest place but at least the water was warm. Shorts, tee shirts, booties, harness, and hard hat made for an easy and rapid dress in. It was only a few minutes after we left the Chief that I made the jump. Arne lowered the camera.

The visibility was close to five feet, excellent for where we were. When I dropped down to the propeller the damage was evident and dramatic. Two of the four blades had curled tips that were deflected six inches +/- and about three feet in length. The other two blades were chewed up along the outer edges, but I didn't see any deflection. Looked like we had a shot. My fear was if the deflections were too deep into the blade section our hydraulics saws wouldn't be able to make the cuts and they'd be drydock bound. After blowing' off a roll of film I asked Arne to pull up my slack. Time to see the Chief Engineer and launch the crew and gear out of Boston. If they made the 11:00A nonstop they could be in San Juan by 3:00P.

I asked Arne to roll up our dive gear. Didn't want it laying around out here while we waited for the crew. We'd have time to go back to the hotel and get some rest. It would be a long night if the Chief agreed to move forward.

I tracked down Ed Washburn, "Chief, there's bad news and slightly better news. You guys wacked the hell out of that propeller. All four blades were damaged, and you'll be needing a new prop. That's the bad news. The better news is the deflections that will need to be cropped are thin enough in the blade section that we should be able to make the cuts and keep you guys going. The other two blades are chewed up pretty bad, but we can fair those out and restore enough of the geometry to mitigate the cavitation. In a nutshell, if you say go, we'll launch the crew and gear and they can be in San Juan by three o'clock. Our plan would be to start right away and work through the night. By noon tomorrow we should have as much done as possible and get you on your way. We should be able to get enough done to get the vibration down to a minor annoyance rather than bouncing the ship around back there,"

"Do it." Said Ed. "I'll call Davies and let him know. We only have three or four months until we go in for drydocking. If we can make that, he'll be thrilled. We'll be able to tell right away on our run back down to Venezuela."

"OK Chief. I'm making the call. The crew is already on standby, weather's good, so here we go!" I said as I went to make the call from the Marine Terminal. Kai Holleson was waiting for the call and he had Steve Humphries on standby to meet him at Logan.

Not much more we could do until they got there so we rolled back to the hotel after reaching Kai. He had our phone number to reach us at the hotel in San Juan. When they got in, we'd run over to the airport to pick them up, and then off to the port. Both Kai and Steve had been here before, so San Juan was familiar territory. My travel agent made the arrangements for airport pick up at Logan for their tickets to San Juan. Time for a break and wait for the call.

Back at the hotel, we caught an early lunch and hit the rack for a couple of hours. We'd need all the rest we could get to make it through the upcoming all-nighter. I set my alarm for two thirty and dropped out for a couple of hours of sleep. For commercial divers it's a practiced art to be able to sleep anywhere, anytime.

Our work required that we manage time so as to take advantage of those opportunities for rest when out in the field. It's pretty common to be shaken awake in the middle of the night to suit up and have to jump over the side to take your turn in the barrel. In this case, we knew the plan and scope of work would require an all-night action to crop and fair the propeller. We were hopeful of limiting any down time in their schedule.

The phone rang, it was Kai. "Hello there. We're at Muñoz.," short for San Juan Luis Muñoz Marín International Airport, quite a mouthful. How about plain old San Juan Airport ?

"You guys got in early. All the gear make it?" I asked.

Kai said, "Looks like it. We brought extra blades and cup stones based on what you were saying about the damage."

"Good thinking. We'll be down in twenty minutes." I said and hung up.

We found that with careful packing we could use minivans for work vehicles when traveling. Taking care not to do any damage or leak anything like hydraulic oil they served us well and were available virtually everywhere we went. Arne and I piled into the latest minivan rental and headed for the airport.

Steve and Kai were standing outside baggage claim with quite a pile. We loaded up and tried to beat the traffic to the Port in Bayamon, southwest of the airport. It was just before 4:00p as we pulled alongside the *CONSUMER.* Our rented Bobcat to supply hydraulic power for our saws and tools had been delivered and was parked at the stern of the ship. Everybody got right to it, setting up the equipment and getting our dive station hooked up while I went up to find the Chief Engineer, Ed Washburn.

SEA-LAND CONSUMER alongside dock in San Juan

Ed was in the control room down below deck in the engine space. I told him it was going to be a long night, but we hoped to be done by noon tomorrow. We had a lot of work to do and weren't wasting any time. I asked him to get us a power cord for lighting so we could have good visibility on the dock. He said he'd do one better and add a flood light over the side for added help. With that, I quickly returned to the dock and prepared the cameras, tools, and special rigging we needed to secure the hydraulic saw to the propeller blades that needed cropping.

This was not our first time cleaning up propeller damage. It required custom made clamps to bite down on the blade section and hold the heavy hydraulic saw and hoses while we made the saw cuts. The clamps were one of the limiting factors as to how much we would be able to accomplish. That's why it was so critical to get a good look before committing to the scope of work. The thickness of the blade section that we could physically crop was not much more than two inches and were also limited by cut depth of the blades on the hydraulic saw.

All set to go. It would take some time to do the measurements and calculate the cut lines that would be marked for each of the blades that needed to be cropped. It is no simple process and would take way longer to explain than most readers would want to hear about. The geometry of the blade section, figuring the weights of materials removed, and formulas for balancing, we'd have many things to consider, and on and on it goes..

Arne was first in and was tasked with setting the propeller to the best position for saw cutting the first of two blades. We had radio coms with the Chief Engineer in the control room and had him turn the propeller with the jacking gear to turn the propeller shaft without using the engine power. All large ships have this capability and we would need each of the blades set to give the best vertical positioning to use gravity to our advantage to make accurate cuts.

Arne was set to start. "Ok topside. We need to rotate the propeller clockwise a quarter turn to get number one in position."

"Roger that." "Chief, mark us a quarter turn clockwise and dog it off. This will take a while. Let me know when you're done." I said.

"Quarter turn. Roger. Standby."

"Topside. They've engaged the jacking gear. The wheel is turning." Said Arne.

"Orders in for a quarter turn. Confirm the position when the wheel stops." I said.

"Hold that." Said Arne. "That's good." He said. Must have been a good call because I never had to call the Chief.

"Chief, we're all set. Please have somebody on standby in the control room. We'll be needing help rolling that propeller all night long." I said requesting control room monitoring.

"You got it. Good luck !" the Chief signed off turning things over to the Third Engineer, the lucky winner to babysit the divers.

My turn to get in there and lay out the cut lines so we could get that saw running. It was a terribly slow process saw cutting the nickel aluminum bronze alloy underwater (NiBrAl). Each of the blades would likely require four to six hours to complete their cuts, so if I could quickly get the first cut line marked and saw running, there would be plenty of time to get the second blades cut line done and scope out the rest of the work for the cup stones.

That would be a separate process and require a tool change out to a heavy-duty hydraulic grinder to fair in the chewed edges on the other two blades. How much fairing we would do would be a subjective call once we got that started.

It took me half an hour to measure and draw the cut line for the first blade.

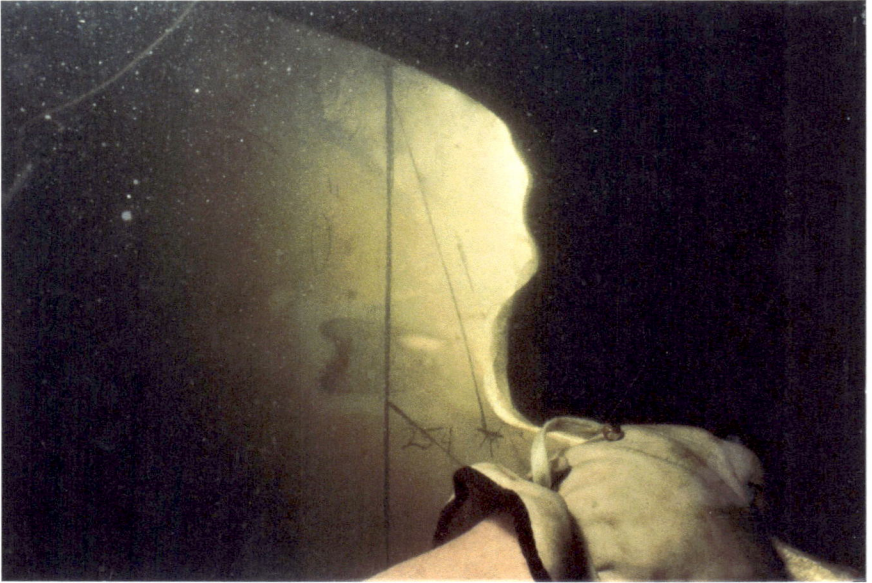

Cut line drawn on damaged blade of Sea-Land Consumer Propeller

I got out, and Arne got back in to set the clamps and saw. Once he got that done we started the saw. He would spend a couple hours standing by watching. You couldn't leave the saw unattended. That lends new meaning to the expression 'watching grass grow.' That would be a speedy event compared to watching the saw and listening to the droning sound of the blade sawing at a nearly imperceptible rate. We'd all get our chance to baby sit that damn saw over the course of the night. The sun was setting, and we'd soon be entering night work.

In a way, it was better working at night. With the ambient sunlight gone the surrounding darkness below allows you to better focus on your work. The helmet lighting floods the work area directly in front of you in a way that it doesn't during the day when competing with the sunlight that invades your surrounds. That part is great, but it doesn't speed up the saw!

While the saw whirred along Kai was in the water as the final few inches were being cut. He attached another special clamp and tag line for the piece we expected would drop off any minute now. The saw itself was secure so when the piece was ready to drop, we would pull up the slack on his dive umbilical and tie off the tag line to a bollard on the dock. Once it let go we would turn off the saw and pull the piece out of the water after everything was secured.

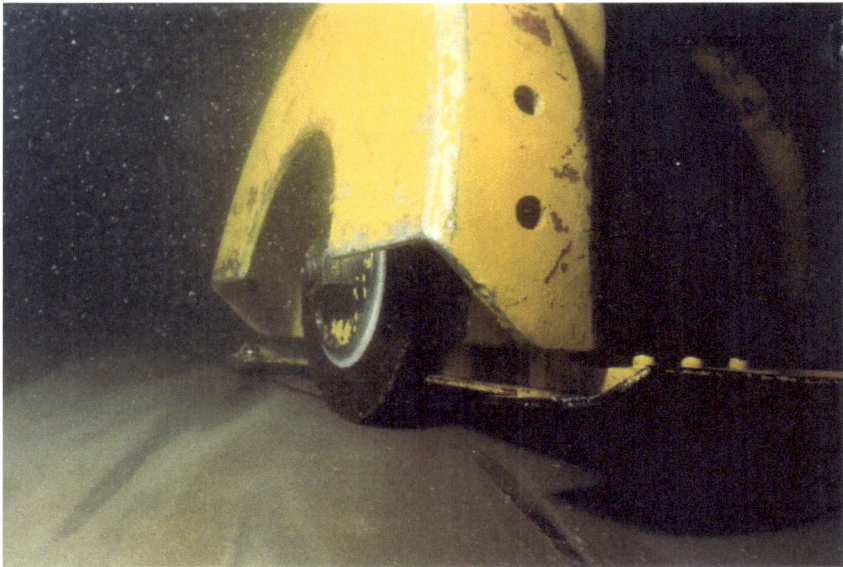

Heavy hydraulic saw used on SEA-LAND CONSUMER to crop damaged blade section

A pop was heard up top as the piece let go. "That's it, topside." Said Kai. We'd already heard the sound through the radio comms.

"How's it look?" I asked

"Like a perfect cut. Sighting the edge, it conforms properly with no deflection visible on the blade section. I'd say this one's good." I'm coming out.

"Roger that. We'll need to wake up our guy in the control room. Time to rotate the wheel again. Before you come up give us a good estimate on the direction and roll for the next cut. Thanks." I said, happy we finally got through the first one. It took over five hours of sawing time. Jeez Louise.

We had to closely weigh the piece we removed. After doing the math, we had up to thirty pounds per blade that could be removed and still be well within operational balance. Seems like a lot but when your propeller weighs up to thirty tons for a ship this size it isn't all that much. Restoring the blade section geometry was paramount since that was the primary cause of the vibration. Two deflected tips were plenty to throw off a bunch of vibration and cavitation while making a hundred turns a minute or better. For large commercial ships, 100 to 125 RPM is generally within operating range for a ship underway. If we could get them enough relief from the vibration to achieve that range of RPMs they'd have a good chance of making their scheduled drydocking in a few months after we got done there.

We managed to get the Engineer to roll the propeller clockwise to the best position for the saw cut of the second blade. Steve was our guy in the barrel getting the equipment moved over and secured. It was closing in on midnight when we started the second cut. This line was slightly longer so we could count on at least another five hours plus of saw time. Could take us until dawn to drop the next piece.

Our minivan would provide shelter and opportunity to rest crew members. With a four-man team we were able to rotate a man to get some rest while one guy worked the saw and two men stood watch topside for support. We'd need that extra bit of rest to carry us through. At the current rate of progress, we were still on track to finish up around lunchtime or slightly after.

Steve would spend the first four-hour shift operating the saw. No doubt about it, we were in for a long night. Coffee was a big help keeping us going. Thank God the ships galley kept a bottomless pot.

We took turns running up and down to keep us supplied. About the time we were ready to drop the next tip it would be close to breakfast time. That, at least, gave us something to look forward to as the saw droned on.

"Hey Steve. Wake up down there. Thought I heard snoring." I joked. It was as monotonous a task as imaginable. Staring at that saw and making sure you kept everything aligned to follow the line marked on the blade was as boring as it gets.

"That could be. Where the hell did we come up with this saw? I could take a pretty good nap and only find us an inch or two farther along. This shit is torture!" He said.

I had to chuckle knowing he was right. "Never know. Maybe you'll hit a soft spot! Gotta pay attention down there."

"Ef you. I know you guys are up there sucking down coffee and telling dirty jokes." Steve said, sounding a little irritated. He'd drawn the short straw for the graveyard shift. Oh well. If we finished up in time, we'd be able to spend an evening in San Juan to decompress before heading back.

"We've got a good chance at hitting the 'Angus' later if you keep after it down there." I teased.

"Oh yeah! I'll be well rested by then!" Steve said, giving himself an attitude adjustment. Now, sawing with a purpose in mind just might get him through the pain of it all.

I was resting Kai as we got deeper into the night. When Steve hit the four-hour mark down below, he should be close to dropping the piece. With any luck, we'd catch a break and hit the galley to re-charge. Working the cup stones to clean up the edges of the other two blades would be physically demanding. It required free handed operation of a heavy hydraulic grinder and using cup stone abrasives that were up to several pounds each depending on which area was being worked on added to the weight. Fortunately, they were easily changed out below so whoever was down there would have a supply in a bag hanging off our staging frame and not losing any time waiting on topside support.

The first signs of the approaching dawn could be seen in the east. Kai had started his shift somewhere around 4:30A and was reporting that he had about two hours left to drop the piece. It wouldn't be long now. I was feeling the effects of pulling an all nighter.. If all continued well, I would rest myself after breakfast while the guys cleaned up the edges below. I needed to be rested to finish up the photography and assess our results. A couple of hours would do it.

"Topside. I'm getting close down here. Shut the saw down while I rig things up to drop this piece." Kai said. Music to my ears.

"Roger that Kai. Let us know when to tighten things up and take in your slack." I said thinking about bacon and eggs and the galley. The sun was up and blazing in the early morning in San Juan. "We're looking good for breakfast if you can get that piece cut through."

"No problem with that. We only have two inches left at the end of the cut. Best guess, ten minutes, tops." Said Kai sounding chipper considering what we'd been through. "OK topside tighten everything up and power up the saw."

The saw was up and running and it was only a few minutes later we heard the piece crack free.

"That's all y'all!" said Kai as we could see the line tighten up with the piece hanging off the bollard. "I'm coming up." It was nearly seven AM. What a night.

The cool air aboard felt great as we made our way to the galley. The Chief Engineer was still there with a coffee in hand.

"How'd you make out?" Ed Washburn asked.

"Got both curled tips cropped and getting ready to clean up the edges of the other blades. The cuts look great. Didn't get that deep into the blade section and we were able to get past the deflections on both blades." I said.

Hydraulic Grinder used on SEA-LAND CONSUMER – Specialized clamp in background

"How much time do you figure you need to finish? The Captain has to schedule the Harbor Pilot and tugs. We're almost done with cargo and need to get out of here. Got my fingers crossed on the vibration problem." He said.

"We should be done by noon if the Captain's looking for a projection." I said. "I'll give you an update around ten o'clock to confirm.

"I'll pass that along. Let's figure a meeting at eleven in my office to get your final take before we sail." The Chief said.

"Looking forward to it" I said as we finished up breakfast and went for one more coffee and sucking up a few more minutes of air conditioning before hitting the steamy weather out on the dock.

For the next three hours we rotated crew in and out every hour or so due to the physical strain of spinning those cup stones and fairing in the rough edges. Once again, restoring the blade geometry being the goal. Where the chunks of bronze had been broken away the face of the blades had small amounts of material that had deflected out from the point of damage. Even small bits extending outside the face of the blades could be impactful when it came to vibration and cavitation.

The actual edges were less of an issue than those areas that lay outside the contour of the blade section. Chewed as they may be, if they conformed to the geometry of the blade they should turn with little to no vibration. Cavitation was another issue. Erosion of the blade surface from the chewed edges could be expected but wouldn't necessarily add anything to the vibration, which was the key element we were addressing. All would be good once they changed out the propeller at the next drydocking I was thinking as I dozed off in the minivan.

Bang!Bang!Bang! on the minivan window. "Hey, wake up in there. It's almost ten o'clock." It was Arne, clearly enjoying himself shocking me back to life.

"Okay, okay. Are we ready for final pics and inspection?" I asked.

"Pretty close. We've done about as much as we can do down there. All the protruding nubs were smoothed out. You should probably get ready to make the jump." He said.

The crew shut down the hydraulics and hauled all the equipment out of the water. When they cleared the gear, they hauled up the two pieces we had hanging off the bollard. I needed to get good pics and measurements for our report before we returned them to the ship. The Sealand Marine Engineers would want the data to check our calculations on the changes to the propeller, post cropping.

I dressed in and did a photo run capturing all the work we completed for the follow up report. Time to get out and wrap things up with Ed Washburn while the crew rolled up all the equipment and packed up the tools. Kai would call in for the pick-up on the Bobcat we used for our hydraulic power supply.

The Chief was up with the Captain discussing the upcoming trip. My timing was perfect. I could give both the latest on the propeller and ask the Chief to let Bill Davies, the Marine Engineer in Port Elizabeth, know as soon as possible on the vibration status.

"We'll know within an hour of clearing the sea buoy, so I can get him a message before four o'clock. He should still be in his office if you call him." Ed Washburn said.

"Would that be the same sea buoy you guys hit the last trip outbound?" I asked sarcastically.

"Yeah, yeah. Everybody's a comedian around here." Said the Captain. It would have been his responsibility that his mate goofed up.

"Well, I think we just might have gotten enough of that cleaned up to keep going. It still might have some level of vibration but I'm willing to bet it's greatly reduced." I said reassuringly.

"We'll see." said the Chief as we shook hands and I got out of there. The tugs were headed down the channel and the Pilot was already aboard.

The crew packed up the minivan and we watched the tugs pull the *SEA-LAND CONSUMER* away from the dock to begin their departure from San Juan harbor.

Time to hit the hotel and rest up for dinner and a Spanish lesson at the 'Angus.' I'd call Bill Davies around four o'clock as Ed Washburn suggested and hoped for good news. Still had time for a nap before making the call, my alarm was set for 3:45.

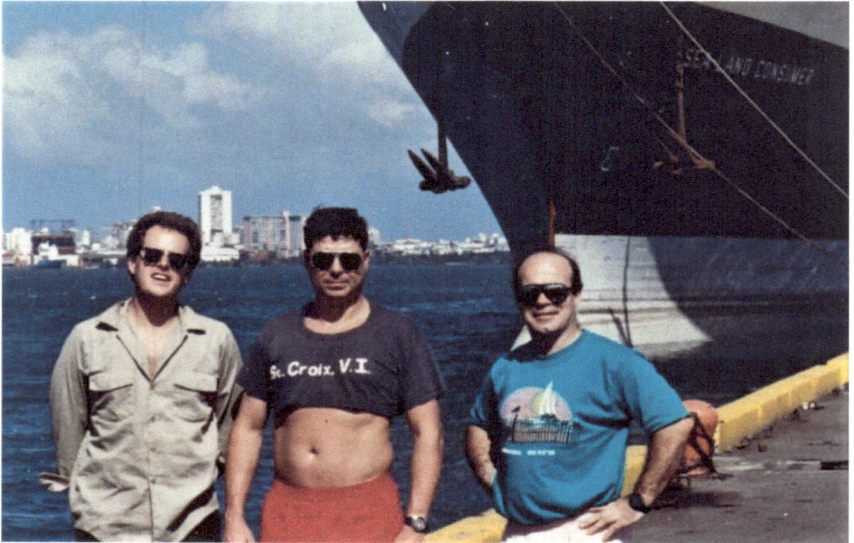

Dive Team - SEA-LAND CONSUMER – Holleson, Humphries, Lee– Photo by Arne Backlund

"Hello Bill. Any word from Ed Washburn?" I asked.

"Hi Chris. Sure did. He was pretty happy. They were making full operational speed with only a fraction of the vibration they had on their trip into San Juan. He'll have more to say after making the run. " Bill said.

"Glad to hear it!. I'm prepared to take another shot at it if we didn't quite get there. Hopefully, that will work and get you guys to drydock.

If there're any issues, let me know. I'd be happy to catch up with them and check it out." I offered.

"Will do. Thanks a lot for the help! I'll update John Katramados. He was worried about shipping a propeller. Not an easy thing to do. At least now he can turn it over to the engineer handling the drydocking and he doesn't have to deal with it. Send me the report when you get back. Have a safe trip." Bill finished up and signed off.

We'd be flying out to Logan in the morning. Time to chill out in San Juan and work on my Spanish. "Hablo espanol ?"

SEA-LAND CONSUMER propeller lying on dock at Sealand Marine Terminal in Port Elizabeth, NJ, after changeout in drydock. Cropped section visible from work performed in Puerto Rico. Story above in Chapter Twelve

CHAPTER THIRTEEN

SEALAND BOTTOM PAINT DILEMMA
Multiple Bottom Paint Failures

❧

At some point, we found ourselves drawn into working on a project to track and document anti-fouling paint failures on a number of SeaLand container ships. There had been major changes to the bottom paint formulas due to environmental concerns. The toxicity of the old standby coatings were discovered to be a major hazard to the waters of the ports and was killing marine life. You might say, that's what they're supposed to do, keep a ship hull free of marine growth. At any rate, we were about to become anti-fouling paint experts

Operating a clean ship was paramount to maintaining a competitive edge in maritime shipping. The cost of fuel is one of the largest expenses in transporting goods by ship. Driving down cost on the engineering and operations side of shipping, allowed the sales teams to offer better rates per ton or container depending on the commodities being shipped.

It took some time for the marine paint suppliers to come up with an alternative that would be less toxic and still give a good result. The first generation of this paint was a multi coat system that worked by gradually wearing away and when a layer got thin enough it would ablate, exposing the next layer below. The theory was that with enough layers, and with each layer providing a measurable period of effectiveness, you could simply calculate how many layers to apply for the ship to reach its next drydocking when the bottom paint would be re-applied. Great idea, as the new paint was well within a reasonable level of toxicity and considered acceptable to mitigate the environmental concerns.

As luck would have it for us, there were serious issues with the new coating system. The layers of paint were peeling off at alarming rates rather than the promised gradual ablation. I was invited to a meeting with the paint vendor and the Senior SeaLand Marine Engineering staff by John Katramados. We would address the issues at their main Marine Engineering office in Port Elizabeth. It was an awkward meeting.

This was a major issue and it boiled down to being either a paint formulation failure or improper preparation of the hull and paint application in the drydock, or maybe some of both. We're talking millions of dollars-worth of liability here. In fairness to the vendor, this was the first generation of the new coating system. They had an impeccable reputation in the industry so there was a real need by them to make things right with SeaLand.

At this point, SeaLand was looking for a path to determine the level of failure on each of the ships. They would be looking for how long until marine growth began to form and affect their fuel consumption and speed. The consensus was that it was a broad-based failure and affected fifteen to twenty percent of the fleet with ships in operation in the trans-Atlantic and Pacific routes that recently completed their normal scheduled drydocking.

In our discussion, having the failure widely spread and involving multiple shipyards led us to believe it was a paint issue rather than drydock application as the root cause. The paint manufacturer's chemists were investigating. Either way they were on the hook and needed speedy action to mitigate the issue.

Any corrective action would require sand blasting and applying new coating once they'd corrected the formulas. Problem was that all the ships were in service and carrying cargo and containers world-wide.

There was no easy way to interrupt the schedules and send the ships to drydock for repainting. Just planning normal dry dockings was a feat in itself.

After much conversation about paint formulation and speculating how things got this messed up, the conversation turned to how SeaLand would monitor the condition of each of the impacted ships and track the degree of failure. That's where we came in.

The paint vendor agreed to pay for our services, and we agreed to develop a cost-effective way to meet the need for SeaLand and keep fair pricing to the paint vendor. This was going to be a scramble to set up the baseline for each ship and length of time between inspections. There was a lot to consider and I'd have to develop a scope of work document for SeaLand and work with the Marine Engineers on scheduling.

After the paint vendors left the meeting, John Katramados asked me to stay to discuss our plan of attack. SeaLand operated fifty-five large containerships.

"Gentlemen, we have a big problem here." He said.

"No kidding!" Exclaimed Bill Davies. "How'd we get this far into it without hearing anything is what I want to know. We've cycled nearly a quarter of the fleet through the drydocking schedules applying this paint, even some of the Atlantic Class. We've positively identified nine ships so far. How do we know there aren't more out there?"

There was a lot of nodding at the table. Everyone was contemplating the potential scale of the problem, painfully aware of the consequences. I took the opportunity to chime in.

"I heard the paint guys talking about monitoring the failure. We'd be able to climb right on that piece to help you establish a baseline. We can do a visual sweep of the bottom of each ship that was recently drydocked and painted as they cycle through our propeller program.

That should capture all of the ships within six months. Another thing, it might just be that not every ship has the same degree of failure." I said.

"Sure, and the moon is made of green cheese! We're screwed on this one. What if the failure is worse than we thought? We'll be growing a garden on those hulls in no time and our performance will turn to shit." Said Jack Rodgers, Port Engineer.

"Let's just take this mess and break it down to what ships, where we can inspect them to get that baseline. We need to see where we stand. Leeward over here can scramble their guys to at least get that for us." Said John K.

John turned to me and said, "We'll get you a list of ships and schedules for where and when they'll be Stateside. We'll handle your paperwork and invoicing and add that to our claim with the paint vendor. I'll call you later to discuss once we have that pulled together. I think we're done for the moment. Thanks for coming today."

With that I got up and thanked John and the gang and left. What a meeting. For us it was great news, more work, and a bunch of travel. Time to get the scope of work put together and add a bunch of new dates on the calendar.

When I got back to town there were major logistic issues to consider. If there was any good news, it was that most of the ships that had been through drydock and wearing the new paint were on the Atlantic side of things serving the European routes and the smaller ships plying the Caribbean and South American routes. Thankfully, they hadn't started much of the West Coast or Asian fleet.

The Atlantic fleet would be available for inspection in Boston, Port Elizabeth, New Jersey and Port Everglades, Florida. The Caribbean and South American Fleet would all be inspected in San Juan, Puerto

Rico, the transshipment hub to the south. The good news was the ports were all familiar and visited often for ongoing service.

File Photo: SEA-LAND INTEGRITY, Port Everglades Florida

I called Arne Backlund to fill him in. "Sounds like a lot of swimming! I'm gonna need new Jet Fins!" he joked.

"Don't worry. They still make 'em!" I said. We had an inside joke from Portland, Maine. I was blamed for losing a brand-new pair of SCUBAPRO JETFINS, allegedly having floated away after improperly tying them to the bottom of the dive ladder before coming out. When I climbed down the ladder after a break there were no fins hanging on the bottom rung. Still a mystery how that happened. My thought was it was a practical joke by the crew to mess with my head but no sign of them. At lunchtime we checked out the local dive shop to pick up new fins. So much for the practical joke conspiracy!

I asked the sales guy for a new pair of JETFINS. He said, "They don't make JETFINS anymore." That got a howl of laughter from the crew. I was sure they were in on it and I was being punked somehow but no, the guy insisted they no longer made rubber fins. I looked up at a wall full of day glow colored plastic fins with racing stripes and lost my cool.

"Don't give me that shit! They still make rubber fins! My middle name is Fin!." With that the crew was nearly in tears laughing. "OK. Give me that electric blue pair of racing fins." and out we went.

I asked Arne to try them out. He said they felt like you were wearing a pair of roofing shingles on your feet and shredded them in one day. We nailed them to the wall in the shop when we got back. There was a lesson there somewhere, and I had a new nickname for a while, FIN. It still gets a chuckle when the story of the missing fins comes up.

Back to Sealand's paint failure. "When do we start?" Arne asked.

"Just as soon as I get the list of ships and schedules. Probably early next week. John Katramados wants to get a baseline ASAP of each ship. We'll work out a photographic inspection plan and a way to quantify the failure on each ship. I'm still thinking on that one. Initially it will be a 'blow and go' exercise. We can go black with a two-man team and inspect each of the suspect ships. It won't cause any attention. With the exception of the Captain and Chief Engineer, nobody will know we were even there." I said with confidence. "From there, we should be able to monitor the ships as they rotate through their normal propeller polishing schedules. At least that's the plan I'm cooking. Any ideas?"

"Nope! Sounds like a plan." Said Arne.

Now it would be a matter of penning up the plan and preparing a workable schedule. I gave our travel agent in Hamilton a courtesy call. They'd been incredibly helpful with handling our travel arrangements and bailing us out when things went haywire out in the field from some distant location. One phone call and they'd have tickets waiting at some airport to save the day. We ran up quite a monthly tab and this could be another expensive mad dash!

John Katramados got us the list of ships and schedules. Turns out that the magic number was eleven ships total. That gave me what was needed to match them up to our usual rotation for propeller work and which ones we'd have to make special ship calls for.

Two of the ships were operating out of the west coast with long transpacific runs. They would need to be attended when they showed up in LA. The other nine were transatlantic and Caribbean with easier scheduling. This might not be too bad from our perspective.

With our maintenance programs we were getting a good look at each ship every six months. I called John K to discuss a few things before sending out a plan.

"Hello there John. I've been going through the list and schedules and think we might be able to get all the data we need with only a few special visits. Most of the ships can fit into our propeller service program unless you want to have us hit 'em all sooner than later." I said.

"My concern is that we don't have a good handle on the degree of failure and how big an impact on speed and fuel consumption we're dealing with." He responded

"Your call. My bet is that it will take some time before any measurable loss in performance will show up. If the flat bottom coating fails, it is likely to have a very slow impact from marine growth. The real issue will be the bow, flat sides and turn of the bilge that has more sunlight exposure and could grow sea grass causing a drag on the hull.

"I agree." Said John. "How would you propose to handle that?" he asked.

"Well, the marine growth should be easy to track by the Captain or Chief Engineer by checking the ship performance. May be as simple as looking over the side when in port, especially at the bulbous bow and side shell along the waterline. We have the capability to do a quick clean up around the edges with a small, easily portable hull cleaning machine that just so happens to run off the same hydraulic power supply we use for the propeller work. It would boil down to shipping an extra crate and hiring a small workboat to support the work."

Marine growth on side shell of Atlantic Class ship from failing anti-fouling coating

"That could work. Put it in the plan and get back to me with your schedules. I'll forward to the Port Engineers." John said. "Thanks for the call."

"Will do. Thanks John."

I went to work preparing a simple schedule and outline for limited hull cleaning if required. Made sense to me to have the hull cleaning machines shipped with the equipment for each ship call just in case. We could always rustle up a workboat and it would add handsomely to the billings if and when we needed to do a little clean up.

Over the next six months we tracked and documented the eleven ships. There was plenty to look at with the coatings peeling off but there was little to no impact. We figured they would start to see growth and performance issues later in their cycles, twelve to eighteen months out of drydock.

We weren't disappointed. All eleven ships required cleaning of their bows, sides, and stern quarters after a year out of drydock. As predicted, the flat bottom areas of the eleven ships stayed mostly free of marine growth, even with the high degree of failure.

Looking at our results, we easily saved Sea-Land millions of dollars by adding to an already existing maintenance program and preventing an overreaction to the failure. It didn't hurt to have the additional scope of work and a little extra on the billing side.

Good news for the paint vendor and SeaLand. Our extra work kept them from having any operational issues and on schedule for their normal drydockings. SeaLand and the paint vendor would work out their issues and apply new coatings as each of the vessels rotated through.

CHAPTER FOURTEEN

SEALAND DISCOVERY- HULL FRACTURE

Main Discharge Deflector, San Juan PR

꿍

Not all our ship calls were big adventures, but some have interesting side notes that are worth story telling. This is one of those tales.

SEA-LAND DISCOVERY was a container ship that was redeployed from the West Coast to the Atlantic Fleet to add more capacity. Increases in South American trade led SeaLand to move the ship to handle the elevated demand for US goods heading south. Those ships cycled through San Juan as the primary transshipment point.

When the ship left LA and departed for the Panama Canal crossing, a report was forwarded to New Jersey and landed on John Katramados's desk warning of a critical issue that needed to be addressed as soon as the ship arrived.

The report contained photos of a hull fracture on the port side main discharge. The photos were poor quality, but the crack was visible. There was no ruler in the pictures to show the size, but the photos were dramatic close ups. The west coast Sealand Marine Engineers conclusions were that the crack posed a high risk of propagating and penetrating the hull. The result could cause a flooding of the engine room and must be repaired as soon as possible.

When the issue came to light in Port Elizabeth, I got another special call from John K.

"Good morning. Got another head scratcher for you." John started. "We just transferred one of our ships to San Juan for our South

American service and got a report of a hull fracture with a warning and recommendation for immediate attention. It came with photos, but they are not clear. The report left me with more questions than answers, especially with the location. I need you to run down there and check it out when the ship arrives."

"Sure thing." I said. San Juan was one of my favorite places. "When will she be arriving?"

"Should be arriving at San Juan in about a week. I'll have the Port Engineer give you a call and confirm." He said.

"Great. I'll make the trip and get you some good photos that'll show what you're up against. If it does require repair, San Juan is a great place to get it done." I said.

"Let's plan on inspecting the crack and get a second look before we do anything. If it needs attention we'll catch it the next time in unless you see it as a high risk to continue." John replied.

"Sounds like a plan. We'll get you a better look at it, inside and out. Thanks John." We signed off and hung up.

The day after my conversation with John K, I received a social call from one of my World Class Diver pals, Basketball Jones.

Billy, 'Basketball' Jones was from Philadelphia and a remarkable character. He once explained in great detail how much he hated Philadelphia in a colorful rant.

He said, "You know how much I hate Philadelphia? I'm gonna buy a Philly Cheese Steak, hike west and keep on going until someone asks, 'What the fuck is that?! I'll take that Philly Cheese Steak, throw it on the ground and call the place home!"

"Hey Basketball, I've got a 'blow and go' inspection coming up in San Juan. You want to make the trip?" I asked, only needing one guy to help me out and no real work involved.

"Sure. I'm in. What are we up to and when ?" Basketball asked.

"Not much. That's why I asked. Some Jackass from LA sent SeaLand a bogus report looking to scalp 'em for a repair job." I said.

"Scumbags ! I love San Juan." He said.

'I'll have my travel agent set up a ticket from Philly and FEDX it to you. I'm going down a day ahead of the ship arrival to enjoy that Caribbean sunshine." I said.

"Know what you mean, brother. See you down there!"

The ship was due in on a Saturday morning leaving a perfect opportunity to fly down Friday, get the diving piece done with plenty of time to hang out Saturday night and fly back Sunday morning.

I picked up Basketball at the San Juan airport Friday night after renting a couple of tanks for the air supply in the morning. Typically, we racked up SCUBA tanks for breathing air for surface supplied operations when we were out of town. With this job, two standard tanks was plenty.

Our hotel was next to the airport, so we opted to hang out and stay away from downtown, at least until Saturday night. The El San Juan Hotel was just down the street from where we were staying. It had an excellent choice of small restaurants and a killer casino. It was a must-see kind of place if you were in San Juan. The ESJ was an incredibly classy looking hotel with heavy carved mahogany everywhere you looked and had the largest crystal chandeliers I've ever seen hanging in the enormous lobby leading to the casino. They claimed they were the largest in the world at the time.

It had a great casino and special restaurants with themed food offerings in elegant surrounds. The sound of the one-armed bandits dinging in the background of the oversized lounge had a hypnotic effect, beckoning all to enter.

We enjoyed the El San Juan Friday night, but Saturday morning arrived early as we made the trip to the port, arriving just after eight o'clock. *SEA-LAND DISCOVERY* was already at the dock with cargo operations about to begin. She was tied up starboard side to the dock leaving the area of concern on the outboard side on the stern quarter.

Basketball and I boarded the ship and tracked down the Chief Engineer. He didn't look familiar but was friendly enough. He had a copy of the report and led us to a side port that could be opened to use for dive access. We had to hump the gear through the ship down to the engine room and set up next to the hatch. Not that big of a deal. I brought a hundred- and fifty-foot short dive umbilical. That, my Superlight, and a couple of tanks and we were in business. After setting up a ladder we were ready to go.

Working in the Caribbean is not the same as New York or LA. Here, when you suit up it consists of a tee shirt, swim trunks and wetsuit booties. A diving harness with a bail out bottle for safety, a five-pound weight belt and harness round out the dress. Clamp on the Superlight and make the jump.

Basketball got the Nikonos and strobe ready as I climbed down the ladder. He lowered me the camera and we began the inspection. The main discharge was just forward of our location and not much more than fifteen feet down the side shell. It was easy to find and the water visibility was better than ten feet. Great for photos.

When I located the discharge, the first thing that impressed me was how small it was. After working on Supertankers and thousand-foot-long containerships, this was a puny opening, twenty-four inches in diameter plus or minus.

The infamous 'crack' was visible at the bottom of a doubler plate on the outer shell of the ship. The doubler plate was square and reinforced the surrounding area where the heavy discharge piping penetrated the hull. At the corner of the connection was a tiny imperfection of the weld that may have had a half inch fracture. By appearance it was an old fabrication defect and not a structural failure condition. What d'ya know? John K would be happy to hear about this.

Small Crack - Deflector Plate - Main Cooling Discharge – SEA-LAND DISCOVERY

"What do ya got down there?" asked Basketball. "The Chief wants to hear after that report he got out in LA."

"Well, it took me a minute to find the problem because of how small the effing thing is, half inch maybe. Doesn't look like a fracture but more like a welding issue when they installed the doubler plate surrounding the discharge."

Just as I was finishing my sentence I felt something like a bee sting or serious bug bite on the end of my 'Jolly Roger.' It was excruciatingly painful causing an uncontrollable outburst. "Holy shit!" I said while pulling down my swim trunks and waving away what I assumed to be a fragment of a jellyfish tentacle. That seemed to stop the pain, and I pulled myself back together.

"What the hell's going on ? You all right down there?" asked Basketball.

"Yeah. Nothing to worry about." I said still suffering the pain and worst of all, location.

I continued with my narrative, slamming the lousy report and findings as nothing more than an attempt to rip off Sealand. After a couple of more pics I asked Basketball to haul up the camera. I was coming out.

It was a short climb up the ladder into the side port. Basketball helped me take off my diving helmet and harness. The Chief Engineer was there, and as I began to fill him in on the results, that damn thing was still in my swim trunks and gave me another horrific bite. I quickly excused myself, spun around and ripped my trunks down to inspect the damage. I couldn't believe my eyes. There was a small black bug like creature attached to the end of the worst imaginable location for a man! I pinched it off and threw it on the deck, stomping on the damn thing in my wetsuit booties. In the meantime, watching the spectacle Basketball and the Chief, broke out laughing.

"What the fuck was that?" said Basketball as I was pulling my trunks back up.

"Don't ask. I was attacked by a vicious sea creature. I got the son of a bitch and stomped the shit out of it! I apologize for the impromptu striptease. Save your dollar bills for the strip bar!" I said, beginning to laugh at how ridiculous this looked and suddenly realizing I had destroyed the evidence. What if something really bad happens down there after the bite. I've got nothing to show! I decided it was best not to contemplate. Oh well. I'd have to re-think my diving attire for the Caribbean, at least for the bottoms in San Juan harbor. Wouldn't make that mistake again!

At least we were done early with plenty of time to kick back in San Juan. We rolled up the gear and signed off with the Chief Engineer. He said he'd call John K with the good news. I asked him to tell John the photos and report would be in his hands in a couple of days. No repairs needed here.

By the time we got back to the hotel there was plenty of time for a late lunch and siesta before heading out to explore the town. Our flight didn't leave until mid-morning. Plenty of time tonight to hit the Condado or maybe a nightclub I heard about called Peggy Sue's. Reportedly it was a hopping place on the edge of Old San Juan.

After our siesta, Basketball asked "What do you want to do." Simple enough question with a lot of options.

"How about we hit the El San Juan hotel across the street for dinner again? We can hit the trail to Peggy Sue's on the way to the old town later?" I asked.

"Sounds like a great plan. Let's hit it." He said.

Being San Juan, there wouldn't be much going on until way later in the evening. The El San Juan Hotel was a great call to start out. The food was excellent, and we enjoyed the lounge the night before.

We got a drink and sat in the lobby at the ESJ hotel. As it got later, there seemed to be a change in the guests in the lounge. We were now clearly under dressed as we watched an endless parade of local beauties as they drifted in and out of the casino. I began to wonder if they were professionals. Anyway, we had come to get something to eat at the China Town Restaurant down the hall from the casino and left it at that.

It would be a few hours until we needed to head downtown, so we hit the casino after an excellent meal in China Town. Once inside the casino, with the constant dinging of the bells from the one-armed bandits and free drinks, it helped us pass the time nicely while waiting to leave for Peggy Sue's.

Ten o'clock, time to head downtown. When we got to Peggy Sue's, the place was getting busy. We parked the rental car a couple of blocks down, for ease of departure later. We strolled over to the entrance to check things out, when a stretch limo pulled up and a bunch of young ladies piled out, clearly ready for a night on the town.

Basketball is one of those guys with animal magnetism when it comes to women, something all men envy. He had no problem wading in to find out what the occasion was for such a group.

He stepped up to one of the girls and said "Good evening ladies. What brings you to Peggy Sue's tonight?"

They all giggled and said they were there for a bachelorette party for their friend who was about to get married to some famous Major League Baseball player from Puerto Rico. They introduced the bride to be, and then asked what we were doing at Peggy Sue's tonight?

"We came here to meet you guys." Said Basketball getting another round of giggles.

The seeming leader of the bachelorette party said "Great ! We're looking for help. We need chaperones to keep from being harassed."

Bachelorette Party San Juan – Author and Basketball Jones do Chaperone Duty

"We're your guys!" said Basketball, without missing a beat. We were considerably older which is probably why we were a perfect fit for the job. Well, we weren't disappointed.

They piled into Peggy Sue's, paid our cover charge, and introduced us as their bodyguards. Guess we got a promotion.

Once inside it was party time. They set us up with the bartender. If we needed drinks they'd be on their tab.

"Jesús Basketball. Bodyguards? We could get killed down here! Guess you gotta go sometime." I said laughing in disbelief at our amazing luck. Five minutes earlier or five minutes later we would have missed our chance to serve.

"Yeah, why not. Makes for a cheap night out. Besides, after your little episode earlier it might take your mind off your injuries. Look at all those losers scoping them out already. We just might have to step in and do our duty." He chuckled.

"I know what kind of duty you're looking for! This group could get you in trouble." I said.

"You never know. I hope so." He said drinking his Corona.

The girls were winding up, hitting the dance floor, and tossing back shots that were being served by wandering wait staff. They partied way into the night as we hovered nearby keeping an eye on things and enjoying the sights.

At some point they decided to pull Basketball and me onto the dance floor to mix it up. Clearly they were feeling no pain and having a great time. We had to oblige and hit the dance floor. It was a dizzying experience swirling around with the whole bachelorette party. I could feel the eyes following our moves from the shadows of the club and wondered how many wanted to take us on later. At this point my cares faded and the party continued.

Basketball finally said to me "Hey man, I've got a bad knee. It's time to take a break."

"Better let the ladies know. They're still going strong!" I said.

He went over to the leader of the pack feigning a limp and said something that caused the whole gang to erupt in laughter.

"What'd you say over there that got that wild response?" I asked.

"Ah just some wise crack about what kind of trouble the groom was in on his wedding night, her unbridled stamina just might cause a sports injury and ruin his career, or something like that." He said

"That's hilarious! Damn near killed us." I said as we sat down at a nearby table.

The club was starting to thin out as they continued to party on. I was feeling myself starting to fade.

"Basketball. We've got flights to catch. Probably ought to get out of here." I said.

"Yeah. Things are winding down. I'll check in with the ladies and see what's up." He said.

Just as Basketball was getting up the whole bachelorette group was headed our way.

"Thanks Guys for looking out for us! We had a great time!" the group leader said as we both got hugs from the group. "We've gotta go. Our limo is out front."

We said our goodbyes and out they went.

"I gotta hit the head before we go." I said.

When I got back we headed for the door. Basketball was in the lead. He swung open the door and we were both blinded by the early morning sunshine! I winced in pain as my eyes felt like they were on fire from the blinding light.

"Holy shit! What time is it?" I blurted out. "We have flights around ten o'clock." There was a clock visible on the bank across the street. It was a few minutes past six thirty. "Looks like we pulled an all nighter! Literally."

Basketball laughed and said "Hey it was worth it! We'll sleep on the plane."

"True, but you have a better chance heading back to Philly with a longer flight. I have to change planes in Miami." I said.

"Sorry to hear that." He said sarcastically. "Look at the bright side. The work piece went great. Just don't let it go to your head!"

"Very funny, ha ha."

We had time to run back to the hotel, clean up and get over to the airport. Basketball's flight was scheduled to depart first. There was enough time to catch a coffee and snack before leaving.

"Call me anytime you've got another San Juan get away." Basketball joked.

"Sure thing. Thanks for the help!" I said as he disappeared down the jetway.

CHAPTER FIFTEEN

FIRE ON THE WATER – VLCC SEAL ISLAND

Engine Room Fire - St. Croix

In early October 1994, we were in St. Croix to perform anther *UWILD* survey on the Hess ITB Philadelphia in St. Croix at the HOVIC Marine terminal. We had been doing these on a routine basis and expected this visit would be no different. There was one caveat. One of the two main circulator pumps for the twin engines had a serious seal problem and needed to be replaced while at the dock.

The twelve ITB Class ships (Integrated Tug and Barge), as described at some length in this book during our adventure to the Croatian War, are unique in their two-section design. The aft section referred to as the Tug is engineered as a pontoon. It marries up to the Barge with a robust hydraulic ram system that draws the two sections tightly together forming a ship. When they are in this ship like configuration they qualify for the *UWILD* program. Over the years the program had been a boom for our business.

The X factor for this project was how to safely remove one of the main circulator pumps that supplied cooling water to one of the engines in place below the waterline. The location of the two pumps was roughly centered between the pontoons on the shell plating that transitioned from the bottom, halfway to the surface on the aft section They had the ability to blow ballast and elevate the ship to mitigate issues with water pressure. That would help, but even with ballasting the valves were still six to eight feet below the waterline. Doesn't sound like much but any sort of catastrophic failure could flood the engine room in a hurry.

We were asked to save the best for last. The inspection would come first with the US Coast Guard in attendance with the ITB in a normal ballast state. The Port Engineer had asked me to get with the Chief Engineer on the Philadelphia for direction in assisting with the valve after the Coast Guard was finished. He asked that no mention be made of the valve with the Coast Guard. Made sense, technically it was not in their scope of work and they wanted to keep it that way. Fine with me.

Our travel plans got us into St. Croix the day before the Coast Guard and gave us the time we needed to launch our boat and get set up with the underwater video equipment and do a good full system check before they arrived. With the extra scope of work, we figured the trip would cover the better part of a week.

Our logistics had improved a bunch with the addition of our own boat. A couple of years or so earlier, I was asked to ship a workboat to St. Croix as a favor to the Hess Port Engineer. Brian Swensen had a new guy coming on board who would take up residence on the Island and work for him. He was getting stretched too thin to cover the fleet.

The deal was that they would store and maintain the boat for us and in return, the new guy, Paul Pedretti, would have the use of it to go fishing or for recreation. For me it was a great deal. I could cut loose that expensive boat we hired out of Frederiksted and have our own boat close at hand in the Marine Terminal when we got to town. I had to agree and shipped a twenty-three-foot MAKO with a 225HP Yamaha down to the island.

The arrangement and timing couldn't have been better. I had just gotten into it with the owner of the Charter Boat we hired from Frederiksted.

Susan's fish.

After years of work-related charters, I hired the Frederiksted boat for a personal charter with my wife Susan to go sportfishing. That's when things went terribly wrong. We were vacationing on the Island at the end of one of our many trips to St. Croix. I asked Susan if she would go sport fishing with me. She wasn't much into fishing but said yes. We met Dennis at the Frederiksted pier and loaded out the fishing gear to chase the Wahoo that were running. Susan and I were leaving the next day and if we got lucky planned to pack up a cooler with dry ice and bring it back with us. So off we went.

It was a beautiful day and the color of the water was that amazing Caribbean blue. Trolling for game fish is an exercise in patience, not an easy thing for Susan. She wanted to catch a fish!

After a couple of hours working the west end of St. Croix we hooked up. I sat behind Susan to steady the rod while she reeled away. She was doing great! I figured it was some sort of small tuna. Dennis was looking over the back deck at the water as Susan worked the fish.

"Holy shit!" said Dennis as he leaped to the side of the boat and retrieved a large gaff. "Keep reeling. It's a Wahoo, and a big one at that!" Must have been charging the boat.

Susan continued to reel until the fish got to the boat and Dennis told her to stop while he gaffed the fish to land it. In it came. The Wahoo was at least five feet long, a real beauty ! Susan was elated. She would have her fish to bring back the next day!

Dennis offered to clean and dress out the fish when we got back and hold it for our pick-up in the morning. The airport wasn't far from their shop. Susan wanted to bring it back to the hotel. I nixed that, saying it might end up on the menu at the restaurant. Little did I know

. . . .

Susan's Wahoo St. Croix, USVI

After a pleasant last night on the Island we spun by the shop to pick up the fish. Dennis said he had a problem. The owner of the shop and boat had just left for home in Mobile and packed up Susan's fish for a family gathering. He told Dennis to pack up a few frozen Wahoo steaks from the freezer and give those to us instead.

"That was my fish!" shouted Susan. "He can't do that!"

"Dennis, what the hell! That's unacceptable! I want Tom's number in Mobile. He's going to hear from me on this one. I'm personally gonna rip him a new one for stealing Susan's fish! I'm not paying for a private fishing charter to have him pull a stunt like that!"

Dennis gave me Tom's number, but he was in transit having left a couple of hours ahead of us. My call would have to wait. When I did reach him he basically told me to eff off and the fish always belongs to the boat. We should never have expected to keep it.

I told him to expect one less customer and I was going to make it my life's mission to bad mouth him and his shop any time I had an opportunity. My new MAKO workboat shipped a couple of weeks later out of West Palm Beach on a tramp cargo ship to St. Croix, not long after my call to fire him and in time for our next project in St. Croix.

I made the trip to handle the customs paperwork and take delivery when the new boat arrived in St. Croix. Paul Pedretti and I took the boat out for a local sea trial and worked out the storage details at the Hess terminal.

Paul offered to keep the boat at his house on the Hess property and launch it for us anytime we were in town and needed it. Couldn't argue with that ! Fast forward again to 1994.

ITB PHILADELPHIA continued

The '*PHILADELPHIA*' was already in port and had an aggressive repair plan during this trip to St. Croix. Our *UWILD* piece was first up to clear the deck for the rest of the plan. Some of the work required welding, so the vessel was placed at the far end of the terminal to meet a setback requirement for hot work.

We rallied the day before the inspection and got everything ready to go. By mid-afternoon we were finished and headed back to the Caravelle Hotel in Christiansted. We planned a lazy afternoon and Happy Hour at the Banana Bay Club.

The Banana Bay Club was famous for their Banana Blaster rum drinks and fantastic location on the waterfront. We all lined up on the bar stools just after four o'clock when Happy Hour two for one drinks were happening. For some reason, beers weren't on the two for one deal. Too bad for Steve H., a Budweiser man through and through.

Steve pounded back his first Bud, served at the bar in a can, and ordered another. The rest of us were drinking fruity rum drinks in the collector cups with the Caravelle logo and Banana Blaster theme. I was sitting at the end of the group toward the water with Arne Backlund to my left, Steve next to Arne and Kai on the other side of Steve. Steve got up and excused himself to hit the head.

All of a sudden, Arne reached up and snatched an enormous cockroach that scurried across the glass hanger above the bar where we sat. He lifted Steve's Budweiser can and stuck it underneath. Beer cans have a hollow area on the bottom of each can. There was plenty of room with the hollow space for the cockroach, even with its huge size.

We couldn't believe the catlike reflexes Arne displayed to make that happen as we saw Steve on his way back to the bar.

"Hey Steve." Arne said as Steve sat back on his bar stool.

"What?" Steve grumbled.

"There's a cockroach under your beer." Arne said.

"Yeah right." Said Steve as he picked up his Budweiser.

Just as he lifted the can off the bar, the giant cockroach came out from under and flew right into Steve's face sending him flying backward off the stool, spilling his beer, and cursing out the 'Swede.'

"You son of a bitch!" he yelled. "I'll get you, you bastard!"

The rest of us nearly fell off our bar stools laughing. Arne couldn't have trained that cockroach any better! Meanwhile, Steve dusted himself off and took his place back on the barstool. Eventually he settled down and took the practical joke in stride. We had a big day ahead so it wouldn't be a late night.

Overnight, the *SEAL ISLAND* arrived outside the breakwater and was being brought in by the giant tugboats from the Hess terminal as we arrived for work on the *PHILADELPHIA*. She had lightered in St. Lucia and was drawing fifty-five feet as she cleared the breakwater on her way to Dock One, a half a mile from where we were working. It was a long trip to Valdez and back. Typically, she'd be in port for the next three days to offload and make any crew changes. The officers were all Italian. They had an easy connection from St Croix to Miami and on home to Italy when they got their vacation time.

SEAL ISLAND - Morning of October 8th, 1994 before engine room fire started

The Coast Guard was due at nine o'clock to start the *UWILD* survey work with us on the '*PHILADELPHIA*.' It was just after seven AM. We had plenty of time to check in and get ready for the Coasties. I went aboard the ship to check in and grab another cup of coffee in the galley. The Chief Engineer, Greg Pierce, a Marbleheader, was in there.

"Look who's here, the divers! Must be hard for you guys to be up and here so early! " he said mockingly. I knew Greg well and his brother Mike, my age from Marblehead.

190

"What do you mean? Bright and early as usual! Coasties said nine so here we are. " I said.

"Sure. Must have been a slow night in Christiansted for you guys to be here this early!" he wise cracked.

"You would know! I keep running into your crew downtown whenever you're in port. You spying on us?" I asked. "Good luck with that! We'll be ready to go as soon as the Coast Guard gets settled."

"Good. I need to get them off my ship as soon as possible. Any way to shorten things up?" he asked?

"Hard to say. We could bore them to death and see if that helps." I joked.

"Good point. Drone on and on until they can't take it anymore. Sounds like a good effing plan." He said. "No offence, but I'll be too busy to watch your TV show." He said with a grin.

"None taken. We'll do our usual exciting program!" I said as I turned to head back to the gangway.

"You mean, short program." I heard him say as I walked off.

The ITB fleet were cookie cutter in design. That helped with creating a program that we could blow through methodically and pretty quickly. We'd start at the bow and work our way aft, finishing up on the tug section. With no issues we could wrap up the live video piece in less than four hours based on previous work. According to the Chief Engineer there were no incidents of significance since they left their last drydocking.

At nine o'clock straight up, a car pulled alongside the 'PHILADELPHIA' and a couple of Coast Guard guys got out. I intercepted them before they hit the gangway and introduced myself. Neither of them looked familiar. The taller of the two introduced himself as Bill Edwards, his sidekick was, John McNamara. We made small talk as we boarded the ship to find the Chief Engineer and start the show. This gave me time to discuss our plan and how routine the ITB surveys have been so far.

We caught up with the Chief. He excused himself for not being able to attend the live show but said he'd be available if something came up. I suggested they get a cup of coffee while I got the crew in the water and ready to go.

Kai was first up and with any luck just might get us through the underwater video piece. I lit up the video gear in the control room and after a comm check with Kai, hit the record button and asked him to proceed.

"This is Kai Holleson with Leeward Marine. Today's date is October 6th, 1994. We are beginning a video inspection of the underbody of the *ITB PHILADELPHIA* in accordance with the rules for underwater inspection in lieu of drydocking. In attendance are Bill Edwards and John McNamara from the US Coast Guard. The ship is at the dock in the Hess Marine Terminal in St Croix, US Virgin Islands. Today we will proceed at the bow and work our way aft, following the hull markings and looking at the general condition of the ship. Any issues of concern that may be discovered will be assessed and documented." And on and on he went, droning along per usual. We had already taken a good look at the underside and knew there were no areas of damage or concern on the ship.

Kai had a great speaking voice and abundant experience on the ITB class. He had gone with me to Croatia years earlier to get the *ITB GROTON* out of the war zone. Perfect to get us through in a hurry. So, on and on he went with the Coast Guard guys watching the show. Occasionally they would ask him to zoom in on something or ask questions as he glided along.

Within two hours Kai had completed the forward barge section and was beginning on the pontoons. It was not much past noon, so we decided to continue and wrap up the video. The photographic documentation was already started during our preview work. The final pics would be done when they left and we knew if they had any areas of concern, we needed to pick those up to include in the follow-up report.

By two o'clock we were finished, and Kai was back on the boat. The Chief Engineer came by for a quick update before we rolled up the video. Nothing of concern to report. The Coasties were happy and amazed at the video quality and clarity. They weren't quite done yet. They told the Chief Engineer they needed to check a few other things. The Chief made a wise crack and told them to meet him in his office.

Bill and John thanked us for our help and went out to the dock to thank Kai for the great show. Time for us to roll up and head for the hotel. We knew the next couple of days would be busy working with the Chief changing out that port side sea valve and any other special requests.

ITB Philadelphia ballasted forward to elevate stern for valve repair after UWILD survey

The plan called for an early start to get the real work going. This would be a challenge. Anytime you have to seal off openings in a ship to remove a valve there is always a potential for trouble. This being a small valve in shallow draft gave me less of a concern but that's when you should probably be most on guard.

Dinner and turning in early was the smart move to be ready in the morning. We rallied early and were on site by seven o'clock getting everything ready to go. All the remote video gear and cabling was rolled up, but we kept the camera at the ready on the workboat just in case. We had a mini battery- operated Sony VHS recorder with a five-inch video screen on deck.

When the Chief Engineer had his crew and the valve ready to go, we installed a custom-made plug to seal off the opening. They slowly unbolted the valve and broke the seal, no leak. Good thing. The plug was installed but there was a concern. The hull plating was sloped upward toward the stern and he asked that we standby the whole time they had the opening vulnerable.

The valve was removed, and a blank cover installed on the inside of the engine room removing any risk of flooding. The sea valve for the ITB had to be machined and repaired at the terminal. This could take a day or more to accomplish and test before re-installing. When we rolled up on Friday our plan was to do some maintenance on our boat and gear on Saturday while standing by the *PHILADELPHIA*.

Saturday morning, October 8th, there was no need to hurry so we enjoyed a good breakfast in Christiansted before heading down to the ship. The work on our boat and equipment would require scouring the island for parts and pieces. Even finding simple hardware was a big deal. You won't find any Home Depots in St. Croix. Over time we developed a rating system for parts we needed by how many stops we guessed it would take to find, like nuts and bolts might be a two stopper. Pieces or parts could be many stops, that is if you could find them at all.

Saturday would be no exception. The crew put together a list of things they needed to keep busy on our repairs and as usual, I would be the gofer, go for this, go for that. This was a role I was good at, and I'm sure the crew was happy to get rid of me for a while. Some of the requests seemed suspiciously further down the scale for how many stops were needed to acquire. Hmm, no surprise. Off I went.

After two hours of riding around, stop to stop, chasing down that shopping list, I found most of the items. When I hit the wall with the long shots, I headed back to the Hess Terminal.

When I arrived at the security entrance to the refinery, it was shut down.

"What's going on?" I asked the Security Guard.

"Mr. Lee, we can't let you in at this time." He said.

"I need to get in there. I have a crew working on the *PHILADELPHIA.*" I said.

"Oh man! There's a ship on fire at the dock." He said.

"What dock?" I asked fearing it was our ship.

"Dock One." He replied.

Holy shit! That's the *SEAL ISLAND* supertanker.

"I'm sorry sir. Absolutely no one is allowed in." He said. I had to do a U turn and head out. What could I do? There was no way to reach the crew down there.

Somehow, we never envisioned needing an emergency evac plan in case of a tanker ablaze with us on it. My hope was they cut loose and made a run for it. The reality was, the *SEAL ISLAND* was on fire at the dock, and that was terrifying. Connected to the discharge manifold, the potential for catastrophic damage at the terminal was as big as the quarter mile long tanker tied alongside.

Over four million barrels of crude oil sailed into the terminal on the *SEAL ISLAND*. At this point they were less than half finished discharging, not to mention there were many more million barrels in storage tanks waiting to be refined . The 'what if' scenarios made my head spin and adrenalin flow. I wasn't sure what to do other than get the hell as far away as possible, and that might not be far enough depending on what happened next. I decided the best bet was the Hotel. The crew would call there, if or when they could, should they decide to make a run for it to Frederiksted.

Contemplating the gravity of the circumstances left me with an overwhelming sense of dread and fear imagining a black smoldering hole where there used to be a marine terminal. I sat in my room waiting for the call.

My mind wandered back to a conversation I had with Arne Backlund years earlier. We were at the same berth as the *PHILADELPHIA* leaning on the handrail looking over at a Supertanker discharging as the sun set over the west end.

"Wonder what would happen if they ever had a fire on one of those Supertankers when they were discharging over there?" Asked Arne.

"I can't even imagine. With that much crude oil aboard and gas fumes in the tanks, if one went off if would be like a nuke, and if it got into the refinery there's no telling what the damage could be. Probably blow a pretty big hole over here and beyond. The shock wave alone could kill people." I said figuring that could never happen.

I tried calling the Marine Department at the terminal for an update and got no answer. My guess, they evacuated. The only way to get an answer would be to run by the main gate and ask. Risky business but I had no other choice.

When I pulled into the main gate I asked, "Can you give me an update on the *SEAL ISLAND*?"

"No sir. They're still fighting the fire." He said.

It had been over an hour since my first visit. I told him there was no answer at the Marine Terminal when I called. He suggested coming back in a couple of hours. By then he may have an update. So, back to the Caravelle I went. There was nothing more to do but wait. It was paralyzing. I sat staring out over the harbor in Christiansted wondering if they made a run for it to Frederiksted. If they had, surely I would have heard from them by now. Nothing. . .

At two o'clock I made another run to the main gate. This time when the guard stopped me he said, "Mr. Lee, the fire was in the engine room of the *SEAL ISLAND* and is now contained. They are allowing some people back into the terminal. You may enter now. Be careful." He said waving me through.

Engine room fire? I was incredibly relieved hearing that. The engine room is a sealed space loaded with fire suppression equipment. At least there wouldn't be a black hole out there, and our crew should be safe wherever they were. I made my way over to our ship.

On the way I could see black smoke billowing out of the engine room vents on the *SEAL ISLAND*. I figured the fire must still be raging inside. As I pulled up, the crew were all standing on the dock staring over at the smoking ship.

"Where the fuck have you been? The bar?" Said Steve.

"Yeah, wise guy. What else am I supposed to do while you guys are toasting marsh mellows over here?"

"Funny guy." Said Steve.

"I came back at ten thirty and they wouldn't let me in. When they said there was a ship on fire at Dock One the only thing I could think of was how far the blast would reach if it went off!" I said. "The other thing was, I hoped you guys had cut loose and made a run for it. I had no idea how bad it was."

"We thought about it, but the smoke was coming out of the engine room. " Said Arne. With his experience working on Supertankers, he would know the risk of spreading was limited. Had it been on deck or at the manifold it would have been a different story.

"Have you heard anything from Hess yet?" I asked.

"Not really, other than it was contained in the engine room. The Chief Engineer came out and said to stand down on any work until they knew what the situation was." Arne said.

"OK. I'll be right back. I'm going to see if the Chief has any updates." I said.

I found the Chief in his office. "What's going on Greg? I got locked out at the front gate earlier." I said.

"Unbelievable! I was doing paperwork when the alarm went off. When I looked out the window I saw smoke coming out of the engine room over there. That is the last thing you want to see sitting here." He said.

"Any update from the *SEAL ISLAND*? I need to figure out whether to roll things up and get out of here or standby." I said.

"Not sure. I'll see if Swensen's on his radio."

"Brian Swensen? Philadelphia." He hailed.

"Go Philadelphia." Said Brian.

"Chief Engineer here. Divers want to know whether they should roll up or stand by?" He said.

"Tell them to standby. I'll be over there in ten minutes." Said Brian.

"Roger that. See you in a few." He said.

"You should probably hang here. He's coming right over." The Chief said.

Brian Swensen, Senior Port Engineer, showed up in the Chief's office. He was visibly shaken and smelled of smoke. His hand was trembling when we shook hands.

"You guys should probably roll up for the day. We've got a mess going on." He said.

I had to ask, "What's the word over there?"

"It's bad. They were changing out the fuel filter on the backup generator and didn't relieve the pressure before unbolting the filter cover. Fuel sprayed all over the engine room and caught fire. I was down there but up on the second deck. The fire spread so fast I turned and ran for the rung ladder to the third deck and closest exit hatch to escape the engine room. My work boots were melting on the deck plate as I ran for the door out of there. Wasn't sure I was going to make it. Four men were trapped below and didn't make it out. Not sure yet if there were any other fatalities. So far, it looks like the four may have been it." Brian said, fighting back the emotions of having nearly been killed by the blaze. He had a wife and a couple of kids at home in New Jersey.

"Thank God you made it out of there Brian! I'll get the boys to roll up and check back here in the morning." That's all I could say, shocked by listening to his story and learning of the loss of the crew. This was a huge tragedy and would surely make national and international news.

I could see Brian wanted to speak with the Chief. I signed off and headed to the gangway. The crew rolled up the gear and we headed back to the hotel. That night, we all needed a good meal and a couple drinks to chill out and go over things.

The Banana Bay Club was the first stop after showering up back at the Caravelle. We ordered a round and even Steve upped his drink from Budweiser to Scotch on the rocks. The mood was somber after the crew heard about the loss of life onboard the *SEAL ISLAND*. Not sure how many times you could expect to find yourself next to a Supertanker on fire, but this was the time to go over what happened and how we should handle it if such a thing ever happened again. I broke the ice.

SEAL ISLAND – Ship not repairable after room fire – Scrapped following investigation

"So, I don't think we have any provision for danger pay due to Supertankers on fire." I said. The wise crack got me a nervous chuckle on a bad joke. "Joking aside. I spoke to Brian Swensen in the Chiefs office. It was a hair-raising experience that almost killed him.. He said his work boots were melting on the deck plate as he scrambled to escape the engine room. His hands were shaking when he showed up in the Chief's office." I said.

"What now?" Asked Arne, a man of few words.

"We show up tomorrow and finish up our work. With luck, we'll get the hell out of here when the Chief is happy. I'd like to hear more from you guys about what happened. Me and the Swede had a conversation about this years ago and never believed it would actually happen. Gives me chills knowing how close we came to this disaster. It could have been a whole lot worse, at least for us. Sucks for those four Engineers." I said.

Arne started, "We were just beginning to do what we could while waiting for you to get back when I heard a siren. Sounded like a fire truck. When I looked around I saw a fire engine heading down the dock toward the *SEAL ISLAND* at Dock One, and then another one and then three more. I told Kai, that was the last thing you want to see here, fire engines heading for Dock One. I jumped off the boat so I could see the ship. Black smoke was pouring out of the engine room air vents. I couldn't see anything burning on the deck or dock, so I figured we'd be OK to stay here. The Chief Engineer came out and told us to stand down until they knew more." He said. "We were wondering where you were?"

"You know me. I have a habit of missing all the action! Remember when Kai made his little trip to the middle of the channel in Port Elizabeth when that SeaLand ship blew off the dock? I was at the welding supply house. Maybe we need a different gofer." I said. "I was thinking the worst when they wouldn't let me in and hoped you guys cut loose and took a ride to Frederiksted." I said.

"We thought about it, but the Swede said the engine rooms are sealed and the IGS system should suppress the fire, so the blaze couldn't get to the cargo tanks or manifold." Kai said.

"Sounds reassuring if you're there and see what's going on. I was on the outside and the gate guard had no info." I said. "We need time to digest this and see if we need to add something to our own safety planning."

They all agreed. We hit the Charthouse on the waterfront for 'Rasta Ribs' and called it a day.

Sunday the 9th, we finished up on the *PHILADELPHIA* and left St. Croix Monday morning for the mainland.

Bottles or Cans ?

Steve never learned his lesson at the bar when Arne got him with a cockroach under his beer can. He was a creature of habit and traveled with a small cooler that held a six pack of cans and enough ice to get him through the night.

On the road, we bunked two to a room to save on expenses. Nobody wanted to get stuck with Steve. He had a terrible habit of drinking the melted ice water from his cooler during the night. The sound of jangling ice cubes from his cooler was a guaranteed wake-up call at least a few times a night for whoever drew the short straw and got Steve for a roommate. I exempted myself from the nighttime cube fest by claiming executive privilege.

As luck would have it, we returned to St Croix not long after the fire on the *SEAL ISLAND* to clean a three-hundred- foot barge that Hess had sold to the Saudis. It was an uneventful trip that lasted the better part of a week and we found ourselves once again back at the Banana Bay Club sitting at the bar.

It was a déjà vu moment. We were lined up, just as we'd been weeks ago. Once again, Steve went to the head leaving his beer unattended. I'll be damned! Arne reached up and snatched another gigantic cockroach above the bar and stuck it under Steve's beer can. This time the Bartender and a few patrons had witnessed the event and sat waiting for Steve to get back and meet his new friend.

Steve came back from the head, sat down, and started eating his cheeseburger that had arrived in his absence. We all watched his every move as he slowly ate his cheeseburger. He didn't pick up his damn beer.

Finally, Steve realized everyone was looking at him but continued to finish his sandwich. He then went to pick up his beer. The whole bar waited for the cockroach to fly out from under as it had the last time this happened. He raised the can to drink and the giant cockroach just sat there as the crowd howled with laughter!

"Backlund! I'm going to kill you!" Steve said.

Steve Humphries

Arne denied having done the dastardly deed while stepping back beyond Steve's reach. The cockroach sat for so long under the ice-cold beer can it was paralyzed and unable to move. Steve should have been happy it didn't fly in his face and knock him off his bar stool like the last time.

When I could finally speak, after laughing, I said, "Steve, try switching to bottles when you drink at the bar, at least if the Swede's around!

He has a way with cockroaches!" I could hardly get it out before the laughter erupted again.

Cheeseburger in Paradise

I was beginning to wonder about Steve. Why was he such an easy mark for all the practical joking that went on with our traveling road show? When writing this Arne reminded me about the one I missed. The best one with Steve. Same bar, I had arrived a day late for some reason and missed the event.

There seems to be a pattern here. They went to the bar; Steve goes to the head and . . . You'd think he'd be more on guard but once again . . .   Steve ordered his favorite cheeseburger and while he went to the head, leaving it unwatched, Arne opened the bun and slipped a bar napkin under the burger. Steve came back and ate the whole damn thing!

"Hey Steve." Said Arne.

"What." Steve grumbled again.

"How was that cheeseburger?" He asked.

"Good." Said Steve. He never noticed the napkin and Arne never told him!

Arne still laughs when he tells this one. Can't believe I missed it!

Engine room fire story link for *SEAL ISLAND* can be found on the references page #286.

CHAPTER SIXTEEN

SEALAND ATLANTIC - LEAKY SHIP

Propeller Shaft Seal Failure - Boston

Worlds First Underwater Replacement

For years we had been maintaining the propellers on the SeaLand fleet. Our program had operated with regular intervals for cleaning and polishing of their props every six months during their active cycle for maximum fuel savings. The service not only achieved measurable savings but also had the added benefit of a mini survey done each time we made a ship call. That helped to find anything that might've been going bad down under. Finding things before they become a time consuming and costly repair was a big deal. Knowing what they had in advance of a scheduled drydocking helped to keep their cost down by not getting a special surprise when they drained the water from the drydock when the ship reached that point.

The twelve ships of the SeaLand Atlantic Fleet developed a number of issues that required attention and repair. At nine hundred fifty feet in length they were so large they required special stern seals for the gigantic propeller shafts that turned the twenty-six-foot diameter, five bladed, propellers each ship was equipped with.

A mechanical seal wrapped the small length of propeller shaft that extended outside of the hull where it passes through the opening in the stern tube and connects to the propeller. The majority of the shaft inside the engine room was attached to a gigantic diesel engine fifty feet or so forward of the stern tube. The stern seal itself was designed in a way that requires a precision fit of a special band of neoprene material that needed to be vulcanized in the drydock to make the assembly watertight. Done properly, the stern tube would prevent seawater intrusion into the engine room. Should any leakage of seawater occur it would end up on the floor of the engine room and pool in the bilges below.

Unlike an oil tanker, a large containership does not have the ability to handle any substantial water leaking into the engine room. They have no oil separators to process the bilge water and are absolutely not allowed to discharge the untreated water overboard per USCG regulations. Their only remedy is to hold the bilge water and off load it when they reach port somewhere during their voyage. This is where the real story begins on the *SEA-LAND ATLANTIC*.

SEA-LAND ATLANTIC - outbound from Port Everglades – Photo by Author

We had been monitoring an issue with the shaft seal assemblies at the connection to the propeller hubs of the Atlantic Class ships. The outer seals were wearing down and closing the gap between the hubs of the propellers and the fixed seal assemblies attached to the stern tube of the ships risking metal to metal contact. The seal material was much like brake shoes on a car with the exception that the design allowed the propeller to rotate against the seal.

SeaLand had asked us to come up with solutions to get them to their normal drydockings where they could address the issue. During our inspections we saw the heavy metal lifting lugs on the assembly were dangerously close to making contact with the propeller mounted seat on every rotation. (Photo below shows the lifting lug partially machined to create clearance)

What we came up with was to grind away material from each lifting lug allowing them to pass by each other while rotating. It would give them adequate clearance and was an easy fix. We would simply make enough adjustment to get by until our next visit and have the ability to make further adjustments if needed. There was a limit to how many times we could do this before contact would be inevitable.

Inside Rope Guard: propeller shaft seal assembly - lifting lug trimmed

John Katramados, Senior Marine Engineer, called me to discuss a new problem with one of the ships, the *SEA-LAND ATLANTIC*. She was taking on water through the stern tube and was flooding several tons a day of seawater as she left Port Elizabeth heading out to make her northern Europe run. He said this was an urgent matter and asked that I meet him, and his Port Engineer assigned to the ship as soon as possible. I flew into Newark Airport early the next day and made the trip to the other side of the NJ Turnpike to SeaLand.

When I arrived at the Marine Terminal, John K and Bill Davies were in the conference room and had drawings on the table and a brief report from the Chief Engineer.

"Good morning gentlemen." I said, entering the room. "Sounds like you've got a leaker."

"Sure do. I think that seal assembly is making metal to metal contact like we discussed. The Chief engineer said the water is getting past the seal and pumping into the engine room." John said.

"Pumping? How do you mean pumping?" I asked.

"He described it as more than weeping and was pulsing each time water came through the seal." Said Bill Davies.

"Sounds to me like the lifting lugs are making contact flexing the assembly casing. That could cause the pulsing or pumping as he described." I said.

"That's what we figure. I pulled your last report to look at the photos of that seal condition. It looks like the worst of the group. Take a look. I think we've reached the end on this one." John said as he passed over my last report. Darn good-looking report I thought to myself. He was right. The space had closed in and was likely to make hard contact soon.

"I think you're right." I said as Steve Johnson showed up. He was the assigned engineer and didn't say anything more than hello when he stepped in.

"We asked you down here to see if we can brainstorm a solution. The leak is so significant that upper management has asked that we look into drydocking the ship. That would be a huge expense and throw a wrench in our cargo scheduling." John said. "I brought the drawings of the assembly and documents from the manufacturer to see if that helps."

The drawings were very detailed and clearly showed the two-part outer seal materials that wrapped the propeller shaft and required the neoprene vulcanization during drydock.

"John, we have a set of those parts in the warehouse for an upcoming drydocking next month. I can run over there and get them if you'd like." Said Steve Johnson.

Before John could answer I said, "That would be great!" John agreed.

"Why don't you run down there with Steve and check things out. We can huddle up later after you see them." John suggested.

"Sounds like a plan. Let's go." I said and off we went.

The warehouse was located at the north end of the terminal and was loaded with every imaginable part needed to keep ships operating. Everything from spare propellers to replacement generators, and anchors lying with piles of di-lock chain piled up around them. Everything I wandered past was huge. Steve made his way to what looked like a storeroom and found the pair of seal elements.

"So, Steve, did you ever see them replace one of these in the dock?" I asked.

"Nope. The manufacturer flies in a team of guys who handle all the seal replacement stuff. The locals handle the welding work to remove and replace the rope guard when they finish up. Nothing for me to see, especially considering everything else going on in the drydock I need to supervise. It's a marathon to get a ship out of drydock and back in service." He said.

"I can only imagine." I said. "So, when I look at these two pieces they fit together perfectly when you lay them on the deck. Once in place, the paperwork says they wrap the material with a flat band of neoprene and vulcanize the piece together where they meet up, completing the rubber seal."

"That's right." Steve said.

"If we go through this, step by step, apart from that special vulcanized connection, everything is mechanical to make this happen. Is that right, at least for the seal assembly?" I asked.

"Yup." Steve said.

"Hmm. What if we split the neoprene band and pre-attached it to each of the two halves? If we do that right, there should be an excellent rubber to rubber seal created by using slightly longer pieces of neoprene which we can squeeze together when we re-insert them into the assembly seat. That could make a good enough seal to slow the water down and with a new outer seal running against the hub of the propeller, it would eliminate the metal to metal contact problem. What do you think?" I asked.

"I think it's a winner! I'll get ahold of Bill Davies and see if we can re-group." Steve said.

"Bill, I think we've got something. See if John's available. We'll be back there in fifteen minutes." Said Steve.

"Let's go. Bill sounded happy to hear we've got an idea. Drydocking is the last effing thing I want to deal with."

Back in the conference room, Steve took the lead explaining our idea at a high level. John K and Bill Davies thought it was a great idea. There was one issue they were concerned with. They'd need a buy in from the manufacturer in order for upper management to move forward. John said he'd get a hold of them and set up a face to face meeting as soon as possible. We needed to be ready with something by the time the ship got back from Europe.

"Good job guys." Said John K looking over at Steve and me. "The manufacturer is British. Not sure who they'll have to cover this, but I plan to get them here early next week. We don't have much time to plan this." He said. "What do you need from us to make this happen?" John asked me.

"I'll need to put together a scope of work and lay out how to make this happen. We'll need a bunch of rigging and be ready to burn off the old rope guard to get at it. We can pre-make a two-piece rope guard cover to close things up when we're done. That'll save a bunch of time. If we plan this out right we'll get this completed while they're discharging cargo in South Boston. It may take a few hours longer than their normal schedule in port. Time well spent!"

"Ya, and if things don't go well we'll need a drydock on standby." John said.

"We'll get it done. If they can do that in the drydock, we can do that sitting at the dock." I said confidently.

"Sure, but Steve will get us a backup. I'm not quite ready to retire yet!" He said jokingly. John wasn't far off from retiring and this would be a feather in his cap if we pulled this off. "I'll call you with the meeting schedule after I get a hold of the Brits. Thanks for making the trip." With that I left to get a plan put together and see how we'd rig things up. Steve got me a drawing for the rope guard, so we'd have something to go by to make the new cover.

When I got back from Port Elizabeth, I called Arne Backlund to go over the fabrication piece for the replacement rope guard. We'd use six-inch-wide by three eighth inch flat bar and have it rolled to bend it as close as possible to the drawing Steve gave us. It would be in two pieces and bolt together over the existing rope guard. Once attached, it would be welded in place making it a semi-permanent fixture. Easier said than done. Piece of cake, Arne said.

My plan had six steps: High level description below

1 – Rig the stern to handle the parts we'd be removing and replacing

2 – Burn off the outer four inches of the existing rope guard to expose the existing seal assembly

3 – Unbolt and remove all of the retaining pieces attached to the propeller hub that make up the rotor for the seal

4 – Insert two new seal pieces with pre-attached neoprene bands in the assembly seat

5 – Reinstall retaining parts and safety wire the new bolts following correct torqueing of each one.

6 – Attach new prefabricated rope guard sections and securely weld before removing all rigging

I faxed a copy of my plan and scope of work to John Katramados. He called and said it sounded good to him. He had a meeting set for the following Tuesday. The manufacturer had a Rep flying in from the UK and someone else from Chicago. I sensed we were in for a rough ride with those guys. I wouldn't be disappointed.

Tuesday, ten o'clock, I was back in the conference room in Port Elizabeth with John Katramados when the seal guys showed up. There was a bunch of them. Six guys filed in and took seats on the far side of the conference table.

John looked at me and whispered, "I'll be right back. We need more bodies in here!"

He returned with Bill Davies, Steve Johnson and two other guys, evening the count. There was a vibe in the air. John K had told me these guys were a pain in the ass and this would be a contentious meeting.

After introductions, John K started, "We're here gentlemen to discuss how it is, your seal failed on the *ATLANTIC* and what we're going to do about it. Our engineers have come up with a plan to replace the seal underwater. We've asked you here to provide us your opinion and to support this effort. Charles, I believe you said you'd speak on behalf of your company and your experts will provide support. Is that correct?" John asked.

"Yes. Thank you John. As you know, our company has developed this seal to meet the needs of operators with some of the largest ships today. Frankly, we do not support this plan and feel this will need to be done in the drydock. I understand there is one nearby that may be able to help. Is that right?" He began.

"There is." Replied John K, seemingly annoyed by the dismissive comments and tone that Charles had taken. "We're here to flush this out and see if you have anything to offer in support of our efforts. Having to drydock the *ATLANTIC* due to your seal failure is an extremely costly matter not to mention scheduling cargo. Is your company ready to pay for that?" He said testily.

"I don't think that is in our contract. Part replacement is free, of course, if there are any defects." Said Charles.

"Thanks. That's why we need to have this conversation. If you're not paying, I'm expecting cooperation." Said John K. It was getting hot in there. I saw their guys squirming in their seats.

"I've brought the team to provide support and describe their opinions on the subject. I'll turn this over to them to provide details and discussion of the design and so on. Harold, will you please start off for us." Charles finished.

Sealand Marine Office, conference room, top right, where critical meeting was held about stern seal replacement on SEA-LAND ATLANTIC with manufacturer

For the next hour, their team droned on and on about their seal design and the process for installation and on to the final vulcanizing of the rubber. In the end, each man had his reason why we should not attempt any of this underwater.

"Well John. That's our position and advice as to your plan. We cannot support it. Not only that, I hate to say it, but it will void your warranty if you move forward with this." Said Charles.

John K rocked back in his chair. It was my turn to chime in.

"Gentlemen, thank you for the detailed presentation. I've listened to all the reasons why we shouldn't attempt this plan. It seems to me, that we can carry out every aspect of changing this out underwater with the exception of the vulcanizing of the neoprene seal. Would you agree?" I asked.

Heads were nodding across the conference table as Charles said "There are many potential pitfalls along the way given the limitations of working underwater, this is not my specialty, but the vulcanizing of the neoprene seal is the final process to insure the seal assembly is water tight." His team now looked like a bunch of bobble heads across the table when I continued.

"We've considered this entire process and it appears to all boil down to the vulcanization of the neoprene. That outer seal in the assembly is static, and basically provides the watertight lip seal on the inside of the assembly while the propeller hub turns against the outer seal. The seal material is much like a very thick brake shoe on a car. If my analogy is close to correct, our answer is to split the neoprene and pre-attach the pieces to the two sections of the outer seal. When pressed back in their proper seat on the assembly forward of the propeller the precision fit of neoprene to neoprene will effectively seal off the stern tube from the rest of the assembly as intended stopping the leak. The new thick outer seal will also stop the metal to metal contact that caused the problem in the first place and keep the *ATLANTIC* on her normal drydocking schedule. We have made our recommendation to Sealand and provided them with a scope of work plan and schedule to fit with their usual cargo operations in Boston. Our plan calls for being wrapped up before the tugs show up with the Harbor Pilots to take her back out to sea."

John Ks turn, "We're going to do this, with or without your support. As for the warrantee, what good is it, spare parts? Seriously. I'll let you tell our upper management that as the ship sails off to drydock and see how fast they find a new seal vendor!" John said. He was pissed but kept his composure.

"Well, alright John. But if you don't mind we'd like to send someone to attend. Would that be OK with you?" He said.

John looked my way. I gave him a subtle nod. "Ok. We'll get you the schedule. We plan to do this at the dock in Boston."

"One last thing John." Charles said as he reached into his pocket and pulled out a business card. "I'm sure these are fine chaps you have here, but I'd like to recommend a company from the UK that is familiar with our products and can provide diving services." As he slid the card across the conference table.

At that, John glared at him and said, "That won't be necessary." He got up and let the card sit there, like a bad smell at the table. He hailed his Admin to escort them out. I heard him mumble under his breath "Damn Brits . . ."

It was a done deal. We would make this happen.

World First - Underwater Stern Seal Replacement

When I walked out of the meeting with all those seal manufacturer reps and my pals at SeaLand, I knew we had a 'never before attempted' challenge. As I saw it, if it can be done in the drydock, we can do it underwater.' The reality was that this was high stakes poker by my friend John Katramados. I was humbled and honored by his faith and confidence in our ability to pull them through this. I can still conjure up the mental image of that business card sitting, untouched, on the conference table.

There were a lot of things to do and not a lot of time until our ship was at the outer sea buoy in Boston. The Harbor Pilots would guide the ship into the South Boston container terminal, and it would be showtime.

I asked Arne Backlund to track down the steel flat bar and find a shop capable of rolling it to the diameter we needed. We'd have them split the ring and weld the mating flanges that would bolt together to fit up the rope guard extension after we replaced the seal. It may seem like a simple thing, but after a long night blowing bubbles and getting all the tough stuff done, this would be the final challenge. Getting the fit up right and welding the cover over the new seal was a bigger deal than you might think. It was the last layer of protection to keep rope or any other material from entanglement around the stern seal and had to be right and tight.

Our rigging plan would be another key to time management. The better prepared we were, the shorter the time we'd need in the water to finish the job. Fortunately, there is an incredibly robust lifting eye permanently welded to the hull directly above the propeller. This is an aid used by a shipyard when changing out the propeller. For us, it was exactly what we needed to remove and replace the pieces during the change out. The rest of our plan would require a selection of come a longs and rope lines for hand hauling pieces to and from the dock.

Paul Mercaldi, as a former Navy Diver added an important detail we'd overlooked. With all the parts and pieces, we'd be handling, the last thing we needed was to drop anything to the bottom or worse yet, come up short when reassembling the stern seal. We wouldn't have a collection of spares. He recommended a rigid container be secured below the work zone to hold the parts. The added value of which was in the unlikely event we dropped something, a weighted line from that container would hang directly to the bottom and would make recovery a simple search and not an impossible task. The soft bottom and muck was a great place to lose things. The drop line would give us a bullseye on the bottom to use for reference. The visibility was likely to be low to zero once we got things underway, and nighttime work would increase the value of this simple set up.

The work zone in the water around the stern seal would be limited, so most everything would be done by one diver at a time. The plan would be to have a second man dressed in topside, and at the ready if another set of hands were needed below.

The week before the ship arrival in Boston, I met Steve Johnson at the SeaLand warehouse in Port Elizabeth to prepare the two halves of the replacement seal. We carefully measured and cut the two pieces of flat rubber seal and attached them to the new parts with contact cement, a type of rubber glue, and screwed the ends in place with tiny stainless steel screws to keep them sticking out about an eighth of an inch to make a compression seal when inserted in the seal assembly. I drove the parts back to Boston with me.

The plan was set, parts in house, we were as ready as we could be. When we got the call, the ship would be arriving early afternoon at the sea buoy in a couple of days. Great, by the time they were settled at the dock it would be late afternoon. We'd need the better part of an hour to get everything hooked up and ready to start. No way to begin anything until the tugs had the ship alongside with docking lines set and Customs cleared.

Our team included five men, Paul Mercaldi, Arne Backlund, Kai Holleson, Steve Humphries, and me. Steve Johnson from Sealand pulled in just as the *ATLANTIC* made the final turn into the terminal. The seal manufacturer tapped a guy from Chicago to attend. Larry Green would be arriving in the early evening, not long after we were underway. He had plenty of time. We'd be at it for hours before getting to the actual seal replacement.

When the ship docked, Steve radioed the Chief Engineer. They needed a little time to clear customs and then he was coming down to the dock. We would set up and then wait for the Chief before we started.

The Chief Engineer made his way down the gangway. "Hey there boys! What's going on? Looks like a party!" He said. Not sure why he was so chipper.

"How was your trip?" Steve Johnson asked.

"Could have been better if we weren't bailing out the bilge from all that seawater! Hope you guys can fix this. I hate drydocks." He said.

"That's the plan." I said. His name was Tom. Don't think I ever knew his last name, but he was always a good guy with a great attitude.

"That damn thing was pumping away the whole time we were steaming back and forth across the Atlantic. At lower RPMs it slows down dramatically. When you make cruising speed it's a mess down there. We're getting tired of containing all that water." He said.

"That's what we're here for!" I said confidently.

FILE PHOTO: SEA-LAND ATLANTIC docked in Boston. Diving equipment in white box truck

I asked Paul to get Arne dressed in and start burning off that rope guard section while I went onboard with the Chief and Steve Johnson to make sure there were no issues with the emergency cofferdam the ship had to control flooding in the event of a catastrophic seal failure. I guess if you remove it after we pull the old seal, that will qualify as a failure . . .

"Last time this was inspected it worked fine and passed the test. That was about six months ago." The Chief said as he closed off the unit when we were there at the stern tube. The massive propeller shaft passed through the cofferdam fitted to the stern tube. "There we go. Should be ready for you guys. I'll have the mate keep an eye on it when you pull the old seal. Steve, give me heads up thirty minutes before you pull it to get a man down there." He asked.

"Sure thing. It's going to be a few hours I'm guessing." He said looking my way. I nodded yes.

Steve stayed on board with the Chief as I made my way back to the dock. Arne was in the water when I got there and was already burning away with BROCO rods . Wouldn't take long with Arne. He would be our main burning and welding guy. Kai was next up, working on the mechanical piece.

Arne split the back end of the rope guard four inches at the top and bottom and removed the two halves. They weighed about fifty pounds or so and were hand hauled with a rope line as they swung free. Arne called out just before each section cut free. When both sections were on deck, Paul had him return topside. Kai was dressed in and ready. As soon as Arne reached the dock, he stripped out of the helmet and handed it over for a quick wipe down and dry liner. Kai clamped on the Superlight and jumped off the dock, dropping ten feet before hitting the water.

Kai got the rigging set and hung the parts container and drop line. Paul had already put together the tool bag he'd need to cut the wires and unbolt the retaining parts. It would take some time to disassemble the parts. It had to be slow and deliberate, no room for error or dropped parts. Kai retrieved the tool bag from Paul and started in disassembling the rotor pieces on the propeller hub. I had great confidence in Kai's ability.

The sun had set, and it was dark as a car pulled into our location at the stern of the *ATLANTIC*. It was Larry Green, the seal guy rep.

"Hello there. Sorry I'm late. It was hell getting out of Chicago." He said. "What did I miss?"

"Hey there Larry. Not much. We've got the rope guard section removed and our guy just started the mechanical work taking the assembly apart. This will take a while. The only tools that fit are hand tools." I said.

He looked at the rope guard sections, and the good cuts Arne had made. "Wow. Nice work!" He said. The replacement sections lay next to the burned off parts and he could see we weren't goofing around here. "Can I get a look at the new seal parts?" he asked.

"Sure." I said. "We have them in the van."

Larry followed me over to the work van. It was dark, but Larry could see the pieces. He picked one up and asked, "How'd you attach the rubber seal? I see the small screws."

"We used good old-fashioned contact cement. The pieces only need to stay put until they're in their happy place!" I said sarcastically.

"I like that slight overcut. If it fits it should give enough compression to stop any water flow." He said.

"That's the idea. When we get to that point, I'm dressing in to make the fit up. If there are any problems, I'll need to see firsthand, but if your drawings are any good, and the parts are right they should just pop back in place." I said. "If they don't, Paul will have to turn down my comms to muffle the stream of obscenities. Seriously, these effing pieces will fit like a glove!" I would be next in the barrel when Kai finished up in a couple of hours.

"I like your confidence, but between you and me, our company expects you to fail and has a crew on standby to meet the ship in drydock." He said.

"They'll be disappointed then!" I said. "If you want to get a cup of coffee, we can hit the galley on the *ATLANTIC*. We've got plenty of time."

With that, we hit the long gangway and on to the galley. We had a conversation about the issues they'd been having with their seal. He implied there were larger concerns beyond what we were up to tonight. I didn't press, but felt they were up against it with the other eleven SeaLand ships and maybe had other clients affected. He asked what Leeward Marine had been up to. I guessed it was part of his mission to scope us out. I took the time to spin a couple of tales. The one about getting that Hess tanker out of the Croatian War was a real eye opener for Larry.

"Holy shit!" He said. "How the hell did you pull that off?"

"Well, I gave you the short story." I replied. "Truth is, we had a lot of help on the logistics, and a lot of 'Luck of the Irish' to pull it off. I'd need a lot more time to tell the whole story." I said, sure he'd take this story back with him if his management asked who the hell we were.

Larry and I finally made our way back to the dock to observe the progress. Kai was giving a good narrative while he worked away at dismantling the assembly. When he finished taking things apart, he would take photos and then pull the old pieces out before coming up. Larry listened in as I wandered over to get my gear bag and made sure the stills camera checked out, had new batteries in the strobe and a fresh roll of film loaded. Paul would lower the camera to Kai when he was ready. That would be my cue to dress in. Time dragged on as Kai continued. He had a challenge with the cramped space and hand tools to break everything loose.

Thank God patience was one of his strong suits. The hour was getting later and later. There was at least another six hours or more of work once the new pieces were set, to button things up and weld on the new rope guard sections. Another all-nighter. We were good at these.

Prior to changing, existing seal located between lifting lug and stainless cap bolt

"OK topside. The last pieces are in the bucket. I'm coming back for the camera." Said Kai. Paul came over to the van for the camera and gave me the heads up to get ready. I'd want to compare the two old sections and compare them to the replacements before I made the jump to replace them.

Paul lowered Kai the camera and started a photo log to track the subject matter later. I dressed in and stood by waiting for Kai to come back with the pieces. He'd leave the camera down there for me.

"Alright topside. Coming back to the ladder with the pieces. Have someone drop me a line to tie them off." Kai said.

Arne grabbed a light rope line and hauled the pieces up as Kai climbed out. He laid them next to the new pieces for inspection. There was a dramatic difference. The new sections were much thicker, showing just how much wear had occurred. The new pieces were more than twice as thick. Kai assured me there would be clearance provided they were the same diameter. With the pieces side by side we could see they were. Larry had approval from SeaLand to take one with him for the seal manufacturer to examine. The other would remain with SeaLand as evidence.

Alrighty then. My time to set the new seals. When Paul was ready, I made the jump.

"I'm going to take a quick look before dragging those pieces down here. When I come back have them rigged and drop them to me one at a time." I said.

"Roger that." Paul replied.

I was amazed at the amount of work Kai had done and the great cuts Arne had made. The fit up for the rope guard would not be a showstopper. Grabbing the camera, I took a couple of my own pics. Paul recorded the details and added me to the log.

"Ready for the new parts." I said. "I'll take both with me and have a go at it."

"Roger that. Standby." Said Paul. "They're hanging in the water." Came over the comms a few moments later.

"Is Larry there?" I asked.

"Sure is." Paul had him answer on the comms.

"Alright. It's showtime." I said swimming my way back to the stern seal with the new pieces. They would be installed vertically, one on the port side and the other on starboard. The starboard piece was the money piece. If it fit right, the rest was a piece of cake.

"Installing the port side section." I said. There was an audible 'foomp' sound as the piece pressed into the seat. "Great fit! I need to take a photo before setting the starboard section." Paul made the notes. Each flash of the strobe was highly visible topside at night as I finished a couple more photos.

"Here we go topside. Starboard piece going in." I said. The piece was not easy to get past the first obstacle of the slightly overcut rubber seal. Once I got it properly aligned I gave it a good push. 'Foomp,' the seal popped into place. "It's in there! Another great fit!" I said. "I'm going to take a few more photos and come up." We'd take a short break before tackling the next phase of getting everything re-installed. It was just past midnight as I reached the deck. Larry was standing there as Paul took the helmet from me and unclipped my harness.

"I guess that does it." Said Larry.

"I guess so." I said. "Now we'll have to see how she does on her trip to Port Elizabeth later today. I'm feeling pretty good about it."

"I gotta say you guys did a great job. My company was sure we'd see this in the drydock." He said.

"You probably will. Just not until it's due." I said getting a chuckle out of him.

"Like you said, we'll see." Larry said.

Steve Johnson had been on the *ATLANTIC* napping and missed the show. We tracked him down and got him to the dock before the seal guy took off. I wanted to make sure it was Steve who handed off the old piece they were promised.

"Christ! I must have been exhausted." Said Steve. "I wanted to see this. Oh well, we pulled it off! John Katramados said he wouldn't be going to bed until he heard back from us. I better go make that call. It's going on one o'clock. Great job!"

"Don't leave yet. We need to hand off one of the pieces to Larry. I figured you should have first choice and give him the piece." I said.

Steve inspected both pieces and handed one over to Larry. "Here you go. Thanks for coming Larry." Said Steve as he headed for the payphone a hundred yards down.

Time for us to get back to it. If all went well we should be done, and all rolled up before the tugs are scheduled at eleven o'clock.

"I'm getting out of here." Said Larry. "We should be hearing from SeaLand later. From what you said I'm going to report this as a success. I'm sure my office will be thrilled to hear it!" he said sarcastically. "Thanks for getting this done."

"You're welcome. Thanks for coming by. Have a safe trip back to Chicago." And with that Larry headed out.

Steve was making his way back from the payphone. He said, "John was ecstatic! He said they were hanging pretty far out on this one, and with eleven more to go this was a huge accomplishment and gave him options if this ever happened to another ship in the Class. Said he's leaving them a voicemail in Port Elizabeth and planning to sleep like a baby. Last thing he said was to give you guys a big thanks for getting the job done. He knew you would!"

"Thanks Steve. We've got another six hours or better to button things up. No need for you to hang around." I said.

"I agree. "I'm going back on board and racking out. Great job!" He said as he turned toward the gangway.

Paul knew we had a long way to go and asked everyone to get back to it. I offered to run out to Dunkin Donuts in Southey for coffee and doughnuts. The crew liked that idea. The place was not far outside the terminal. I asked Paul to take a break. Kai would be next in to put everything back together. Arne would be well rested and ready when it was time to re-install the rope guard. He would complete the job and de-rig the site as we pulled out. Off I went to Dunkin Donuts.

It was almost two o'clock when Kai was ready to get back at it. Paul was getting nervous about the time. He knew how things slowed down the later it got and was painfully aware of our schedule. Not to worry, Kai would motor through his piece and make way for Arne.

By four o'clock Kai had it bolted back together and properly torqued. It wouldn't take long to safety wire the hardware. It was time for Arne to show off his skills again and get us out of there.

It was likely we would need another guy assisting to get the heavy bands properly placed and welded. Steve H had been a member of the team to help with all the topside work and as standby for assisting if Arne needed it. Rested or not, I would have Steve dress in and help get the pieces set while Arne tack welded them in place. When that was done, Steve could come out. He'd make dive pay for the day and that was twice that of tending or topside support. He'd be happy, long night or not.

Steve helped guide the pieces for Arne and beat them into place with a ten-pound sledgehammer while Arne tack welded them in place.

"We're good to go Topside. The new pieces fit pretty good. I can make this work. Thank Steve for the help when he gets out." Arne was ready to run some rod and get us home.

It would take quite a bit of welding to make sure that the new section of rope guard would stay put. You can just imagine how much seawater rushes through that space with the ship making way at twenty-five knots crossing the Atlantic Ocean.

Just past nine Arne said, "Last rod Topside. Make it hot!" referring to the single pole knife switch used to power up the underwater rod holder that energizes the welding rods. The switch was opened and closed for safety every time Arne added another rod. He used a bunch on this job.

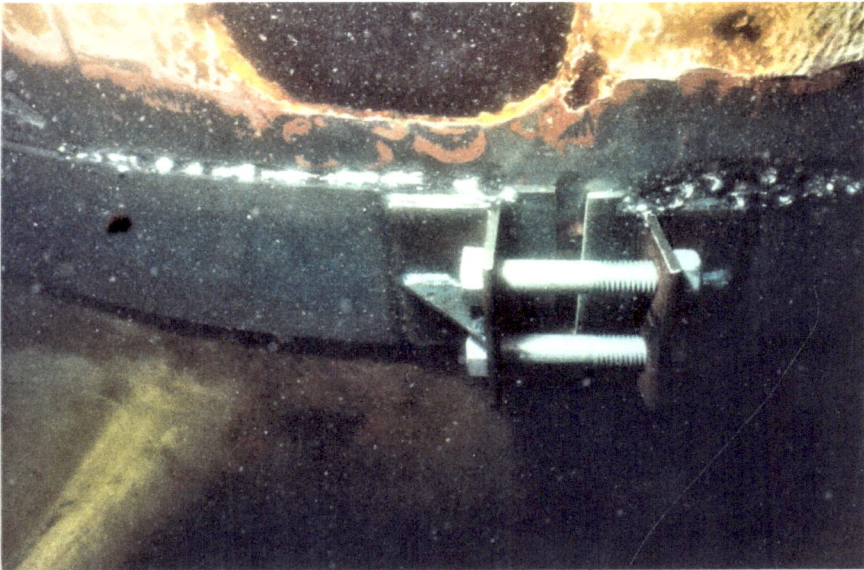

Rope guard replacement, view from underside of rope guard – bolted and welded

Before he cut loose he took photos of his work. No need for me to check up on his welding. When he was younger, he was an ace welder in Sweden building Supertankers before taking up Commercial Diving.

He finished up the photography and began the de-rigging underwater. Paul, Steve, and Kai hauled everything up. We were done and had Arne back on the dock by ten o'clock. After a round of high fives we rolled up the dive gear and welding machinery

Steve Johnson had rolled by earlier before taking off to Port Elizabeth. He asked me to sign off with the Chief Engineer before we left. After a hearty round of handshakes and thanks to the crew he left the terminal.

I was ready to get out of there and go home to bed. All-nighters were always pretty stressful. I found the Chief Engineer in his office waiting for the Boston Harbor Pilot and tugboats to show up and lead the ship out of port. He thanked me and said he'd know within minutes of clearing the outer sea buoy how we'd done. I assured him it had to be better than what he had before. He said he'd call John Katramados once they got underway.

Mid-afternoon, I got a call from John K. "Great job!" He said. "Just heard from the Chief Engineer. He said it leaks less than the last time they left the drydock over a year ago! He was really happy. No more pumping bilge water and I don't have to head to the drydock. I'll guarantee our senior management will be very pleased."

John asked us to re-inspect the stern seal when she returned to Boston from her European run. We did. It looked just like we left her. I did the inspection with Paul's help and forwarded the report . . .

That was the end for this one. There were eleven more ships in the class we continued to monitor and adjust to keep them from suffering the same fate as the *ATLANTIC*. She would be the only changeout we'd have to make.

Never did hear another word from the seal manufacturer.

CHAPTER SEVENTEEN

MT CABRITE - DREDGE FROM HELL

Main Scoop Inlet Sea Valve Failure – Port of Long Beach

Sometime in early October 1995, I received a call from Brian Swensen about a sea valve issue on the *MT CABRITE* Supertanker. They discovered the problem after she arrived at St. Croix when they were unable to close the valve in order to drain the *condenser* for routine inspection.

MT CABRITE in St Croix prior to departure for LA and Valdez, AK

The sea valve controls the flow of cooling water for the gigantic steam engine. The *condenser*, located in the engine room, is the heat exchanger for the system that 'condenses' the superheated steam from the boiler back into water in a closed loop system that generates the power to turn steam into propulsion. The steam drives a turbine that powers the drive shaft and a thirty-foot diameter propeller up to a hundred revolutions per minute as the 'Supertanker' makes way to and from St Croix to Valdez Alaska.

Inside the condenser a honeycomb of tubes pass seawater from the inlet scoop through the forty-feet-long by ten feet in diameter cylinder to the overboard discharge on the opposite side of the ship.

Cooling tubes inside 'condenser' with marine fouling visible – must be kept clear

When the honeycomb in the condenser gets clogged with marine life or debris sucked through the inlet it restricts the cooling flow and can cause overheating of the enormous boiler that provides the steam.

The opening to the inlet scoop does not have much protection from the outside. There are long steel flatbars bolted four-inches or so apart running fore and aft filling the nearly four-by eight-foot opening. The open spacing between the bars allows marine life or debris to pass through with relative ease into the condenser and clog the tubing.

The *CABRITE* had no overheating issues in St. Croix, at least not yet. Fortunately, they developed a preventative maintenance program after we repaired a sea valve on a Hess Supertanker in the past.

When this happened on the *VLCC SEAL ISLAND* years earlier they were unable to seal off the condenser. With the valve completely closed seawater continued to flood into the condenser and drain onto the engine room floor into the bilge below.

To accomplish the cleaning process for the condenser requires men to enter the chambers on each end and ream the tubing with very long pipe cleaners. They can only enter the condenser vessel when it is completely drained of seawater. Without being able to drain the system and complete their task cleaning the cooling tubes they could be at risk of overheating the boiler and causing an emergency drydocking. In a nutshell, no cooling, no steam, no propulsion.

We were hired to do an inspection up the pipe inside the scoop inlet and check the condition of the butterfly valve on the *SEAL ISLAND*. The piping from outside of the hull to the valve is approximately four feet in diameter and travels upward at a forty five degree angle forty feet plus or minus to the valve The valve operates by opening and closing a round disc known as the 'butterfly' a quarter turn each way inside the valve chamber to open and close the flow. I did the inspection and found that the seal was badly damaged on the butterfly. As a result, they would never be able to achieve a watertight seal until it was replaced. At this point we ginned up a plan to replace the valve seal underwater. This had never been attempted before and would be a world's first if they agreed to move forward with our plan.

It was a really big deal and had everybody's attention at Amerada Hess. We developed a detailed scope of work and after convincing a number of nervous Marine Engineers got the go ahead to proceed. The challenges and large safety concerns were overcome, and we succeeded with changing out the seal and solving their problem.

For the *CABRITE* we agreed to catch up to her in LA in about three weeks and check it out while they were picking up stores there on their way to Valdez, Alaska.

Brian informed us that he had heard the problem was most likely 'mechanical.' Being unable to completely close the valve they needed an inspection before taking the next step. Either an obstruction would need to be cleared, or they would have to make an adjustment to the valve stem. The stem adjustment could re-center the butterfly disc inside the valve chamber and allow it to seat properly. It sounded like it might be a straightforward fix.

He loaded out our specialized cover on the *MT CABRITE* in St Croix before they left for Valdez. We custom made it for sealing the outside of those ships. Brian felt we may have need for it on the upcoming project at the Port of LA. It was always kept in storage in St. Croix at the Marine Terminal for safe keeping.

For this trip I planned to hire a local company to assist me and charter a workboat. It would save on logistics by using local assets and equipment. The way I figured it; I'd be more of a supervisor than part of the dive team. Having been there and done that a number of times over the years gave me the experience I needed to make this an easy go. It was highly unlikely to require any seal replacement work.

I tracked down a company that could provide a four-man team, fully equipped, for support along with a thirty-foot workboat to use for the project. They would have an air compressor and diving umbilicals along with a Superlight and a couple of Kirby Morgan Band Masks for back up. All I would bring was my personal Superlight and camera gear.

The *MT CABRITE* was due to arrive on Wednesday, November 2nd at the anchorage in LA. There would be no customs delays, so we expected immediate access once she was at anchor. Everything was all set as I made my travel arrangements to LAX to arrive on Tuesday, the day before.

It was an early flight out of Tampa that got me to LAX by noon local time. I called Steve Roberts, the owner/operator of the small diving company out of Long Beach. He said they were all set. I asked him to meet me in Long Beach midafternoon to go over the scope of work and plan the load out of the workboat on Wednesday.

Brian Swensen confirmed the arrival for the 2nd and gave me the number and contact for the ships chandler that would be providing provisions, and the best way to track the ship and anchorage location. When I checked in with the Chandler he said they were due around three o'clock in the afternoon and were showing an outer anchorage location, that would be good for us and should provide pretty decent water quality.

Steve and I met up at his shop and went over the details. He said they had experience with working on ships, but not so much on Supertankers. I assured him the only real difference was the size, all the other parts are basically the same. Where we needed to work was a bit of a challenge, as the opening was about the size of a house door in the middle of a ships flat bottom over a thousand-feet-long and three hundred feet wide.

"Holy shit!" said Steve. "How do you ever find something that small down there?" He asked.

"Luck!" I chuckled in jest "You just have to think of the flat area of the bottom as a gigantic grid pattern with each piece of the grid fifty-foot long and ten foot wide. The grid lines are the weld seams of the ten by fifty plates used to construct the outer shell of the hull. Not that hard to find something if you can find the right plate section and follow the seams." I said. "We've been all over these ships and know the routing to find the main scoop where our work begins."

"Great!' said Steve. "Glad we have that worked out. My guys are pretty good at finding their way around."

"Won't be too bad. Once we locate the correct weld bead at the water line, we slide down to the flat bottom and follow the road map from there." I said.

With that, it was time to look over the gear and work out the rally time and place down at the port. We'd meet at the workboat at noon based on a three o'clock arrival at the outer anchorage. I wrapped things up and found a hotel near the port to hang out until we'd meet up. Being rested up was a really good idea before taking on a beast like the *MT CABRITE*.

The morning of November 2nd was uneventful. It was another perfect day in Southern California. I made sure to eat a hearty breakfast and hit a convenience store for food and drinks to drag out on the workboat. It would be another tough go, but we were ready. The boat was only twenty minutes away and easy to find. I had spent a bunch of time working in the LA area early in my career, so it was no problem to find my way around the waterfront.

When I arrived, the dive crew was already there setting up on the workboat. Steve Roberts introduced me to the team and boat operator who was a pal of his. So far so good. I hit the pay phone that was close by and called the Ships Chandler for the anchorage details. He said there'd been a change. The *MT CABRITE* was being moved to another location and he gave me the number locator for the area. Didn't think that much of it at the time. Steve and his boat guy would know where to go.

"Steve, the Ships Chandler says they moved the anchorage location." I said.

"Oh ya? What was the number?" Asked the Boat guy. I gave him the number and he said, "Oh shit. That's way closer in, and south of their original location. Probably no more than a mile west of the gigantic land reclamation project expanding the port for a new giant container facility. I'm not sure with being only a mile off the dredging, what kind of visibility you'll have out there. My guess, lousy." He said.

MT CABRITE at inner anchorage, close to shore in Long Beach CA November 2nd, 1995

Hearing that gave me pause for thought, as in 'I thought I wouldn't have to do any diving work.' The kind of work we were doing required at least some visibility to carry out the task, especially with a green crew. Oh well, it was time to get going. The Boat Captain pulled away from the dock and headed down the channel toward the harbor. As we rounded the corner in the channel, I could see the dredging operation and quay rock boundary for the new port expansion. It was a vast area with an enormous pumping operation. The dredge piping led far into the area from a huge dredge roaring away just north of the reclamation zone. The closer we got, the dirtier the water looked. The visibility was going to be poor at best.

I asked our boat Captain to take a ride-by and get a closer look at the impact of the dredging. My concern was rising, but visibility is a relative thing. There are different levels of zero viz. California zero viz is typically anything under three feet. We always joked about that when working in the dirty waters of the ports in the northeast. Joking aside, even muddy water usually leaves you a matter of inches and could be as good as a foot, plenty good enough to get things done.

Not far away was the *MT CABRITE*. At twelve-hundred-feet long and three hundred feet wide there's nowhere to hide. The ships ladder boarding access was on the starboard side. We hailed the ship as we came alongside, and I stepped off onto the small landing at the base of the ships ladder. Steve followed me and we made our way up to meet with the Captain and Chief Engineer. Paul Pedretti, Hess Port Engineer, was already aboard and waiting when we reached the Captains office.

"Hello there gentleman." Said Paul. He introduced us to the Captain and Chief Engineer. "I've briefed the Captain and Chief about our plan so there's no reason to hold you guys up."

"Thanks Paul. We'll get tied alongside and take a run through that piping up through the butterfly valve to look for any obvious signs of damage or debris." I said. "With any luck it shouldn't take that long. We'll hit you back on the radio with results. How's the boat running?" I asked, referring to our workboat that Paul had been borrowing to go fishing in St. Croix where he lived.

"Running great! Got a big Wahoo a few days ago!" He said. "Hail us on channel ten and we'll find a clear channel to chit chat."

"Fair enough. We're on the way. Please make sure they hang the 'diver in the water' sign on the main controls. Thanks." I said as we turned away and headed for the gangway. The workboat was there for us on our return.

We had lines dropped over the side at the right location to position ourselves near the beginning weld seam that would be our guide to find the scoop. There would be no way around it. I'd have to dress in to run a tag line from the workboat to the grating bars covering the opening to the main scoop. With crappy visibility, it would be impossible to direct someone to find it who's never previously been below to see it. Oh well. Once that was set we should be able to make progress.

Where we tied up left us just under two hundred feet from the scoop. The ship was on its ballast leg on their way to Valdez. That's a light draft condition, drawing about forty foot, plus or minus, in the stern. That would help us having a shallower draft but wouldn't help any with the visibility. On their way back from Valdez loaded with crude, they'd be underway drawing seventy-five feet or more.

Starting the road map to the scoop would begin by locating the correct weld bead at the waterline. From there, I'd be making a vertical drop to the turn of the bilge and onto the flat bottom. Once I made it to the flat bottom, it was a simple count of the cross welds until reaching the tenth one. At the tenth longitudinal weld, I'd need to stop, and turn to the right to follow the weld forward about eight feet and stop again. Turning to the left, the scoop will be found six to eight feet directly in front of me to port. Simple enough, especially if you've done it a few times.

It was five o'clock by the time we settled in, and I began getting suited up. We had a three-hundred-foot air umbilical to reach the scoop and I needed at least a two-hundred-foot soft line to use for a down line to attach to the bars covering the scoop. That would allow us to run back and forth to the scoop location without getting lost. Once we were ready I asked Steve to hail the ship and let them know we were commencing diving. When he confirmed the notification, I clamped on my helmet and jumped from the back deck of the workboat into the water.

The first thing I noticed; the water was black. I had an intensely bright helmet light that was no help. When I put my hand on my faceplate I couldn't even see the outline of my fingers. This was an extreme disadvantage. When you think about the size of this behemoth of a ship, that makes you feel like a blind man trying to find a needle in a haystack, but the haystack is more like a hay field! Good luck with that!

Thank God I've done this so many times. To succeed, I'd just have to close my eyes and paint a grid map in my mind and exercise good focus as I navigated my way through the pitch-black water to the grating covering the inlet.

"How's the visibility down there?" Asked Steve as I was blowing bubbles collecting my thoughts before grabbing the tag line to run down to the scoop.

Protective bars covering opening to main scoop. Not visible November 2nd

"What visibility? The visibility sucks! This is a true black out condition. Not my idea of happy days down here." I said sarcastically. "I can't see the outline of my fingers on my faceplate. All I know is there's a big son of a bitch of a ship somewhere around here." I said trying to make a joke out of it. "You have that tagline ready?"

"Ready to go." He said.

"OK. I'll slide over along the waterline and start my blind man's trip to the scoop opening. Let it out as I go but don't leave a lot of slack in the water in case I need to pull it for directional confirmation if I get turned around."

"Roger that." Said Steve.

I found the correct vertical weld at the waterline and started my descent. It was a little unnerving sliding down the weld bead, clearing my ears along the way until I felt the curve of the bilge. Seemed like a really long drop to reach the flat area. A few feet under the turn was the first longitudinal seam.

"OK topside. I'm on the flat bottom crossing over seam number one. Nine more to go." I said. Nine equals ninety feet, a pretty far distance in the pitch dark.

"Roger that." Said Steve. "I'm starting a log."

"Thank you sir." I said sliding my way to port. "Crossing number two." I continued, three, four, five and so on until I reached the tenth seam. So far so good I thought.

"OK topside. Reached seam ten. Turning right to head forward along this seam ten feet." I said using a wingspan with my arms as a five-foot rule. "Ready to make the turn to port and reach out to the scoop. If I counted right it should be only a few feet away.."

I would release my constant touch of the weld and surge ahead the short distance to the bars covering the scoop. "Here we go." I said jetting forward.

240

All of a sudden my whole body was pummeled by a large and very powerful blast of hot water. It blew me off the hull twisting and tumbling through the darkness. It was a huge rush of water that forced me a good distance deeper based on the squeezing I felt in my ears.

I suffered a complete loss of spatial orientation. There was no way to tell up from down. The loud banging and noises from the ship that reached my ears was omnidirectional in the water rendering my sense of sound useless for orientation. Only by having the workboat take up my slack and drag me back to the outside of the Supertanker would I be able to re-establish control.

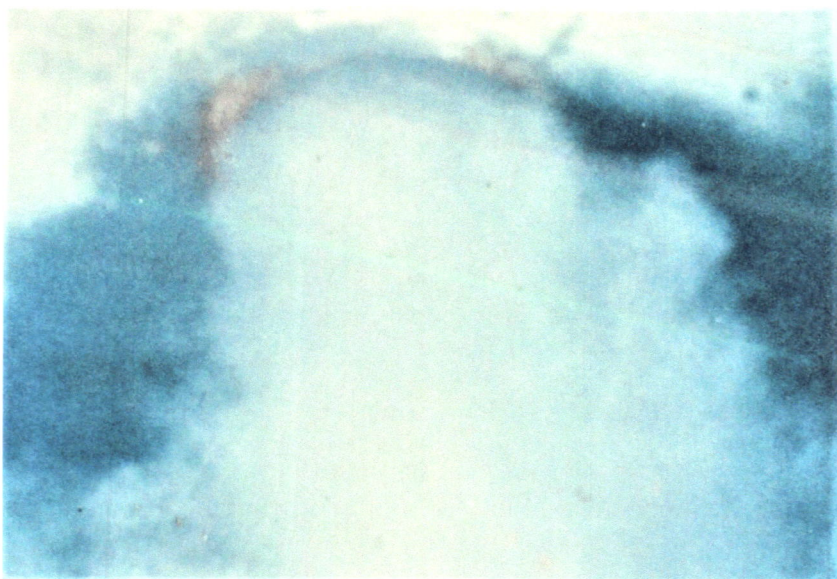

High volume discharge from generator on bottom of Supertanker – Photo by Author

"Take up my slack." I called out. "I need to come up and start over." I said keeping the long string of obscenities to myself. What the hell was that? I thought, trying to conjure a mental image of the scoop and surrounding area while kicking upward to re-establish contact with the ship hull once they had a strain on my umbilical. Had to be a major pump discharge that blew me off the hull. My best guess was it was the cooling water from the back-up generator. Damn! I had forgotten about that. In the Caribbean you see it clearly as you approach the bars of the scoop.

They pulled me back to the turn of the bilge where I asked them to stop while I cleared my ears and ascended. What the reader needs to know is how loud it was underneath the engine room. Typically, something ignored when you're working and have a good command of your surroundings. In this case, everything seemed louder, machines thumping away and clanging coming from some unknown source. A whole angry world of unseen machine monsters living above your head. It all added to the horrific venue of the pitch-black water. Most people would probably find the environment terrifying.

Back at the surface, I wandered over and found my starting point. "Here we go again Topside." I said beginning the slide down the weld seam, around the turn, one, two, three . . . ten. "Back at the tenth seam. Let's try this again." I said moving slightly forward from the last position and made my leap of faith. Bahwoosh, there I went again tumbling through space. Shit! "Take up my slack God damn it!" I said. "Blew me off again. Haul me back until I say stop." There was absolutely no way to re-orient myself once I lost my touch point.

"You alright down there ?" asked Steve sensing how irritated and tense I sounded.

"Ya. I'm OK, just a little pissed! There's a good-sized discharge between me and the scoop. I think it's getting ahold of my umbilical and dragging me into the discharge stream. They say the third time's the charm. Guess we'll find out." I said with this little exercise wearing me out. Thinking about it, if I passed over the tenth seam five or six feet and turned forward to the right that might allow me to make the leap and keep me and my hose out of harm's way. I know this is the right location even though I failed to remember the discharge.

"Here we go, third try." I said trying to sound cool and calm despite how pissed I was. They probably wondered what kind of knuckle head I was after I told them I knew just where the scoop was! They'd get their chance in the barrel. California divers cry like babies when they have three foot viz. They'll be crying for their Mothers when they get under this beast!

Couldn't wait to hear what they had to say about this real zero viz! The last guy I brought back east for a job in the Delaware River jumped in and said, "Holy shit! This really is zero viz." as he sucked down a K sized air cylinder in fifteen minutes. That's two hundred and fifty cubic feet of air, the equivalent of over three scuba tanks. We figured that just might be a world record!

In the meantime, I made it back to the tenth seam and moved a wingspan farther to port. "Making the turn Topside. Here we go!" I said making the leap forward. "Hallelujah! Gotcha you son of a bitch!" I said as I grabbed the bars and tied on the tag line.

"OK Topside. Take in the slack on the tag line and then leave it slacked off slightly. Let me know when you got that, and I'll take the straight shot back to the workboat." Jeez Louise.

"Good to go." Came the word from above. By the time I got back to the boat I was sure glad to have a gang there to get to work. I needed a break after all that exercise.

I asked Steve to have one of his guys go down there and loosen six bars and leave them hanging on one bolt, leaving the second bolt in its original hole. We couldn't afford to lose one. It would give me enough room to swim through the opening in the hull and up the pipe to inspect the butterfly valve.

Thankfully, I would have time to rest up after my recent ordeal before taking on the next little horror show. This was not a job for anyone with claustrophobia. I can't imagine much worse conditions in which to work underwater.

Steve's guy made the jump and after making a wise crack about working in a mud puddle, he went below and did what I asked. Took him a while but he was back on deck in thirty minutes. My turn.

Back I went into the darkness. I just couldn't wait to swim that forty feet up the pipe to the butterfly valve. I'll know I've found it when I bang my head. This would be a real challenge to do any meaningful inspection. If there was no obstruction, I could feel the valve seat for any improper contact from not closing properly. I'd bring the stills camera and get some photos by using a special diopter and strobe. I could take a portrait in a mud puddle with that thing. Just no seeing anything until getting the film developed later.

It sure was great having that line to pull myself back to that damn scoop. I felt the hanging bars and slipped my way through into the pipe leading to the valve. Sure enough, I banged my head on the butterfly and began feeling my way around. I couldn't see anything but there was no obstruction of the valve. That meant it would need a stem adjustment from inside the engine room.

The valve itself was about the size of a Volkswagen and it would take really large tools and burly crewmen to make any adjustments. OK by me. At least no seal replacement. I'd return to our workboat and have a conversation with Paul Pedretti and ask what he wanted to do. We had the cover aboard so we could seal the opening so they could drain the condenser. If they opened the inspection port on the side, he could get a look at how much of a mess they had in there. With the cover on they could at least get a temp seal to drain the condenser and put someone in if it needed cleaning.

I asked Steve to take up my slack as I made my way back to the boat. I handed up my stills camera and climbed out. Time to call Pedretti.

"*MT CABRITE*, Leeward Marine." I hailed.

"Go to channel 70." Said Paul Pedretti.

"Roger that." I said switching to channel 70. "Paul, I got a good look at the butterfly valve. Actually, I never saw it but felt it. The visibility was horrible. The dredging they're doing turned everything into a mud puddle."

"Great. What did you 'feel'?" He asked.

"It feels clear, but it was difficult to tell by feeling if there was any hard contact on the seat. This must be a stem adjustment issue like you thought. Question is, what's next for you?" I asked.

"Let's throw the cover on down there and drain the condenser. Might as well get a look inside while we're here. If it's not bad we just might be able to make it back to St. Croix and get a better shot at adjusting." He said.

"OK. It'll take twenty or thirty minutes to get that installed so you can drain the condenser. You'll have to let us know if it's sealing alright once you get it drained. We'll hail you on 70 as soon as its tight." I said.

"OK. Standing by." Said Paul giving us our marching orders.

Steve's guys muckled the cover down there and buttoned it up after loosely bolting the bars back in place and then installing the cover. It was attached with J bolts that hooked on the bars to hold it in place. When they opened the condenser the extreme water pressure pressed the cover tight to the hull and they'd be able to tighten the nuts to make a good watertight seal.

"OK Paul. We're all set down here. Cover's on. Go ahead and drain the condenser and let me know when you're done." I said.

"It'll take about twenty minutes." Paul said.

"Roger that. We'll stand by on 70."

"Leeward Marine, *MT CABRITE.*" It was Paul back at us a short time later. "The seal is holding. The condenser is drained. We're opening the port for inspection. Standby. We may want to move you to inspect the butterfly valve going through the access port here in the engine room."

"OK, Paul. Do you want me to come up and discuss?" I asked.

Paul said, "Give me a few minutes to check things out."

"Leeward Marine. Standing by on 70." I responded.

If we had to shift to the engine room and work through the access port window on the end of the condenser, that was a big deal. We had to use specialized safety protocols in case of emergency, not the least of which was cutting the diving umbilical and stranding me inside until they did a rescue from the outside after removing the cover. This would be a very bad time with a green crew to take that kind of risk.

To reach the butterfly valve from the engine room, I would have to squeeze through the access port, dress into an eight-inch wetsuit and coveralls for openers My crew would then have to pass my helmet through the opening. From there, I would have to tend myself and enter the inlet pipe that remained full of water after they drained the condenser.

The pipe lay at a forty-five-degree angle leading forward and downward until it reached the valve about twenty feet down. It would require me to make a head-first entry into the water filled pipe to approach the valve and have good position to inspect the butterfly. They could open and close the valve with me watching to see where it was hanging up, that is if I could see anything at all in that mud water. If so, they should be able to make small adjustments and re-test until we had it properly seated again.

This whole thing could get out of control I thought, just as the radio crackled to life. "Leeward Marine. *MT CABRITE*." It was Paul again.

"Go *CABRITE*." I responded.

"Hey, we've got an issue here. I need you to come down and have a look at the condenser." Paul said.

"Roger that. Be there in ten minutes." I said, motioning to our boat Captain.

Steve had the crew make sure everything was onboard before releasing the lines to shift back to the ship's gangway. I stepped off and made my way up with Steve in tow. We made our way down to the engine room and found Paul Pedretti.

"What's going on?" I asked.

"We really need to have you inside there for us to make the adjustments to that valve stem." He said. "One problem. We seem to have steam bypassing the system and still feeding through the condenser. I'm not sure it's safe to put you in there. You need to check this out before we do anything else here." He said.

Oh shit, I thought, looking back at Steve. "Let me get a look in there." I said stepping past Paul to get a look. It was hot as hell in there. The steam must be blowing past a shut off valve on the other side of the condenser. Without cooling water running through the condenser the steam would super heat the coils inside causing the air temperature to skyrocket where I needed to operate. My opinion was that it was unsafe, and beyond the level for diving operations. I pointed my light down to see the water at the top of the inlet pipe. It looked like a mud puddle. It would be a fool's errand to attempt entry into the chamber.

"Paul, the water in that pipe will give us a zero viz condition. Without being able to see, it will be really hard to assist. The temp inside there is well over a hundred degrees with steam still feeding through the condenser. Without cooling the temperature will continue to rise. If that steam can't be shut off it has the potential to be lethal. The air would be unbreathable while inside the condenser, especially when I go to remove my helmet. This is way past the limits for safe operation, even with our special safety protocols." I said.

"That's what I thought, but I figured you should see what we're up against should anyone ask later." He said.

"Hey, thanks for thinking of me!" I joked. Paul laughed and Steve didn't know what to say. He wasn't laughing. Probably thought we were both nuts.

"Alright. I'm calling it. You guys can pack it up. The condenser looks clean so we should be able to make the trip." We were done according to Paul.

I looked at Steve and said, "Only one thing left to do. We have to retrieve the cover and make sure it gets back on the ship."

"That's right. I'll get some guys on deck to haul that back aboard. We need to drag it back with us to St. Croix." Said Paul.

Steve and I signed off with Paul and offered to give him a lift back to port if he needed one. He said he planned to continue on to Valdez and make sure the ship made it. The steam valve blow by was a big concern and if steam fitters were called for in Valdez, he'd need to be there. Made sense. We said our goodbyes and headed for the gangway.

Steve had one of his guys make the jump to remove the cover from the scoop inlet. Wouldn't take too long but it was important to reattach the bars and tighten the bolts securely before heading back. I recommended attaching the down line to the cover and swimming it back to keep it from hanging up. Once clear of the flat bottom, the crew hauled it over to the workboat.

They got the cover back on the deck and tied it off for the men on the ship to haul it back aboard. It was getting late as we headed back to the Port of Long Beach. The good news was I didn't have much with me other than a gear bag and helmet. My cameras traveled as luggage. I couldn't wait to hit the hotel and crash out. The only thing left was to square up with Steve and be on my way.

I had a red eye flight back to Tampa on the 3rd. It would get me back to my house around ten in the morning. On the flight back I had time to think about all the risks and dangers associated with this ship call. Seemed like most of my work lately had considerably bigger challenges with much greater risks then they used to. The work paid well, but at what cost? The old saying, 'The greater the risk the bigger the reward,' is only true if you're around to enjoy it . . .

VLGG "MT. GABRITE"
UNDERWATER INSPECTION
AND SERVICE OF MAIN SCOOP
INJECTION VALVE
NOVEMBER 2,3, 1995

Title Block from report on MT CABRITE

*Author's Photo: MT CABRITE at **outer** anchorage – Port of LA, 1992*

CHAPTER EIGHTEEN

WESTERN LION - THE SHEEN

Coast Guard Orders Supertanker Ejected from US Waters Siting Oil Sheen - Valdez

⚊⚊≈⚊⚊

The first oil tanker to load crude oil in Valdez took place in early August 1977 following the completion of the pipeline from Prudhoe Bay and construction of the Valdez Marine Terminal. The *ARCO JUNEAU* was loaded and transported its crude oil cargo to the Cherry Point Refinery in Washington State. This was the opening of an endless line of tankers to follow, sending countless millions of barrels south to feed the insatiable need for oil in the US.

The waters through Prince William Sound were carefully charted with the US Coast Guard standing watch protecting the pristine coastline. That was the promise made when the Trans-Alaska Pipeline project was approved.

On March 24th, 1989, the nine hundred and eighty-seven-foot tanker EXXON VALDEZ piled onto Bligh Reef and spilled 10.8 million gallons of crude oil into Prince William Sound.

The disaster changed the world. The environmental impact was of a scale never seen before and led to new regulations with severe penalties for violations. The shock of the disaster would be far reaching. The shipping industry would propose changes to ship designs and construction that eventually led to the rise of double hull tankers. The industry was given a ten-year grace period to convert to double bottom ships and ultimately full double hull designs to protect the public and the environment.

The Coast Guard was ordered to step up their patrols of all tankers entering and exiting Prince William Sound. Their arsenal included aircraft and helicopters to watch over the long entry from the Pacific Ocean through the Sound and into the Alyeska Marine Terminal in Port Valdez.

FILE PHOTO: EXXON VALDEZ tanker prior to incident in Valdez

With an eagle-eye, they were looking for any evidence of leaking oil from ships, inbound or outbound from Valdez. It is here where our *WESTERN LION* story begins.

We had worked on all of the Maritime Overseas LION Class ships under long term charter to Hess in St Croix. They operated the *NORTHERN, SOUTHERN, , EASTERN*, and *WESTERN LION*. The ships were all the same design of twelve-hundred-foot-long supertankers, considerably larger than the *EXXON VALDEZ*.

It was mid-November in 1995 when I got a phone call from my old friends at Maritime Overseas. It was an awkward conversation with Joe March, Senior Marine Engineer for Maritime Overseas He was unwilling to discuss their problem over the phone but made it clear they had an urgent need.

"Hello there, Joe. How're you doing?" I asked.

"Ah, I've been hanging in there, battling this damn disease." He said. Joe had been battling cancer now for two years and things weren't going well. "I'm afraid we have a problem of a delicate nature and Keith Duncan asked me to invite you to the office to discuss." Joe said cryptically.

"What's up?" I asked.

"That's the problem. We need to discuss this in person. This is a highly confidential matter and Keith asked that we meet here and not exchange any other details until we meet." Joe said. "Can you be here tomorrow?"

Jeez Louise, this was a first. With a total blackout of details this had to be a real beauty. "Tomorrow? I can if I catch an early flight out of Tampa."

"Great." Said Joe. "It'll be good to see you again my friend." He said as we signed off.

What the hell was that? I wondered to myself. He didn't mention anything about the problem, or which ship they were worried about. I'd have to wait until tomorrow to find out. Susan wouldn't be happy. We had dinner plans for Friday night. I wouldn't get back in time after my meeting to keep our date. This was going to cost me.

I was able to book a seven AM nonstop on November 10th to LaGuardia. Maritime Overseas had offices in the Grace Building in Midtown Manhattan where they occupied two full floors.   The

Marine Department was on the lower of the two with Keith Duncan, VP of Shipping, and his team sharing the space. Joe asked me to call after I landed to confirm a meeting time.

The flight was on time. I called Joe and I arrived at the Grace Building just after one o'clock. Keith would be available at one thirty.

I introduced myself to the receptionist. She rang Joe and announced my arrival. He showed up moments later.

"Hello there, my friend!" Joe said with a broad grin and a hearty handshake.. "Great to see you!" He said as he led us to his workspace, a cramped cube buried in the middle of the office. Space was at a premium in Manhattan. Joe wasn't there much. Most of his time was spent traveling the globe and tending to his ships.

"Great to see you Joe. What the hell is going on? I know this is no social call." I said.

"Well, in a way it is. Keith has made it one!" Joe said jokingly. "We'll wait for Keith to fill you in. There are things going on way above my pay grade. We've got a real corker this time."

While waiting for Keith, we took the time to catch up. Joe had been with me in the Canary Islands back in 1984 when Aquafacs did its first job and performed the world's first inspection inside a Supertanker using divers. Been a long road since then, and I was sad to see that Joe had lost a bunch of weight and was not looking well.

At one thirty, Keith Duncan rounded the corner and was standing in Joe's cube.

Keith extended his hand, "Thanks for coming." He said without a smile. He turned and walked off. Joe got up and he and I followed Keith as he wound his way back to his corner office. "Close the door." He said.

254

"Been a long time since I've been here." I said looking around the room.

"No need, you chaps having been doing great work." He said looking over his black thick rimmed glasses. "I've asked you here because we've got a bloody big cockup going on with the Coast Guard." He said leaning forward in his chair. "The *WESTERN* left a sheen on the water on the way into Valdez." He said. "They were boarded by the Coast Guard when they arrived at the terminal."

FILE PHOTO: ALYESKA TERMINAL- South end of Alaska Pipeline. Supertanker terminal

Oh shit! Here it comes . . . Of all the places, Valdez. That really got my attention! It now made sense why I was here in person. It had only been six years since the *EXXON VALDEZ* incident, and the Coast Guard wasn't playing around up there.

He went on, "When they boarded the ship at the terminal they rounded up the Captain and Chief Engineer in the Captains office and read then the riot act. Leaving a sheen on the water is a major violation with huge fines and potentially other sanctions like being banned from the terminal and could even include jailing the Captain for negligence. The Chief Engineer tracked down his Second on watch and confirmed that they failed to shut off the head tank and left a light sheen all the way from Prince William Sound into the terminal at Valdez." He paused and looked at Joe to pick up the tale.

"Yah, that was the bad news." Said Joe. "The good news is the Coast Guard believed the Engineers story and made them a deal. They could load their cargo of six million barrels and exit the Valdez Marine Terminal. After that, they were banned from entering US waters without providing them an underwater inspection report providing proof the seals were OK and not fouled with fishing line or otherwise damaged." Joe said. Oh Boy, I could see where this was going.

He continued, "That's where you come in, my friend. We need your help to get this inspection done before the ship arrives in St. Croix." That was the final destination to offload at the Hess Refinery and it was in US waters. He looked back at Keith.

"There's a hitch. We only have one shot at it in St. Lucia when she's lightering for St. Croix. St. Lucia is international." Said Keith.

"Great!" I said, speaking too soon. "We've got good conditions down there."

"Not so fast." Joe said. "The last time she went through drydock was in the far east. They welded covers over the inspection windows at the top and bottom of the rope guard to keep out the fishing line and ropes they were prone to get sucked up as they made the trip back and forth to Alaska. Access to the propeller shaft is not possible without removing those covers."

"Uh oh." I said. "That could be a big issue. No burning or welding is allowed in the terminal in St. Lucia. You got any photos from the drydock to see what they did?"

"No, but we have a report. It says the covers were tack welded. This was the far east, for all we know, their idea of a tack weld may not be the same as ours." Joe said with a raised eyebrow.

"There's more." Said Keith. "We don't want any of this to leave the room. The vessel is under long term charter to Hess. This will become a hugely awkward matter should they catch wind of it. We need you to make the trip to St. Lucia, get the survey done and keep as low a profile as possible. Speak to no one about this other than the Captain and Chief Engineer. Joe will work with you and have Mario inform the Captain of our plan." Mario was an elder Italian Marine Engineer who spoke the language. He'd relay the message to the Captain.

"Good luck!" said Keith, standing and shaking my hand ending our meeting. Joe picked up the report and we left for his space to comb through it. Maybe there was something useful in the document.

"Jesus Joe. I was hungry when I got here but I just lost my appetite. Now I see why I needed to be here." I said.

"Not sure how long I'll be around, but this one takes the cake so far!" he said. "You'll need to come up with a plan and meet the ship down there. When you figure this out, call me to discuss. I'll send you the arrival schedule after we hear from the ship later today. I'd love to catch up with a pint, but the doctors say no alcohol, a cruel turn of events!" He said jokingly. "Maybe next time at the Domino Club."

Mt. Pellier Domino Club in the St Croix rainforest was a place we spent many hours hanging out eating Cynthia's smoked kingfish and enjoying the cool venue at the top of the rainforest. Her husband George served ice cold beer or your favorite tropical drinks. Out back were the world-famous beer drinking pigs. I always felt obliged to buy them a beer on my way out. Always good for a laugh. By Joe's appearance, I'm afraid that was wishful thinking.

There was nothing useful in the report from the drydock. We were on our own and there was no doubt, failure was not an option . . .

It would be a relatively short flight from LaGuardia, and I would arrive back in Tampa in the early evening. My head was full of ideas on how to attack the problem. I would need the weekend to contemplate the situation and hopefully an answer would come to me. After wheels up, I ordered a double shot of Bailey's and dozed off.

Thanksgiving was not far off and after my god-awful trip a little over a week ago to LA, I felt like age was really starting to catch up. Oh well. No way out of this one. I would come up with the plan and drag Paul Mercaldi with me with as little gear as possible to achieve our goal. Not sure how much I wanted to share with Paul prior to the trip. Didn't want to scare him, but I couldn't lie, this was a big deal and about as challenging as it gets. Six million barrels of oil aboard the *WESTERN LION* are steaming to St. Lucia with no guarantee of making it to St. Croix. We would have to succeed to get the *WESTERN* to its final destination, US waters, St. Croix.

FILE PHOTO: WESTERN LION at HOVIC Terminal, St Croix

Two Weeks to Prepare - The WESTERN LION was On Schedule Steaming to St. Lucia

The weekend would bring a good soak in the pool and a Sunday family BBQ. I invited my sister Jean and her husband Paul over. It would be a good time to break the news. Paul would likely be thrilled, especially after a couple of rum and cokes to loosen him up. He loved the Islands, and this would be his first trip to St. Lucia. I would take care not to overly alarm him, but he needed to know how serious this was going to be, not the usual 'rum run' as we used to call our trips to the Caribbean. Before I broke this to Paul, I needed to mull things over. We'd enjoy the Sunday BBQ and get serious Monday morning.

We'd need to be a hundred percent ready. It would be just me and him making the trip. The way I saw this, it was going to be a really long day just to get the covers removed. My hope was that the report of tack welded plates was accurate. Even at that, the only safety compliant tool to cut through the welds would be a high-speed pneumatic tool grinder with cutoff wheels. I planned to buy six tool grinders and a bag load of cut off wheels to pack with the gear. Steel wedges and a good beater would also be needed to break them free. Both of those we would borrow from the ship.

The ships onboard air compressors were enormous and could supply tool and breathing air. We would tee off the supply and run the breathing air through a specialized filtration system before feeding my diving umbilical. The ships air supply would be a reliable source. Other than being unfiltered, it could be easily used with the properly rated filtration cartridges. We'd bring three spares in case the air was a little damp or oily. There wasn't much of a choice.

The combined cubic feet per minute for the high-speed tool grinder and my breathing air supply at seventy feet down was a considerable number if you didn't have an unlimited supply. There was one small safety concern. If we lost air for any reason, the impact would be immediate. My breathing air made a slight hissing sound from a light free flow I used for comfort. It gave me a little breeze inside my helmet. If it stopped, that was the alert for me to check the status and if necessary turn on my tiny bailout bottle. It's amazing how far you can stretch seventeen cubic feet of compressed air. Starting at a depth of seventy feet, it wouldn't last long. With skip breathing, a technique used to conserve air by consciously taking less breathes per minute as you sort out your issues, the seventeen cubic foot bail out bottle would be suitable in case of an emergency loss of air.

We could use a shorter diving umbilical that would pack and ship neatly as luggage. Two hundred feet would be plenty to work with. I would swim a couple hundred yards from the mooring dolphin to the stern of the ship. Then my helmet would be lowered from the deck to me in the water from directly above where I needed it, at the stern seal location. At thirty pounds, I'd hang back until it reached me at the water in case someone forgot how to tie a proper bowline.

Heads up BBQ or the Last Supper

Paul and Jean showed up for our Sunday BBQ. I had already mentioned we had a trip coming up but didn't divulge the details. I knew when he heard St. Lucia all would be good. Little did he know.

"Hello there! Where's the Mt Gay?" asked Paul looking for his favorite rum.

"Sorry man. Only Cruzan here!" He knew that already. At the price, Cruzan was my standard rum stock. At two bucks a bottle I brought many cases back from my ventures to St. Croix. "Thanks for coming. Make yourself a drink!"

Jean was in with Susan helping with the food prep. I was the grill man and Susan was the Master of Planning, when it came to pool parties.

Paul and I grabbed a couple of pool floats and hit the water. I started to fill him in on the next adventure.

"So, how'd you like to make a trip to St. Lucia in a week or so? Don't think you've made one of these trips yet." I said.

"Hell ya!" said Paul. "I've been to Puerto Rico and St. Croix with you guys and Jamaica when I was in the Navy. Never been to St. Lucia."

"Well, we've got a beauty! An inspection of the stern seal on the WESTERN LION. She'll be arriving pretty soon and need this to happen while they're lightering." I said.

"Sign me up!" said Paul. "We need video or just stills?"

"Still working on that one. I figure we can get into the planning tomorrow. There are a couple of special issues. I'd rather not get into today." I said trying to downplay my concern.

"Great! Turn up the music!" He said as the kids showed up and leaped into the pool on top of us.

Paul showed up at eight o'clock Monday morning raring to go. It wouldn't take long for that to subside as I began my story about the 'special' trip I just made to NYC. All was good until I mentioned that the covers would need to be removed from the rope guard before I could take the photos and confirm the condition,

"Holy shit! What the fuck are we going to do?" said Paul. "No burning or welding in oil terminals. Broco rods are out. Jesus!"

"The only thing that makes sense is using the high-speed tool grinders like we used on the Atlantic Class to shave those lifting lugs on the stern seals. They sell small cut off wheels that fit. We should be able to cut the tack welds and drive steel wedges to pop the cover plates off. My biggest fear is whether we find tack welds like the report says or continuous weld beads around each of those covers. No photos were available from their last drydocking in the far east." I said. "The other issue is the cut off wheels are made for use in the dry. Underwater they'll work but you're relying on abrasives only. No heat to speed up the cutting properties. Basically, we'll be cold grinding our way through. That will be a really slow go for sure, even at over 20,000 RPMs. It's wearing me out thinking about it!"

"We better get a bunch of those cutoff wheels!" said Paul.

'Ya, and a half dozen tool grinders. They don't do well in salt water." I added. "With SeaLand it was one ship, one tool grinder and that was only used less than thirty minutes per ship. These will be in continuous duty, so we need really good luck. Feeling lucky?"

"No. This is starting to sound like a tough trip. Whatever, at least I'll get a trip in to St. Lucia and maybe a bottle of that STRONG RUM you tangled up with down there with the Swede!"

"I hope not. Your liver won't be able to handle it!" I joked.

CHAPTER NINETEEN

WESTERN LION - MISSION IMPOSSIBLE - ST.LUCIA

=⚓=

Ready or Not - Arrival Day Approaches

I called Joe at Maritime Overseas as he requested and filled him in on our plan of attack. He made a couple of suggestions and confirmed the ship would be able to provide tools and air supply with no problem. He would have Mario reach out to the Chief Engineer and have them get the items I requested pulled together and on deck when they arrived in St. Lucia.

"Joe, I hope you don't need those covers back!" I joked. "When those sons of bitches pop free they'll be heading to the bottom." That got a chuckle out of him.

"No, no. They won't miss them. Let's just hope those welds are what they say. You know where we're at with the inspection, the ship can't go anywhere until you're done. That doesn't mean to take your time!" he said laughing. I didn't think that was funny. "If that ship finishes lightering before you're done the Chief will have to come up with something to say about the delayed departure. Hess will be asking. They don't like Supertankers hanging around, especially when they're expected at the refinery. That could get dicey if we run too long after discharging. We'll have to keep our fingers crossed. It's all you kid!"

"Thanks Joe. I appreciate the confidence. What's the arrival schedule at St. Lucia?" I asked.

"Next Saturday the 6th, should be alongside by late afternoon." Said Joe.

"Great! A night job! Hey, there's one more thing. I need you to fax me a work request that I can use for getting through Security at the terminal." I said.

"You got it! Give me a few minutes. I'll get that done right now. Good luck!" said Joe signing off.

"Thanks. Piece of cake!" I hoped.

FILE PHOTO: WESTERN LION, fully loaded heading for St Lucia, Drafting 75 feet

Last chance logistics before take off

Paul and I got together and packed up the gear and tools we'd bring to St. Lucia. Using a checklist, we methodically walked through every detail and all the items we'd need to pack. Film, batteries, cameras, and spares including a second camera and comm box. The good news was that the water visibility would be terrific at the terminal. That would be a huge help.

I had my travel agent get us flights to the island on Thursday, January 4th , two days before the ship arrival. That would give us a cushion in case there were any baggage problems plus time to unpack and test everything. We also needed enough time to get our diving permit for St Lucia in case anyone at the terminal asked for it.

We had to pack light, by relative standards, but it was still a bunch of moving parts. The cases we used for shipping were designed for the military to ship specialized weapons. Cam locks and other security features made these perfect for our traveling road show. They were made out of indestructible ABS plastic, one of the most durable and lightweight materials available. Measuring three and a half feet long, two-feet-wide and eighteen inches deep, they held roughly ten cubic feet per trunk.

I hand carried my Superlight helmet in a bowling ball bag due to its size and shape. It had to be removed from its carry bag to fit in the overhead bin on most airplanes. That always got a lot a strange looks from the other passengers. I always kept it with me when I traveled. You can improvise with almost anything except the damn Superlight. Without it you were toast.

Thursday January 4th arrived, and my wife Susan drove me and Paul to Sarasota Airport. We caught the ten o'clock American Eagle flight to Miami and connected from there directly to Hewanorra International Airport on the south east end of St. Lucia. It was a great flight with no hitches. All our gear and luggage arrived without incident. Took some time to clear customs with all the diving gear and cameras. Not too bad during pre-911 days.

After picking up our rental car, we hit the road for the hotel thirty miles north in Castries. That would be the closest city to the Hess St. Lucia Terminal. They were near the water and had a nice pool and Jacuzzi. We'd hang out and hit the Jacuzzi after dinner. Figured I could use it for a little stress relief. Didn't work.

My anxiety was rising, waiting for the ship to arrive. It took a good nightcap at the bar to dull the senses enough to slow my racing mind, and not allow any creeping thoughts of doubt to undermine my confidence. I couldn't escape hearing Joe March's final words in the back of my mind, 'It's all you kid.' There was no plan 'B.'

Friday morning, we needed to obtain our permit to dive in St Lucia and then we'd be ready for the ship's arrival on Saturday. It was game on, shaking out all the gear in the back area of the hotel parking lot. Using the checklist and a good head scratch we made sure nothing had been overlooked. We were ready.

After an early evening Friday, we had a lazy start on Saturday. The *WESTERN LION* wasn't due until late afternoon so there was plenty of time for a good breakfast at the hotel with plenty of coffee to get cranked up. To avoid any access issues at the terminal we left at two o'clock for the thirty-minute drive from the hotel on the north side of Castries to the Hess St. Lucia Terminal located on the westside of the island, south of the City.

The facility itself was for storage only. It had fourteen large storage tanks built by Hess expressly for Supertankers use.

St Lucia storage facility for offloading two million barrels of crude oil from Western Lion to meet 55' draft requirement for St Croix,

The *WESTERN LION* needed to reduce the depth of their draft to fifty-five feet from seventy or better on arrival from Valdez to discharge at the Hess Refinery in St. Croix. The volume was around two million barrels, plus or minus, that had to be discharged to meet the requirements to enter the St. Croix terminal.

In St Lucia there was only one dock for Supertanker discharge available. It doubled for use by smaller tankers to shuttle the excess crude from the Supertankers back to the refinery. It was quite an operation set up by Leon Hess. We called it 'The St. Croix two step.' It allowed Hess to operate foreign flagged Supertankers to carry Alaskan Crude to St. Lucia and avoid the Jones Act.

To better understand the unusual setup in St Lucia, a brief history of the law will help. The 'Jones Act' is a hundred-year old federal law that regulates commerce in the United States. It requires goods shipped between U.S. ports to be transported on ships that are built, owned, and operated by United States citizens or permanent residents.

The 'Jones Act,' by definition, would require all Alaskan crude leaving Valdez, a US port, for delivery to another US port be compliant with the statute. By having deliveries of crude oil to the Hess owned refinery in St. Croix making their first port of call in St. Lucia to discharge allowed Hess to circumvent the law. It was hugely controversial and caused a lot of heartburn and lawsuits with the US Merchant Marines and their Union.. Thankfully, we didn't have a dog in that fight.

So, there we were as the *WESTERN LION* appeared at the outside marker where the Hess tugs would take the ship under tow and tie her off to the mooring dolphins. That was quite a sight. It was a monster of a ship and looked completely out of place stuffed in that cove in St. Lucia. It's amazing that they had that kind of depth to dock something that big.

The tugboat horns blared as they signaled back and forth carefully moving the tanker into position, aligning the ship with the discharge manifold. Dock workers standing by on the mooring dolphins handled the wire rope mooring lines and secured the ship. With a couple of final toots, the tugs departed. There would be a brief delay before we could board the vessel due to the St. Lucia customs process. Not that big of a deal. We made the gangway around five thirty in the afternoon.

The *WESTERN LION* was crewed with Italian officers and Engineers along with Filipino Able-Bodied Seamen (ABs). We asked for help handling our trunks. The gangway was a steep ship ladder type and we needed more horsepower to drag the cases on board than we could muster. Besides, I needed to reserve my strength for later.

Four Filipinos made the trek and safely transported everything aboard. They rolled our equipment on a four wheeled cart the six hundred feet aft to the location we had selected to set up our dive station. Now the fun would begin.

Paul uncrated everything while I went up to meet the Captain and Chief Engineer. They had been briefed by Mario, so much of what we needed was already on deck and coiled awaiting our arrival.. After a few minutes of pleasantries, I went back down and worked with Paul to set up the equipment.

Paul methodically laid out the air lines from the ship to our filtration system and had the diving station nearly finished by the time I returned. My Superlight helmet was the last piece to be added and coms tested. The second air line would connect to our tool grinders. Once I had that in hand, with a bucket full of cut off wheels down below, Paul wouldn't have to do much unless we needed to change out the tool if it wore out or broke during use. He'd haul it up, throw another grinder online and toss it back in. We tied multiple down lines to the handrail to lower tools and diving gear to me after I swam from the mooring dolphin to the stern.

The sun was going down as we completed setting the stage. Time to make my way down and get the show on the road, more like show in the water. It would be a long night ahead.

The only thing I carried with me down the gangway was a pair of jet fins. My neck dam, the collar that the Superlight attaches to, was around my neck as I climbed down the ladder and entered the water. Everything else would be lowered, and I would finish getting suited up in the water at the stern of the ship. It was docked Port side to, and it was at least a couple of hundred yards from my entry ladder to the stern. Not that long a distance as I began my swim just before eight o'clock.

I looked up and felt really small. That damn ship was enormous, and those creeping doubts began to bubble up. I had to keep those doubts in check and focus on my task. There was no choice here other than success. But still, it was almost surreal that this Behemoth was going nowhere until I finished our mission.

I hailed Paul as I got close enough to where I could see him hanging over the rail, and he could hear me shouting from below. "OK Paul. Get my Superlight and harness on the hang line and lower it down until I tell you to stop. Make sure you turn on the air before sending it my way."

"Roger that." He said. The helmet was starting its descent a few seconds later.

"All stop." I said as I positioned myself below the helmet that was suspended a foot above. "Slowly lower away until I say stop." The helmet slowly lowered into the water over my head. "All stop." I clamped the helmet in place, cracked the air valve slightly and untied the rope. "Com check." I asked.

"All good." Said Paul. "You want the stills camera?" He asked.

"Yes, and the twenty-five-foot soft line I left with it. I'll drop down and do a blow by before we drag the tools down here."

"Roger that." Paul said lowering the camera.

The *WESTERN LION* was drafting just over seventy-five feet, so our work area would be starting around sixty foot to the center of the cap nut at the end of the propeller shaft. It was getting dark, but the water clarity was amazing. Like a giant aquarium, it gave me an eerie view, gliding my way to the propeller. I made a landing just forward of the thirty-foot diameter propeller.

I got my first view of the cover on the topside of the stern tube. It was one hundred percent welded. No tack welds here. I muttered a long stream of obscenities under my breath. Paul could hear me but couldn't understand what I said.

"What's going on down there?" Paul asked. "I can't understand what you're saying."

"Ya, you're not supposed to." I said. "The top cover has a full effing weld. I'm sliding around to the bottom to check that one.. Ah, it's the same, shit!" I could have easily cut loose a good rip, but 'shit' summed it up well. No sense in crying about it. Both Joe and I suspected as much. Anything else would have been too lucky.

"What do you want next?" asked Paul.

"A crying towel! Throw a bunch of cut off discs and a small crescent wrench in the metal bucket and tie it to the air hose for the tool grinder. Make sure everything is safety wired up and get ready to lower it down. I'm wrapping the stern tube with that soft line to hang tools on. Let me know when you're ready."

"Roger that." He said as I was hanging my camera off on the tie line. I surfaced to handle the bucket when it got into the water to avoid it from tipping and dumping the discs. The tool grinder would follow along with me until I got the bucket tied off below the stern tube.

"Ready to lower the bucket?" asked Paul.

"Go ahead. Slack off the line when I get it. I may be making a fast descent if it's heavy in the water." The bucket was on the heavy side and I dropped the fifty plus feet in a hurry, making a landing on top of the stern tube where I established my balance before tying it off. Jeezus that was quite a ride. Good thing my ears clear easily I thought.

"I'm all set down here. Better get a chair. This is gonna be a while!" I said, arranging the hoses and positioning myself to start on the top cover. I'd have to develop a technique and have Paul time how long it took per inch of cut weld so we could make a rough projection of what we were up against.

Tool in hand I said, "Paul, for the first few inches I want you to time this. Knowing that, we can multiply it by the total weld bead length of both covers to come up with a guess on tool time to get the covers off. The inspection part will be a piece of cake."

"I like the piece of cake thing." Paul said.

I had a yellow lumber crayon with me to mark the cover and track my progress. Other than time, the high-speed tool grinder didn't require much physical strength. More like a dentist tool than serious grinder.

Marking the starting point at the twelve o'clock position at the forwardmost edge of the plate, I began cutting. The high-pitched whirring sound penetrated the water and filled my helmet. When I called it like a dental tool, that was exactly what it sounded like. The volume of air discharge from the tool grinder was phenomenal and interfered with keeping a good visual of the cut line. Paul started the timing.

I had marked a point three inches from the starting point. Every time I stopped to examine the progress; it was disappointing. The weld bead was likely three eighths of an inch thick or better and I wasn't getting deep enough yet to break through. My three-inch point was a pipe dream. I would be happy to just make my first break through as Paul chimed in to say we'd been at it twenty minutes.

"Jesus Paul. I haven't even broken through the weld yet at my starting point. I'll keep going and have you mark my first break." I said. ZZZ,ZZZ,ZZZ whirred the tool at twenty thousand RPMs as I continued to work my way through. Seemed like five minutes later I could see the crack between the weld and the underlying stern tube.

"That's it Paul. What do you have for time." I asked.

"You're not going to like it, thirty minutes!" He said.

"Great! Thirty minutes an inch. We've got to do better than that. Each cover has four feet of weld plus or minus. That's ninety-six inches. At thirty minutes an inch that's forty-eight hours! How many cut off wheels did we bring?" I asked sarcastically. There was no way we could take that long! I needed to come up with a solution.

From my experience in marine construction, I learned a lot about steel. If I could make enough points around the plate to drive steel wedges between the covers and the heavy plating of the stern seal, it might be possible to gain a big advantage and fracture the welds. With that in mind I decided to make a series of short cuts and expose enough to drive a series of wedges and continue my way around the cover until I had a few set that could be hammered with a heavy sledge hammer. I explained my idea to Paul. His response was something like 'good luck with that.' That's all I could hope for.

On and on I worked on one side of the top cover until I felt it was time to try a steel wedge. I asked Paul to lower a second bucket with a ten-pound hammer and half a dozen steel wedges, and to stop when

I said so. The visibility was so clear, I could simply look over and see when the bucket was at my elevation. I would have him slack it off after I got ahold of the line and swing it into place beneath the stern tube on my tool line next to the cut off wheels.

"Lower away." I said to Paul. "All stop." I said when the bucket was straight over to port. "This bucket is going to be friggin heavy, so don't just let go when I start pulling on it. Slack off slowly and I'll hump the thing back over." The ship was three-hundred-feet wide amidships and narrowed up to about a hundred and fifty wide where we were. That would leave me seventy-five feet to muckle the hammer and wedges over to the stern tube.

I grabbed onto the line and said, "OK. Start slacking it off." I started kicking my way over with all I could muster with my jet fins and wasn't going to make it. "All stop!" I said huffing and puffing as I let the bucket swing free.

"What's up?" asked Paul.

"It's too heavy to swim it over. I need another hand line. It needs to be at least a hundred-feet-long. See if you can get one of our helpers to track down a mooring toss line with a monkey fist. They should have a bunch of those. I'll use it to pull the bucket to me from the stern tube. When I wrap my leg in the line holding the tools I'll drag it over. You can finish slacking it once I get started." I said. A monkey fist is a special round knot about the size of a baseball with a weight inserted into its core, usually a large steel nut. There is a loop on the end that gets attached to a long, light rope that they use to hurl from the deck to waiting workers below to drag the heavy steel cabled mooring lines to the bollards below. The weighted monkey fist gives the rope enough heft to carry it in flight the long distance to the dock.

"Roger that. Standby." Paul said.

It was only a couple minutes later when he chimed back in, "They had one right here at the stern for the aft mooring lines. I'll unroll it and lower you the monkey fist and you can rig it up."

"Great. Lower away when you're ready." I could see the monkey fist off to port. "All stop. Let it go when I give you a tug on the line." I pulled on the line and Paul let it go. I tied the monkey fist around the bucket line and took the slack end over to the stern tube and secured myself.

"OK. Don't start slacking until I say so. I'm going to start pulling it over." I said as the bucket started to swing my way. It was amazing how easy it was when you're not free falling with a dead weight. "OK. Slack it off. Make sure you have the end tied off to the handrail." I said. "Ok. I've got it."

With the hammer and wedges I now had a mission and determination. That was the good news. The bad news was it would take over four hours more to get the top plate ready to drive the wedges and attempt to break it free. I hoped Paul wasn't sleeping up there. Sure had enough time.

"Alrighty." I said grabbing the hammer and my first wedge. "I'm trying the first wedge." It had a very thin edge that I could drive into the cut weld bead. I had angled the cuts in a way that would best allow for this operation. My fingers were crossed.

The ten pounder was heavy, but by choking all the way up to the hammer I was able to start pounding the wedge into the cut. Great news, it took hold. Didn't get much penetration, but after getting a few installed I could work my way around.

About thirty minutes later, the wedges were installed, and I began hitting hard on the wedges starting from one side and hoping to begin cracking my way along. Finally, after a real slam I heard something pop. Sure enough, the weld had cracked, and the break line was better than ten inches long. That's when I knew we'd get through this!

"Paul, not sure if you could hear it, but we cracked through and have a ten-inch break. It left enough of an air gap to drive another wedge, and maybe get this son of a bitch off of here!" I said.

"Great news!" He said. "What about the other cover?" He asked.

"Don't be a party pooper! One plate at a time. Besides, I figured out a little better technique, and it's been saving us time during the last part of my prep on this one. With luck we can knock off some time on the next one. Stand by, while I hammer the shit out of this one!" I said.

Two more wedges went into place and I hit hard on the one next to the first one and worked both striking blows as hard as I could swinging a hammer underwater. POW, it snapped free. I scrambled to collect the wedges so they wouldn't end up on the bottom.

"That's it for the first one!" I slid it over on the stern tube and grabbed the camera hoping I could get everything we needed for the Coast Guard from the one opening. Unfortunately, no luck. It was so massive inside the rope guard and with limited views from the top there was no way we could get enough to cover the report.

I kicked the cover over the side of the stern tube to the bottom of the bay and said, "Paul, I've got good news and bad news again. Good news is the propeller shaft is clear and oil free. The bad news is we can't get enough through the one opening to satisfy the need. The Coast Guard will want to see the top and bottom of the propeller shaft at a minimum."

"That sucks! It's well after midnight!" He said.

"Is that all? The night's still young!" I said. Truth is I was really starting to feel it and had a new concern. My bottom time was going to be a problem when we finished. I'd be way over the line into the exceptional exposure range. The nearest chamber was in Puerto Rico if I got any kind of a hit from too much in gassed nitrogen. There was always a risk of blowing a bubble in the blood stream and causing an embolism. Just another great thing to contemplate while hammering away down there.

Enough crying, back to work. "I think this next one will be quicker. The welding in the drydock would have been overhead. Probably not as good penetration and more brittle. It least that's what I'm hoping."

"Just keep at it. Everything up here is holding together." Said Paul trying to add some encouragement.

I was right about the welds on the lower cover. They were much easier to cut through and I was ready for wedges by three o'clock in the morning. This time I didn't give a shit what happened to the plate or wedges once this cover popped off. I was worn out and things seemed to be moving in slow motion. I started driving the wedges, no small feat working overhead with a ten-pound hammer. I was able to stabilize myself by standing on the rope loop around the stern tube to gain purchase on the hammer without it dragging me to the bottom. Just don't miss . . .

Finally, POW, the plate popped off and the wedges flew. I watched the plate as it drifted back and forth on its way to the bottom. I didn't drop the ten-pound hammer although I probably should have. I was out of breath and nearly hyperventilating as the plate faded into the depths.

"OK Paul. Both covers are gone. I need to take a break before taking the photos and measurements inside the rope guard. Give me five minutes and then give me a heads up."

"You got it." He said.

I laid on top of the stern tube and breathed deeply until Paul signaled my break was over. I was spent. "Alright. I need you to get out our air tables and calculate my bottom time. I know I'm well over the line down here. Check the exceptional exposure air tables. In the meantime, I'll take the photos."

I could see clearly now, with the bottom cover gone. With a good set of photos, I could put together a great looking report. There was no line around the propeller shaft, and it looked to be in great condition. Nothing really to measure, so all I would need to provide before leaving the ship was a well worded hand-written report for the Coast Guard, with the promise of the follow up report and photos to be sent as soon as possible. I would send that to Joe in New York for them to handle. All I needed was to get them cleared for St. Croix and now we were ready, kind of.

"I've got bad news." Said Paul. "I can't find you on the air tables. You've been down there over seven hours. What do you want to do?" He asked.

"Shit! I knew it. However, the ship has been discharging crude and coming up. Where I'm working now should be a little shallower than when we started. I'm done down here, so we can start hauling everything up. Have one of the guys run down and read the hull marking with the draft numbers back here on the stern. When we have that, I can figure out a plan."

"Roger that." Said Paul.

We started hauling up the gear and de-rigging the ship. The runner came back and said the hull marking showed the ship sitting at sixty-five feet by the stern. I was surprised it had come up ten feet since they started discharging. That allowed me to use a fifty-foot average, over time, to use for a baseline to set up a conservative in-water decompression before coming up. That's not the way they teach it in

Diving School. Averaging is not allowed when calculating bottom time

I drifted over to the outer edge of the ship and looked up at the shimmering water on the surface fifty feet above me. The lighting on the ship brightly illuminated everything, including me in the water below. All the while I knew my problem was serious and I couldn't come up.

I cranked my air valve and gave myself a good vent, it was time to check out how I felt. Other than being totally exhausted, not too bad. I asked Paul to prepare a knot line for me to hang on, with knots set at ten-foot intervals. He could re-use the line with the monkey fist and tie four knots starting ten feet up from the monkey fist. I had an idea that taking somewhere between thirty and forty-five minutes I should be ready to come out. It would depend on how I felt as I hung out, literally, and made my way up the drop line.

Paul got the line rigged up and lowered the monkey fist to me. I asked him to stop and tie the line to the handrail while I ascended to the first knot at forty feet and held it chest high. "Give me a time check in twenty minutes. I figured, with all the factors considered, I can safely surface in under an hour. We'll use twenty at forty, fifteen at thirty, ten at twenty and ten at ten feet for in water decompression. Water temp is warm enough, and after fifty-five minutes off gassing, it should be safe to come up." I said. There were unknowns here, and a big risk if I got it wrong. With all my years of experience, I was left with guess work in the bowels of the Caribbean to make the right choice. Nobody but me to blame if things went badly.

Hanging there on the line, resting, and breathing calmly, I nearly fell asleep. I caught myself as my grip loosened. I clipped off to the line to avoid another surprise. If I was able to cat nap on the way up, it would allow me to re-charge a bit before the final push to get out of the water. Couldn't see anything wrong with that.

Paul clocked my ascent and when I got to twenty feet my mind wandered back to reality. I had to get out of here, and back up on the ship to write the report. After that, help roll up the gear and then get out of there. The one good thing was the thought of a good night sleep at the hotel. We'd stay the night and not take any further risks by flying right after an exceptional exposure underwater event.

Suddenly, I got a mental jolt. The cove where the terminal is located, was full of Hammerhead Sharks! Not my imagination, I've seen them swirling around, swimming slowly as they circumnavigated the cove. From up on the bluff, we could see them every time we worked at the terminal. So, here I was, about to make a long swim back to the mooring dolphin in the middle of the night, with a cove full of sharks. What better way to finish the job. It was time for a decision, swim to the shore and climb up the quay rock to the road leading to the ship or return with a six-hundred-foot swim to the original entry point.

Paul signaled my time was up at ten feet and asked what I wanted to do. "I'm gonna swim to the quay rock and climb out on the road. It looks shorter. I'll tie off the Superlight and when I say so, you can haul it up. I'll swim to the shore and meet you back on the ship." I said.

"Roger that." Paul said. "It doesn't look much shorter going that way."

"Ya, but at least I won't have to climb that long rung ladder to get out." I answered. "OK. My helmets off. Haul it up." I said as I cleared my head. Up it went.

I looked at the shore and thought, *Goddamn that's a long swim.* Just me in my tee shirt and shorts, with a pair of jet fins, and maybe joined by some other fins. As I began the slow swim, the thought of those Hammerheads kept playing in my head. What a way to go, eaten by a Hammerhead in St. Lucia! I told myself, just focus.

In all my years of commercial diving, I've never had any concern about sharks, or any other danger outside the task at hand, and now I had this worry rattling around in my head? There was something wrong. Maybe a crack in my mental armor or was I just deliriously tired.

After my black water ordeal in LA a couple weeks earlier and now this, maybe my old Irish Grandmother was right in her warning that bad things happen in threes. This would be number two. Would I be ready for number three?

As I continued my swim to the quay rock, the theme of the movie JAWS began to play in my mind. . . . Enough of that, I thought. Which was it? Fear of the unknown, or simply delusions from exhaustion? Either one was unacceptable. I climbed out on the rocks and made my way up to the road.

Standing there dripping wet, I was staring back at the *WESTERN LION* when it hit me, the realization that the job was complete. I turned and slammed my jet fins down on the road. This would be my final ship call. There was no room for fear in this line of work. I had come to question my mental toughness and even the desire to continue as a commercial diver. Hammerhead Sharks? Seriously? It had to be a sign it was time to hang it up.

Picking up my fins and slowly walking back over to the ship my mental focus began to return. Boarding the gangway, the reality of the moment set in; we had succeeded. The *WESTERN LION* would be clear to re-enter US waters. The only thing left was to scribble out a findings letter which Joe could send to the Coast Guard.

With any luck, Hess would never hear about the Valdez saga. Now, how much to charge for exposing myself to so much danger? Something to contemplate while enjoying my Baileys on the rocks on the trip back to Miami.

I was certain it was time to move on, but it was best for now to savor the moment and enjoy the success of a nearly impossible mission.

WESTERN LION discharging crude oil at the terminal in St Croix following the lightering in St Lucia

This would be the last ship call for LEEWARD MARINE. . .

Sunset over Buck Island - St. Croix – Photo by Author - Taken from Cormorant Beach Club

EPILOGUE

One Door Closes - Another Door Opens

⚓

The *WESTERN LION* made her schedule to discharge her four million barrels of crude. As far as I know, no one was aware of the saga to restore her compliance with the Coast Guard to re-enter US waters. Whether Hess found out or not, no longer concerned me, as I had made up my mind and was turning the page. No more diving.

Not sure if it's 'Luck of the Irish,' or only plain luck, but my life has been full of adventure and driven more by luck than any planning of the life ahead of me. I had drifted along with the tide and finally at age forty-two, found it was time to toss the anchor and leave the wilds of commercial diving to all the youngsters who dared take the plunge and challenge the abyss. I had and survived to tell my tales.

Looking Forward

Once again, I'd have to stick my finger in the wind and see where it blows. The one sure thing, I'd be off to the next great adventure. But, where do you start after all those years, or do you? Maybe it was as simple as taking some time, and just continuing on down the trail wherever it leads. If there's one thing I've learned, there is little in life that one actually controls, or better yet, wants to control. For me it's better to soldier on and see what comes next.

One day with my feet up and a copy of the Sunday paper in my lap, I found myself drawn to the help wanted ads. It was early Spring in 1996 and time for me to see what people actually did for a living.

After all the years of working out on the fringes, job hunting was a foreign thing and yet here I sat. The skills I had were varied and leaned heavily toward construction and engineering. So, there it was, 'STEEL ERECTING' 'Construction Supervisor Wanted,' steel erecting, must have a minimum of five years' experience and valid Florida Driving License. Good pay. Call 941-blah blah blah. . .

Time to call and see what's up. The Company was even headquartered in my adopted town, Sarasota. When I showed up, there wasn't a piece of steel anywhere in sight. No cranes, trucks, or the usual trappings you'd expect to find at a construction company doing steel work. All I saw was a field full of huge wooden reels. I was confused and checked the address on the ad. Huh, this was the place.

Upon entering the office, I was met by the owner. The steel erecting, they were doing was for TELECOM. The steel was for towers, and the giant wooden reels were coax cable, which would run up the towers and power the antennas. Welcome to the birth of Cell Phones, PCS. (Personal Communications Services)

Was it possible I had just fallen into the next big thing with another frontier needing pioneers? What do you know? It was, and the development of cell phones would ultimately go on to change the world. The next great adventure had just begun, and there I was right in the middle of it. It would become my next great adventure!

Oceans Ahead

It is here the working trail will finally end for me in 2019 after twenty-two years and several thousand towers and cells sites constructed. It has been a truly amazing ride, and an honor to have worked with so many fine people along the way.

As for me, once again I'll drift along with the tide that has provided me so much opportunity and continue to keep a line in the water. You never know what might strike that line!

I may pen a story or two about my times spent in Telecom or a few short stories between the tides of my adventures in Commercial Diving before my memory fades. So as the door closes on telecom and facing the next chapter in life a new door opens to the fresh breezes and calm waters that lie ahead.

Author, Retired, fishing for Peacock Bass in the Amazon Rain Forest, Brazil

REFERENCES

Government of Virgin Islands v. Roberts, 756 F. Supp. 898 (D.V.I. 1991)

https://law.justia.com/cases/federal/district/courts/FSupp/756/898/2291710/

GTS Admiral W.M. Callaghan." GTS Admiral W.M. Callaghan | MARAD

https://www.maritime.dot.gov/content/gts-admiral-wm-callaghan

National Transportation Safety Board Marine Accident Report: Engine Room Fire on Board the Liberian Tankship Seal Island While Moored at the Amerada Hess Oil Terminal in St. Croix, U.S. Virgin Islands, October 8, 1994. NTIS

https://ntrl.ntis.gov/NTRL/dashboard/searchResults/titleDetail/PB95916404.xhtml

LEE BROTHERS – Jay, Scott, Dana, Greg, and Chris (Author) left to right in 2013. The last photo of all five Marblehead LEE Brothers together. One for the ages with Brown's Island and Little Harbor in the background. Photo taken in front of Brother Greg's house on Peaches Point.

www.ingramcontent.com/pod-product-compliance
Lightning Source LLC
Chambersburg PA
CBHW042000090426
42811CB00031B/1965/J